# Enterprise
# Software Security

# Enterprise
# Software Security

## A Confluence of Disciplines

Kenneth R. van Wyk
Mark G. Graff
Dan S. Peters
Diana L. Burley, Ph.D.

**ᵥᵥ Addison-Wesley**

Upper Saddle River, NJ • Boston • Indianapolis • San Francisco

New York • Toronto • Montreal • London • Munich • Paris • Madrid

Capetown • Sydney • Tokyo • Singapore • Mexico City

For information about buying this title in bulk quantities, or for special sales opportunities (which may include electronic versions; custom cover designs; and content particular to your business, training goals, marketing focus, or branding interests), please contact our corporate sales department at corpsales@pearsoned.com or (800) 382-3419.

For government sales inquiries, please contact governmentsales@pearsoned.com.

For questions about sales outside the U.S., please contact international@pearsoned.com.

Visit us on the Web: informit.com/aw

Library of Congress Control Number: 2014950276

ISBN-13: 978-0-321-60411-8
ISBN-10: 0-321-60411-3

Text printed in the United States on recycled paper at RR Donnelley in Crawfordsville, IN.

First printing: December 2014

I want to dedicate this book to my wife and my parents,
for believing in me and encouraging me.
—Kenneth R. van Wyk

I want to thank my old friend KRvW once again for his
trust and patience, as well as for the
astounding insight that launched this adventure.
—Mark G. Graff

My work is dedicated to my family and to
childhood memories about my grandparents.
—Dan Peters

To my family for their unwavering support.
—Diana L. Burley, Ph.D.

# Contents

# Acknowledgments

**From Kenneth R. van Wyk:**

Thanks of course to my authoring team. We come from a pretty diverse set of backgrounds and experiences—by design—and I'm proud of what we've put together here. Together we proudly wave the flag of confluence and hope many will join in.

Likewise, our tech reviewers have been fabulous: Danny Smith (who has been on a couple of my review teams now), Bill Reynolds, Derrick Scholl, Andrew van der Stock, and Kevin Wall. Like the authors, you represent a diverse set of experiences, and we value greatly all your suggestions. I hope we've done them justice. If we haven't, it certainly isn't your fault!

I also want to send out a special thanks to my mom and dad. My dad, who as a schoolboy was captured by the sounds of those Rolls Royce Merlin and Griffin engines in their Spitfires and Hurricanes as they flew over his grade school. He later went on to be a 747 pilot at what was at the time one of the biggest and most respected airlines on the planet. He encouraged me in everything I did. Every hobby, everything. He always encouraged me to soar, whether it meant competing or simply pushing myself to the limits of my abilities. I'm forever grateful for that encouragement.

And my mom, who not once, not twice, but three times followed her husband and moved to three different continents. She was a farm girl from rural South Africa, where English was anything but the primary language. And then, she not only learned English, but became an English professor at a U.S. university. I often consider how I would react to being, say, a French professor to French students, and it gives me chills.

How could I fail, given such amazing examples! Thanks, Mom and Dad. I love you both.

**From Mark G. Graff:**

I want to thank my old friend KRvW once again for his trust and patience, as well as for the astounding insight that launched this adventure (maybe better: his "trust, insight, and astounding patience"). To Diana and

Dan: There would be no book without your skills and dedication; I feel rescued. To my family: Wow—look what we did! Finally, love and fond regards to fellow security practitioners/sufferers around the world.

## From Dan S. Peters:

I feel proud to be part of this exquisite author group and to able to contribute my knowledge and experience to this book project. Even though I could anticipate ahead of time all the stress related to book writing, it was a very easy decision for me to take part in the project once I talked to Ken and Mark about it. The arguments were simply so convincing and aligned so well with my vision of the situation that I could not resist the temptation. Together with Diana, the four of us formed a well-rounded team, complementing each other's vision, knowledge, and passion for the subject of software security. I believe that the confluence book would not be possible based on the experiences of individual authors, and could only be born out of such collaboration.

My family, of course, deserves appreciation as well, as they often had to cope with weekend calls and late-night shifts while I was trying to move forward on an especially stubborn subject. They had to deal with my frustrations about writer's block and continued encouraging me in this endeavor through all these weeks, months, and (alas) years. Thank you!

## From Diana L. Burley:

Thank you to this amazing team of authors. Ken and Mark, our synergy was apparent from the start, and I was honored to work alongside you as your vision turned into our vision and then into our reality. Dan, your ability to hone in on the technical details of every discussion sharpened us all. Our collaboration is a call to action. To the educators who will answer this call, the future begins with you. Let the message of confluence permeate your classrooms as you develop the next generation of security professionals.

To my family—my children, who inspire me every day to push beyond traditional boundaries and challenge the status quo; my parents, who instilled in me the need to disrupt accepted thought patterns by crafting arguments that blend academic rigor (from my mother, the college professor and administrator) with practical wisdom (from my father, the corporate executive); my brother, whose belief in me carried me through the late nights; and my best friend, who makes each day *always better*!

# About the Authors

**Kenneth R. van Wyk** is a career security guy, having started with Carnegie Mellon University's CERT/CC in the late 1980s and subsequently worked for the United States Department of Defense and in several senior technologist roles in the commercial sector. He is the co-author of two popular O'Reilly and Associates books on incident response and secure coding. He now owns and runs KRvW Associates, LLC, a software security consulting and training practice in Virginia, USA.

**Mark G. Graff** is the CISO of NASDAQ OMX. Formerly the chief cybersecurity strategist at Lawrence Livermore National Laboratory, he has appeared as an expert witness on computer security before Congress and analyzed electronic voting machine software security for the state of California. A past chairman of the International Forum of Incident Response and Security Teams (FIRST), Graff has lectured on risk analysis, the future of cyber security, and privacy before the American Academy for the Advancement of Science, the Federal Communications Commission (FCC), the Pentagon, and many U.S. national security facilities and think tanks.

**Dan S. Peters** has been involved with security for longer than he had first expected when he stumbled into this field out of curiosity while making a good living as a consultant and a commercial software developer. Many security disciplines are exciting to him, but mobile security has been the most intriguing topic as of late. Before working on this book, Dan repeatedly shared his passion for security in conference presentations and numerous publications.

**Diana L. Burley, Ph.D.,** is an award-winning cyber-security workforce expert who has been honored by the U.S. Federal CIO Council and was named the CISSE 2014 Cybersecurity Educator of the Year. As a professor, researcher, and consultant on IT use and workforce development for nearly 20 years, she passionately promotes a holistic view of cyber security to influence education, policy, and practice from her home in the Washington, D.C., region.

# Preface

In today's commercial enterprises, information security staffs spend years building walls around their business applications. That's good. Practitioners have known for years, however, that—for a real chance at corporate safety—the enterprise's application programmers must also build security into the business software.

Yet even the powerful combination of a sound perimeter and front-to-back application security might not suffice against the highly sophisticated attacks launched against today's networks. One surprising reason: There is all too often a cultural and physical separation between the software development staff and the information security staff in large enterprises.

This book bridges that gulf. We identify the issues that distinguish and keep the two groups apart, and suggest practical and actionable guidance as to how best to collaboratively address the security needs of the enterprise. This book will help programmers design, write, deploy, and operate better enterprise software applications. It will help network security engineers make better use of the applications' output to drive and adjust manifold security appliances, such as firewalls. But we hope it will achieve much more.

Uniquely drawing ideas from two distinct disciplines, software engineering and network security, this book is intended to point the way to a new, holistic approach to enterprise protection. We envision an integrated program of application development, security appliances, network architecture, and policies and procedures we call "confluence."

It's not just about the perimeter anymore, or even safe software. Recent developments such as the so-called "advanced persistent threat" have breached those barriers. But in this book we show how businesses can move forward by building software that actively contributes to the intrusion detection and response processes. (Today, most extant enterprise software still provides audit logs or event logs of security exceptions, and little more.) Drawing on our case-study files, we show how software should—and can—be made to play a vital active role in protecting an enterprise before, during, and after security incidents. Software can and should take active measures to safeguard customer data, business processes, and other sensitive data within the scope of the application. This approach, so far as we know, has not been addressed to this degree in other publications.

By taking a wide-angle view of security, we show how even parts of the company that are not on the firing line can nevertheless help make the company safer. (See Chapter 9, "The View from the Center," for example, for a discussion of the role of Human Resources in this effort.) And along the way we reintroduce, for the benefit of non-engineers (certainly a majority among today's developers and security practitioners) certain well-understood engineering principles, such as feedback loops and fidelity tests, into the battle. It's a fertile field—a frontier, really: an area of technical ground left unplowed because as a community of technologists we have not sufficiently considered the two disciplines of development and IT security together.

## Moving Targets Are Harder to Hit

Much has changed while we wrote this book. Cloud computing has entered the scene in a massive way, as has mobile. When we started the book, Ken was carrying around one of those dreadful little "smart" phones with a physical keyboard. And then, along came a little company from Cupertino and one from Palo Alto that redefined mobile computing and forever changed the status quo.

These changes have had a huge impact not only on the computing world, but also on our project. A moving target is always harder to hit. But, in another and very real sense, they've underscored the need for such a book. We see small teams of "agile" developers these days diving into projects with sometimes reckless abandon, in search of the next great app. Although this innovation should be embraced and encouraged, we're also cautious when it comes at the expense of making some dreadful security mistakes.

One of the subgoals of this book is to help a new generation of software developers and IT security professionals avoid some of the horrible mistakes we've personally witnessed over the years.

## Origins, Authors, Credentials

This book began over six years ago, in early 2008, with an observation by Ken van Wyk. A principal in a successful security consulting and training company, Ken had noticed an unaddressed need while conducting his "Secure Coding" classes for application developers around the world. Although his students were generally highly skilled at programming, and quickly acquired the technical defensive coding and diagnostic techniques he taught, the nature of "the threat" (and the tricks and mindsets of attackers) involved mostly new concepts. This lacuna hampered the ability of some students to anticipate what an attacker would do. At the same time, in conversations with enterprise security practitioners at some of the same companies he was teaching at, he found that some of the canniest firewall gurus lacked a basic grounding in programming beyond, say, some familiarity with scripting languages, but not higher level programming languages. These same gurus were often frustrated with developers who "didn't get it" when the topic was enterprise security, while they themselves often lacked familiarity with the "business logic" that was a prime mover on the development side of the house. As an old hand in the network security game, Ken saw that a yawning communications gap had opened in the field over the decades he had been working in it.

Ken approached Mark Graff, with whom he had previously collaborated on the successful tome *Secure Coding* (O'Reilly, 2003), and proposed writing a new book that would try to bring the two diverging fields back together. The working title was *Confluence*. Together Mark and Ken worked up a draft outline and successfully pitched the book to their first-choice publisher, Addison-Wesley.

We'll fast-forward the story here, to the point in 2011 when the two original authors realized they needed help if the project was ever going to make the bookstores (or web sites). After a round of recruiting (employing SC-L, the "Secure Coding" website inspired by the book and managed by Ken) and a diligent interview process, two new authors joined the project. Dan Peters (from a large security vendor) and Dr. Diana Burley (from George Washington University) filled out the team, supplying a critical mix of technical and field expertise, strategic thinking, academic precision, and a critical mass of time and energy.

Your four authors combine for about a century of experience in programming, engineering, education, communications, entrepreneurship, management, and security architecture. Our collaborative product examines *each* of these practices in the light of "confluence," the flowing together of heretofore divergent disciplines. Let's take a look.

## Contents

We have arranged topics in this book in a logical order that roughly follows the high-level stages of a classic programming project, and chapter list below reflects that ordering. So after we take a detailed look in Chapter 1, "Introduction to the Problem," at the problem we are trying to solve—the divergence of technical streams that ought to be collaborating—we move into our own little development life cycle with Chapter 2, "Project Inception." While examining confluent design, implementation, testing, deployment, and maintenance, your authors illustrate various points in terms of real-world experience and provide a running example. Wrapping up, we recapitulate the material slightly from a new, integrated point of view, showing how a Chief Information Security Officer at a hypothetical company might undertake to put all the disparate pieces into motion to produce a confluent enterprise.

Generally, of course, we recommend that you read the chapters in order. This is a narrative analysis, not a technical compendium. We provide technical snippets, but mainly what we offer is argument and advice. And although we would be delighted to find that readers find a particular excerpt especially pertinent to their requirements, we have tried our best to write a book that can profitably be *read* in its entirety. It is our testament, in a way: an attempt to shine a light along a path we think leads to a safer and more resilient online world.

## Summing Up

All these years have been a long time to write a book. We stuck with it because we think that there has been a bit of a wrong turn in the evolution of information security. We find ourselves in a cul-de-sac, but we think we see a way out. We hope you will agree. Let's get to it!

# 1    Introduction to the Problem

**Y**our authors have been at "this security stuff" for more than 20 years. At various points during that time, we have been on the front lines of two key struggles, writing secure code and securing enterprises from attack—often after the fact, as a result of incident response operations. Over this time, we have seen good progress in both arenas. Yet when we examine the common software produced today, and the way our enterprises are protected, we find egregious flaws and serious risks. We find mistakes and pitfalls that have been well understood and well documented for many years (even, in some cases, decades). We also see new threats and ingenious new attacks. Worse still, as programmers, enterprise security practitioners, and educators of long standing, your authors share a portion of responsibility for the status quo.

For all these reasons, as we ponder the security predicament all of us in the modern world now face, we feel an urgent responsibility to help make a safer world. This book contains our analysis of today's enterprise software security mess, what we think it means, and our prescription for recovery.

In this first chapter, we describe the lay of the land as we see it—that is, the nature and significance of the problem. We sketch out how we arrived here, with a short history lesson. We diagnose the root cause of the problem, as well as some of the key vulnerabilities that have emerged and the many attacks that those vulnerabilities make possible. Finally, to illustrate these issues as concretely as possible, we introduce a notional application made by a fictional company of our imagination. The story of this little app and its creators' struggles to make it "ready for prime time" will continue throughout the chapters of the book, as we describe our vision of how enterprises—and the software that runs them—can provide a safer foundation for today's Internet-dependent world.

## Our Shared Predicament Today

Just during the short decades of our security careers, our society has become vastly more dependent on the Internet. It's now woven into our commerce, education, news, and entertainment. It's part of our political discourse. To some of us (we know these people, even if you don't) the Internet seems as important as air and water. Many of these people have not known life without the Internet, and to them it is a basic utility—like electricity and water service. So important is the connectivity that Internet access provides that many digital natives (those who have grown up in the age of the Internet) make major work and life decisions based on the ease with which they can connect. The necessity for constant connectivity is a global phenomenon, with one of every three college students worldwide indicating that the Internet is as important to them as water, food, air, and shelter. College students in the U.S. are on par with the global average, whereas nearly two of three college students in Brazil and China indicate this level of importance (see Figure 1.1).

| Among College Students % | Total (n=1441) | US (n=100) | CAN (n=101) | MEX (n=100) | BRA (n=105) | UK (n=100) | FRA (n=100) | DEU (n=100) | SPA (n=103) | ITA (n=100) | RUS (n=100) | IND (n=113) | CHN (n=102) | JPN (n=101) | AUS (n=104) |
|---|---|---|---|---|---|---|---|---|---|---|---|---|---|---|---|
| Yes, it is that important to the way I live my life | 32 | 32 | 19 | 16 | 65 | 22 | 13 | 18 | 50 | 50 | 19 | 41 | 64 | 28 | 18 |
| No, but the Internet is pretty close | 49 | 37 | 58 | 63 | 32 | 44 | 39 | 65 | 37 | 34 | 76 | 53 | 31 | 62 | 49 |
| No, the Internet is not that important in my life | 19 | 31 | 23 | 21 | 3 | 34 | 48 | 17 | 14 | 16 | 5 | 6 | 5 | 10 | 33 |

**Figure 1.1**   Table from the 2011 Cisco Connected World Technology Report—Q: Do you consider the Internet as important to your life as water, food, air, and shelter?

On the dark side—and not by coincidence—Internet-related crime has become a lucrative industry, with more than half a billion dollars of consumer losses in the U.S. alone reported in 2012.[1] And the infrastructures of technologically advanced countries seem alarmingly vulnerable to disruption by the complex and effective attack tools readily available at thousands of web sites. A 2009 automated Google scan identified more than 4,000 malware distribution sites, and the number rises every day. As shown in Figure 1.2 and Figure 1.3, complaints of Internet-related crime to the Internet Crime Complaint Center (IC3), a joint unit of the U.S. Federal Bureau of Investigation (FBI) and the National White Collar Crime Center (NW3C), have risen significantly since the year 2000. And although actual consumer reports have fluctuated over the past several years, dollar-value losses have consistently increased. In 2012, for instance, the adjusted dollar loss associated with consumer complaints rose 8.3% to just over $500 million.[2]

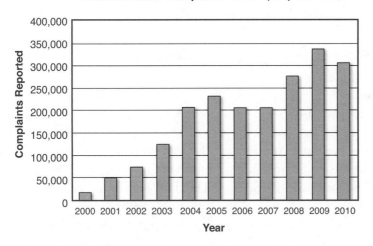

**Figure 1.2** Internet Crime Complaint numbers from 2000 to 2010.

Source: IC3 2010 Annual Report

**Complaint Totals By Year**

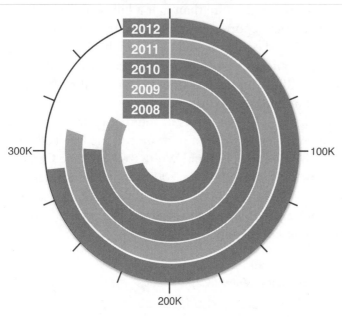

**Figure 1.3**   Internet Crime Complaint numbers from 2008 to 2012.

Source: IC3 2012 Annual Report

So that is the state we find ourselves in. The software we rely on has deep-seated flaws; the means and methods we use to protect our networks and data repositories are weak and porous. Tens of millions of "identities" (in the U.S., that equates to Social Security numbers) have been stolen, either sold or stashed away for further use. The networks and services we rely on so much work well most of the time but, like most of the parts of our complex life today, seem remarkably fragile to those who know the most. If our networks were highways and our applications were bridges, smoke and rubble would be commonplace sights; creaks, cracks, and potholes would be everywhere. And we'd all be driving around this mess on our way to work, to the market, or on our way home.

## Why Are We in This Security Mess?

What other discipline would tolerate such repeated vast failures? It doesn't have to be this way. We are confident the software and security communities can do better. More pragmatically, we simply have to figure out how to do better, or, given the risks, we will soon be overrun by government restrictions and regulations that none of us will be happy with. (And that's the *best* case.)

What can be done? Our argument in this book is that the solution to our current security troubles lies in *confluence*...a flowing together like the rivers shown in Figure 1.4 (the Allegheny on the left and the Monongahela on the right), which flow together to form the Ohio River in Pittsburgh, Pennsylvania.

**Figure 1.4** The confluence of the Allegheny and Monongahela Rivers forming the Ohio River.

Source: www.pittsburghgreenstory.org/images/3_rivers/3_rivers_large_photo.jpg

So how does that concept relate to software security, and how could bringing it about make us safer?

We argue that although the responsibility for implementing security on a particular network resided years ago in a single set of people—the programmers who worked on it—that function today resides in two separate camps: application developers and enterprise security practitioners. What is necessary for effective security today is to once again bring together the work of these two groups, to make the two kinds of security flow together into a whole (see Figure 1.5). In reality, we would like to see a world in which every employee in a company has a fundamental responsibility for security, but for the purposes of this book, we are largely going to focus our attention more directly on developers and security professionals.

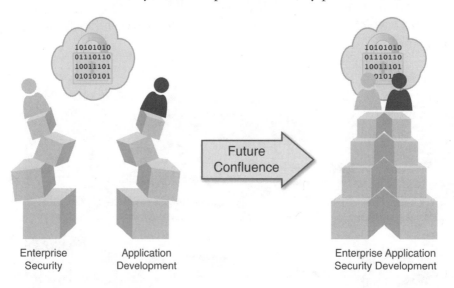

**Figure 1.5**  The two kinds of security need to flow together into one.

In this chapter, we'll make the case for confluence. We'll trace how software security and enterprise security, once unified, forked off from each other and evolved separately. We'll outline, in both cases, how the disciplines are practiced today. And we'll show how the current state of the practice creates the holes and opportunities for failure we see exploited every day. It should be noted that, even though subsequent chapters talk about challenges in the context of internal development within enterprise, these general concepts are broadly applicable and can and should be used (with minor adjustments) by software vendors and developers at all levels.

We'll begin with a short walk through the Internet epochs your authors (and maybe you too) have lived through and worked in so that we can put our current state of affairs into an appropriate context. We haven't arrived where we are today entirely by accident, but perhaps we have done so without sufficient foresight being exercised.

## Ancient History

For quite a few years, the Internet (like its predecessors, ARPANET and NSFNET) was regarded as an academic, scientific community for collaborating on research projects or sharing data. It wasn't that long ago, until 1995 in fact, that commercial activity was *forbidden* on the Internet. Until that time, the National Science Foundation's "Acceptable Use Policy" for the NSFNET backbone prohibited network use for any purpose that was "not in support of Research and Education."[3] In large part due to the nature of the work, the network world was very trusting and open—quite possibly to a fault. But since the Net was relatively small, and no commerce was being done on it, there just didn't seem to be as much focus on security. Most networks at that time relied on either the honor system or a few virtual door locks. After all, it was largely used by professors and researchers with only altruistic motives for the advancement of science, right?

As with most seemingly utopian worlds, however, things were not as they seemed. As the network of individuals grew and the mission of computer networks changed, network security became more important. (For this reason, perhaps, the United States federal government played an important role in the development of network security, especially in the 1980s and early 1990s.)[4] We are not going to try to provide a definitive history, but here are some key early developments in the emergence of software and network security as we see them:

- 1975: J. H. Salzer and M. D. Schroeder lay out basic computer security architecture principles in "The Protection of Information in Computer Systems."[5] The focus is on access control mechanisms and authentication, not on detection of transgressions.

- 1978: Robert Morris and Ken Thompson document the security of encrypted passwords on UNIX systems. As a result, many security teams recommend changing passwords every 30 days. Not much has changed except today's systems are vastly faster at cracking passwords.

- 1980: James P. Anderson authors the seminal work in intrusion detection, *Computer Security Threat Modeling and Surveillance*.[6] Audit trails (log files) are a major concern; that is, the emphasis is on retrospection, not real-time detection or prevention.

- 1985: The U.S. Department of Defense defines various levels of security and the criteria required for certification at each level in the "Orange Book," part of its computer security "Rainbow Series."[7] Still the focus is on host-level authentication and access control, and the ability to reconstruct failure events.[8]

- 1986: Dorothy Denning and Peter Neumann (of SRI) begin development of the Intrusion Detection Expert System (IDES), the first system to perform "intrusion detection" by means of statistical analysis of anomalies.[9]

- 1987: Development begins at the United States Air Force Logic Support Center on the system later known as Haystack, a more advanced statistical anomaly checker that, with the slightly later DIDS (Distributed Intrusion Detection System), became the first security system to take a network (as opposed to host-based) perspective on security events.[10]

- 1987: Larry Wall, a system administrator working at NASA, releases Perl, a general-purpose interpreted programming language that will come to be so commonly used by early Net-savvy "sysadmins" that it will come to be known as "the glue of the Internet" and "the Swiss Army chainsaw" of programming languages.[11]

- 1987–1995: Kevin Mitnick becomes an increasingly well-known and highly sought-after cyber criminal, the highest visibility (certainly to the general public) cyber criminal to date. After several missed attempts, the FBI finally arrests and successfully convicts him of multiple computer crimes in 1995.

- 1988: The release of the "Morris Worm" in November takes down or ties up a significant number (the most prevalent estimate: 10 percent) of the 60,000 or so systems on the nascent Internet, exposing network vulnerabilities to a broad audience for the first time.[12]

- 1989: Cliff Stoll, an astronomer and part-time system administrator at Lawrence Berkeley Laboratory, publishes *The Cuckoo's Egg*, about his long-distance battle (which began in 1986) with a German attacker searching for U.S. government secrets.[13]

The Morris Worm and "Cuckoo's Egg" stories generated a storm of public interest, focusing the attention of many people on network security problems for the first time and, we think, helping to accelerate investment in various security development projects. Observe in our tiny chronology how the pace of remarkable breakthroughs picks up now. Note, too, that in most cases the tools are still being created (often out of sheer necessity) by experienced system administrators *who are also programmers*. That is, if there is this time any effective difference between security software and software security, they are to a large degree still practiced, outside of academia at least, by the same sorts of workers. We feel this will change over time.

- 1989–1992: Multiple government-sponsored security research projects begin to bear fruit, for example, MIDAS, NADIR, and ASIM.[14] Commercial software packages begin to appear, offering automated audit trail reduction and analysis and anomaly detection, for example, ISOA, Clyde Vax Audit, Stalker, CMDS, and NetRanger.[15] The first commercial bastion host firewall package, written by Marcus Ranum, was released as DEC SEAL in 1990.[16]

- 1991: Tim Berners-Lee publishes information on the `alt.hypertext` Internet newsgroup about the new World Wide Web software he has developed at CERN.[17] The Web slowly starts to grow. In an irony that will befuddle security professionals for years, the HyperText Transfer Protocol (HTTP) is defined as a stateless protocol, despite running on TCP, which is stateful. Although this might seem subtle to many, it would prove itself to be a significant security hurdle that still hasn't been fully cleared as of this writing.

- 1992: Bill Cheswick of AT&T Bell Laboratories, a full-time system administrator, publishes "An Evening with Berferd," describing how he "for several months…led [an attacker he nicknamed Berferd] on a merry chase in order to trace his location and learn his techniques."[18] Marcus Ranum, another "sysadmin," designs and implements the TIS Firewall Toolkit and the Gauntlet firewall.[19]

- 1992: Phil Zimmerman releases Pretty Good Privacy (PGP), a free public key cryptography tool for a network of loosely connected people to protect information they share. Zimmerman isn't alone either. Other encryption tools and libraries start appearing during this same timeframe, giving civilian programmers access to excellent cryptography to use in their software.

- 1993: CERN announces that its WWW software will henceforth be free; Marc Andressen's team at the National Center for Supercomputing Applications releases Mosaic, the first graphical web browser.[20]

  In 1995 NSF defunded the NSFNET backbone and competitively redistributed the funds to regional networks, allowing them to buy connectivity through private networks. At that time, the Internet (as it was now called) had more than 50,000 networks across all seven continents and in outer space.[21] This privatization paved the way for electronic commerce—the .com era—to begin. The earliest domains in the .com space were little more than "brochure ware" for their owners: a place to advertise the company's products and services, that is, but not to conduct direct commerce. As we see it, there were two primary obstacles between this state of affairs and the Internet we know today. To pave the way for commerce on the Internet, business owners needed software that could move the goods and the confidence that the Net could faithfully be relied on. After all, tens of thousands of companies suddenly need web-capable application software and network security and along comes tons of free software!

- 1993–1995: Rob McCool writes and releases the NCSA web server httpd; CGI (Common Gateway Interface) functionality is added to httpd; the loose-knit Apache Group releases the Apache web server (which uses NCSA's httpd 1.3 as a base);[22] the first data entry forms feature appears in the HTML 2.0 specification.[23] A more-or-less standardized way to serve dynamic content has arrived.

- 1995: Sun Microsystems releases the source code for Java (version1.0a2, the "full public alpha version") onto the Internet. Tens of thousands of copies are downloaded by developers in a few months.[24] Java technology is woven into the new powerhouse Netscape Navigator web browser. David Bank of *Wired* writes, "While today's Web is mostly a static brew—a grand collection of electronically linked brochures—Java holds the promise of caffeinating the Web, supercharging it with interactive games and animation and thousands of applications programs nobody's even thought of."[25]

- 1995: Dan Farmer and Wietse Venema write and release the controversial SATAN security scanner. Effective at finding outward-facing security holes, and at the same time highly portable and offering a browser interface, SATAN was a fulcrum of sorts. It brought together elements that heretofore had been disparate: network security, system software vulnerabilities, enterprise application software, and the use of new hyper-portable web platforms (PERL, CGI, and HTML).[26]

- 1996: Gary McGraw and Edward Felton write and release the first Java Security book for users to create a comprehensive Java use strategy that accounts for software risks.[27]

- 1997: Gordon Lyon (also known as Fyodor Vaskovich) releases NMAP, a network security scanner that uses host discovery and port scanning to find network vulnerabilities.[28]

- 1998: Martin Roesch releases SNORT, a packet sniffer program that evolved into a network intrusion prevention system;[29] Renaud Deraison releases Nessus as a free remote security scanner.[30]

## All Together Now

Before proceeding, let's take a look back and knit the preceding narrative together a bit so that we can watch two important streams—software security and enterprise security—separate.

In the 1980s and early 1990s, security tools like network firewalls and Intrusion Detection Systems (IDS) started to emerge from the academic research community, and several research projects looked into ways of detecting anomalous or malicious behavior on computer systems. In their academic research incarnations, detection algorithms focused on largely signature-based detection of known bad actions or statistical anomaly detection, based on defining some form of normative state for each object being watched.

It took a few years for commercial IDS products to arrive, but when they did, they were generally available in two flavors: network-based and host-based (see Figure 1.6). So here we see some preliminary indications that the security product folks were attempting to poke inside the actual computer systems where the crown jewels were stored, the application servers. In many cases that your authors personally witnessed, however, the application owners were more than a little reluctant to allow extraneous processes (along with memory, disk, and CPU "footprints") on their production systems.

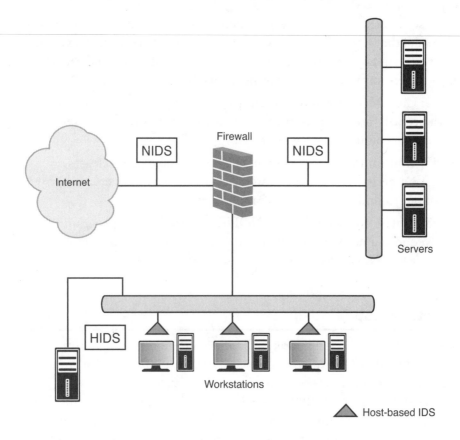

**Figure 1.6** Commercial IDSs were network-based or host-based.

Another step in this evolution was to build elaborate distributed IDS sensor systems with centralized monitoring and updating facilities that would sort through the volumes of data to find indications of security events, as shown in Figure 1.7. What is worth noting is that it was often the network engineers and system administrators who recognized major problems and took it upon themselves to develop these early network security solutions.

All of these network-centric solutions were regarded by the application owners as relatively innocuous and were thus tolerated. However, the downside of this security progress was that it served to create a significant divide between the security team and the application development team. Each team could operate independently to carry out its responsibilities. This is a key problem that surfaced and has still to be properly resolved.

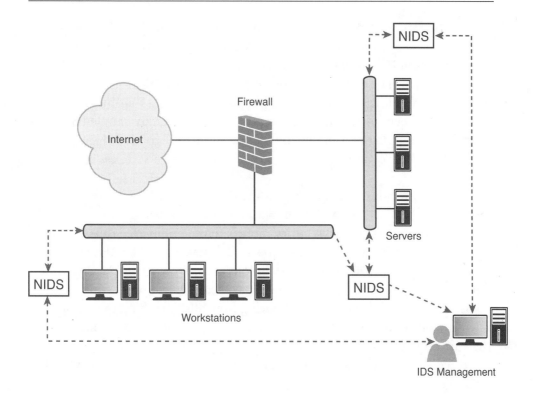

**Figure 1.7**  Distributed IDS sensor systems with centralized monitoring and updating facilities.

A secondary problem also arose. As the security teams became increasingly in charge of the network security components in the data centers, they also became the "data cops" or policy enforcers. That is to say that the application developers had to get permission from the security team to allow their application to talk to the external network. This placed the security team in a policy enforcement position, further dividing the software developers from the security folks, who were now often viewing each other as adversaries instead of colleagues.

Now, bear in mind that during this same period, significant changes were taking place in the software development world, at least in terms of the types of software that were being developed. The Web was thriving, and commerce was jumping onto the bandwagon in huge numbers, with the associated enormous pressures to deliver products. In a very real way, the now-infamous "dot-com boom" period fed this frenzy.

Developers were being pressed as never before to deliver their wares. Companies were using the Net in largely unexplored ways. And all of this was being built on software infrastructures that were mostly untested in the business world. The statelessness of the Web, for example, forced developers to write application components like session cookies that by all rights should have been infrastructure-level API calls. (Seemingly simple functionality like a shopping cart in which to store purchased goods before paying the "cashier," for example, become quite nontrivial in a stateless application world.)

So around about 1998, we argue, the die was cast. Most of the Internet infrastructure we use today was in place, or about to be, and the platforms, methods, technologies, and security models that e-commerce runs on were up and running. Between the pressures to deliver code "yesterday" and the focus on nothing but functionality, copious security errors inevitably were baked into applications and architectures. Meanwhile, on the enterprise security side, specialists were configuring firewalls, installing the latest intrusion detection systems, and trying to find time to integrate and check the various log files.

If we indeed are in a security mess, that—as we see it—is how we got here.

In many ways, the situation is unchanged today from 1998. Yes, there are many new development platforms (C#, Ruby, Python) and network security services and appliances (data loss prevention utilities, spam blockers, security agents), but it's our thesis that the table was set when the crafts diverged. Add in the *cultural* separation between the developers and the enterprise security teams, and the question we should be asking is why there aren't more security flaws in today's apps and networks.

Further, we should add that, if the previous scenario sounds eerily familiar with regard to mobile application development today, we share your concern. Indeed, we see entire communities of developers and companies discovering (for themselves) many of the same problems we've witnessed here. We are seeing many of the software security mistakes of the past coming right back to haunt us in new yet familiar (to some) ways. Why on earth should these come as a surprise to today's software developers?

## The Status Quo: A Great Divide

In today's enterprise data center environments, there is a strong commitment to security, but not always where you'd expect or hope for it to be.

In many production environments, firewalls are considered mandatory, along with IDS and (to a lesser degree) Intrusion Prevention Systems, or IPSs. The good news is that today's firewalls are almost always configured using a positive enforcement approach, meaning that anything that is not explicitly allowed is forbidden, at least when it comes to ingress rules. (Of course, we all know that despite firewall filtering, a great deal of badness flow into our networks via email attachments, connections initiated by internal clients, and countless other means.) Firewall and IDS/IPS monitoring has matured and grown substantially, and is now largely considered to be a well-understood business system.

All of this sounds pretty good, at least on the surface. The dark secret that isn't being addressed here is that the security systems are entirely the domain of the information security team, and generally have little or no direct contact with the enterprise application realm.

There are exceptions to that generalization, as one might expect. Perhaps most notably, enterprise software applications generally do have event logging (often called "auditing") capabilities for logging security-relevant events. So enterprise applications do have at least a little bit of visibility into the security monitoring systems.

In some data environments, this connection between the application-level event logging and the security team is actually quite robust in some senses. Most data center environments, for example, have a standardized event-logging architecture that application software is required to conform to.

It's also worthwhile to note other enterprise-level security services that are commonly found. Centralized antivirus, anti-malware, software firewall, and similar systems are frequently run in the data centers. Similarly, centralized or even federated authentication services including role-based access control, single sign-on, and other security infrastructure components are increasing in popularity. Even public key infrastructure (PKI) services are more commonly found today than just a few years ago, especially for providing single domain server-to-server authentication services.

In other words, security managers have found no shortage of products to spend their security budgets on for many years. That's a good thing, right? Well, not so fast.

A major problem, as we see it, is the significant separation that still exists between the software developers and the security teams. Why is this a problem? Isn't there a healthy "checks and balances" separation that ought to be present?

Here's the issue. By separating these two groups so thoroughly, we're missing out on useful and valuable collaborative benefits. We'll examine some significant examples of this below, but for now, suffice it to say we've been watching the security folks slowly approach—but not quite touch—the applications themselves, in ever-decreasing radii for years.

We corralled the applications into isolated network segments, even giving them names like demilitarized zones (DMZs) and such. We placed instrumentation around the applications themselves in the form of network-based IDSs. We even encroached on "their" turf by trying (largely without success) at putting host-based IDSs on their server platforms. But we have largely left the developers to themselves to do their work.

But they want to be left alone? Perhaps they do, but perhaps not. The problem with this approach is that we've enabled a world of software applications that are fraught with security flaws, many of which we've known about for years.

How can that be the case? Well, the problems are numerous. Let's explore a few of them.

- **Functional specification**

  First and foremost, software developers are trained—incentivized even—to focus on functional specifications of their products. That is to say that they put most of their energy into what a piece of software is intended to do. Security flaws, on the other hand, typically fall into nonfunctional aspects of the software. Software can be absolutely compliant with functional specifications and yet have egregious and trivially exploitable security defects, such as SQL injection implementation bugs in web applications or broken trust model design flaws in the Europay MasterCard Visa (EMV) payment cards used throughout much of the world. This focus on functional specifications is important, but it needs to be greatly broadened to include ensuring that nonfunctional "features" are not possible in software. It's also useful to point out that some development methodologies don't use functional specifications per se, but rather such things as use cases and user stories. No matter what we call them, though, failing to consider what an application should not be able to do leaves room for many bad things to happen.

- **Learn from history**

  Outsiders could easily look at the software industry and think they're incapable of learning from past mistakes. After all, there is no shortage of examples of software security defects today that were first discovered and understood a decade or more ago. At times, it appears as though Santayana's ghost haunts us: Those who fail to learn from history are condemned to repeat it.

- **Lack of knowledge**

  It's a generalization, but we've found it to be all too often the case that software developers lack the knowledge of security issues—vulnerabilities and their associated attacks—whereas security staff members tend to lack a clear understanding of how software really works. This is extremely unfortunate because, as we'll see in detail in this book, there is a natural and indeed vital collaboration that ought to exist between these two groups. Their respective lack of understanding of the other's issues is a major barrier to effective collaboration, and we need to do better.

- **Overly trusting**

  Perhaps it is a result of focusing on functional specifications, but software developers often place trust in things that are not in any way worthy of trust. They trust such things as users, software frameworks, and system libraries without necessarily understanding the ramifications of that trust. The recent OpenSSL "Heartbleed" vulnerability is an example of this kind of trust failure resulting in widespread system security defects.

  The following three problems (complexity, connectivity, and extensibility) are commonly referred to as the Trinity of Trouble.[31]

- **Complexity**

  It's almost never the case these days that an application "system" consists of a single server and a number of client systems that connect to it. Those days are gone. Today's systems far more often consist of a series of servers, each delivering a specific service or set of services, to make up a whole. Many times, these servers and their services span multiple organizational and geographic boundaries. Web applications are often "mashups" of dozens or more individual components. This complexity drives many things, including security, which can often lead to security failures. For one thing, cross-boundary assumptions that prove false are all but inevitable in these sorts of complex scenarios.

- **Connectivity**

  In addition to growing increasingly more complex, today's applications are increasingly connected to disparate components. What's more, many of these components might not share many—if any—of the same security assumptions. Imagine, for example, an online financial system that enables its customers to make stock trades, research stocks, etc. Its servers may well connect via service-oriented architectures (SOA) to systems that simply provide up-to-the-moment stock ticker pricing data on a read-only basis. The security assumptions, sensitivities, and issues between just those two systems alone could be enormously different. Connecting these different security domains into a single application—from the end user's perspective, at least— is quite likely to result in security defects such as vulnerabilities to data injection attacks like SQL injection and cross-site scripting. The transitive trust problems associated with complexity and connectivity often make for an end system that is far too complicated for any single person to thoroughly understand, from both a functionality and a security standpoint.

- **Extensibility**

  Computer application owners, whether at a small or large level, are seldom content with "good enough." We all want to be able to add features, tweak features, remove features, and so on. We want our systems to be extensible to suit our needs. From a very real security perspective, that extensibility fights against us. If it's not implemented securely, we can be allowing dangerous or malicious software into our systems. A recent example of a system extensibility failure happened when Target stores had their credit card payment systems breached due to extensible point of sale (POS) systems getting infected with malware.

- **Antiquated paradigms**

  In security, we often speak of a "castle and moat paradigm" to define an enterprise's perceived security perimeter. This metaphor might be useful for helping people conceptualize a security boundary between the inside world and the outside world, or trusted and untrusted, respectively. On the other hand, the massively distributed nature of today's computing environment creates so many virtual holes in the security perimeter that the stone wall of the metaphorical castle is misleading in the extreme. Any organization that considers its security perimeter to be a solid wall of any sort today is at the very least fooling itself, and more than likely it is downright negligent to entertain that notion.

- **Inadequate security testing**

  Far too many software development organizations we see today do almost nothing in the way of security testing their products. When we do find security testing being done, often it is nothing more than a cursory penetration test done just before the product is shipped, or else merely focused on testing functionality and not nonfunctionality. What far too seldom happens is the sort of rigorous security testing we've come to understand is possible in the software security community.[32] Among other things, a serious security testing program should realistically take into account the abilities of one's attackers. Today's adversaries are often resourced and highly capable.

These are just a few of the things that we have to understand about the current situation in order to figure out how we can fix things and move forward. That's not all there is, though, by any stretch. Even when software security is respectably well executed, we're missing out on opportunities to do better—way better. What's more, in many respects, we're not talking about things that are hugely difficult to do.

As an example, although we've spent a lot of time understanding such things as user identification, authentication, and, to a lesser degree, authorization, that's pretty much where things have stopped. An identified, authenticated, and authorized user of an application is generally allowed to do anything and everything the application is capable of (within the bounds of the data and functions he is authorized to access, at least). What's the big deal?

Imagine an authorized user of a credit card processing system that is co-opted into working with organized crime to steal customer data. The authorized user could log in and extract customer names, credit card numbers, and so on out of the system. In many of today's applications, that authorized user would go about his criminal activity completely unfettered. What's more, the firewall and IDS combinations we described earlier would provide almost no value at all in this scenario. What should we be doing better?

In our experience, we've asked many software developers how they would handle a situation such as the one described here. In nearly every case, the developers' solution set would consist of "logging" the transactions and essentially passing that problem off to someone else—namely, the security team. The security folks would thus have the task of monitoring the activity and making security policy enforcement decisions after the fact. This approach is simply not sufficient for today's business environment. The security team members are not experts in the application's business domain. They are "IT guys." What basis would they have to know that reviewing 200 credit reports in a day as shown in the audit logs is odd? Traditionally they wouldn't. But if the application team worked hand in glove with the security team across the full life cycle, together they could identify activity thresholds, verify application logging integration, configure log reviewers, and have action plans upon threshold alerts. An "oops" is a failure by both teams.

There is a significant opportunity, particularly for enterprise application software, to build security mechanisms directly in the software that could detect, observe, and even curtail this type of criminal activity in many cases. We'll explore this topic at length later.

## What's Wrong with This Picture?

The vast majority of the common attacks against today's software can be addressed substantially with just a relatively small number of security fixes.

There are many papers, web sites, and even books that delve deeply into the different attacks that often work against today's software. It is certainly not our aim to duplicate any of those here, but we do want to take more than a simplistic view at the most common attacks found today. As a reasonable starting point, we've chosen the OWASP Top-10 (2013) list of vulnerabilities maintained by the Open Web Application Security Project (OWASP) (see www.owasp.org). Although the OWASP Top-10 is by definition a list of common defects in web applications, many of the issues are conceptually relevant to other software technologies as well.

Also, we should note that the OWASP list is a list of *vulnerabilities*, while we're discussing their associated *attacks* here.

- **A1: Injection bugs**

  Injection flaws are a general category of application defects that enable an attacker to introduce malicious data into an application that in turn is sent to an interpreted service, such as a SQL database query, an XML store query, or an operating system command interpreter. The malicious data is carefully constructed so that it changes the intent of the call to the interpreted service.

  The classic injection flaw on web applications is an SQL injection. Using SQL injection, an attacker can change the meaning of an SQL database query and even inject arbitrary SQL commands to the database on behalf of the web application's middleware code.

  If unchecked, injection flaws can enable an attacker to execute any arbitrarily chosen input that can run on the target interpreted environment. That can range from data leakage from an SQL database through running privileged command-line programs on a targeted server operating system. The damage potential here is essentially unbounded.

- **A2: Broken authentication and session management**

  A security cornerstone of any application is how it identifies and authenticates its users. As such, authentication mechanisms are popular targets among attackers. Authentication subsystem defects are likely to be discovered in short order.

  A closely related topic for web applications is session management. Since strong authentication and session management are not provided by the Web itself, the developer is forced to do these functions from the ground up. (Most application development frameworks do provide the fundamental underpinnings of authentication and session management, but it is still up to the application developer to make proper use of these primitive constructs.)

As with any technology that is an afterthought, many mistakes have been made in authentication and session management. Exposing a user's authentication credentials in a plain-text (not encrypted) context, for example, can quickly allow an attacker to compromise the user's account and steal information or money, or attack other high-value targets. Predictable session identifiers can also enable an attacker to hijack another user's active session, giving the attacker unauthorized privileges and data access.

- **A3: Cross-site scripting (XSS)**

This attack occurs when an attacker is able to dupe a web application into transporting maliciously formed data to an end victim using a web browser. The data is in the form of a client-side script, entered in standard HTML format. XSS attacks can take one of two primary forms: a stored XSS attack or a reflected XSS attack. Both are dangerous in their own right and for different reasons, but the underlying concept is the same.

A stored XSS attack can take place when the attacker has the ability to enter data on a web site, and then that data later gets replayed into an unsuspecting user's browser. The time between the data being stored and the data being replayed can be anything from a few moments to years. Thus, stored XSS attacks have been likened to digital mine fields. A reflected XSS attack, on the other hand, takes place when the malicious script gets played back instantly into a victim's browser. Of course, the attacker's goal isn't to immediately send a script to his own browser, but to get the script into a victim's browser. Thus, reflected XSS attacks are normally combined with alternative delivery mechanisms, such as email messages containing image requests that in turn generate requests to vulnerable URLs. Both forms of XSS attacks are highly effective mechanisms for an attacker to run a script in a victim's browser. A good question to ask about XSS is how much damage can be done with a client-side script.

- **A4: Insecure direct object reference**

Often, web applications contain references to actual objects—filenames, account numbers, customer IDs—that can be easily attacked via client-side manipulation. Since any data coming from the client side is under the control of the user, any data references are subject to tampering, even if they are hidden from the direct view of the user, such as in hidden HTML parameters and cookies.

Thus, any data that refers to an actual object can be altered, and if the data is left unchecked, the attacker can trick the application into referring to a data element other than what the developer intended.

This attack has often been used to trick web applications into divulging data out of victims' accounts, reading unintended files on server-side operating systems, and so on.

- **A5: Security misconfiguration**

At a simplistic level, a security misconfiguration can result in any error in configuring the functional or security aspects of a system—usually a server. This can include failing to set a folder to be read-only and allowing an attacker to make unauthorized changes, for example.

Attacks against such misconfigurations are rampant, and trivially automated; most vulnerability scanners include tests for every well-publicized security flaw, many of which fall into this category of security misconfigurations.

Things start to get a bit more difficult when we include all of an application's components into what we consider to be a server configuration issue. For example, application frameworks, dynamic libraries, and such are generally declared and included with software by the developers at build time.

However, when new framework releases come out—at times due to security updates—those frameworks almost never get timely updates in application software, because that would involve complete rebuilds of the application(s), along with testing and such. Further, those rebuilds would be done by developers, not by data center operations staff. In our experience, that sort of update is exceedingly rare to find in production data operations environments. Nonetheless, even framework-derived application flaws of this sort would fall into the category of a server misconfiguration.

- **A6: Sensitive data exposure**

Whether at rest or in transit, many web applications expose sensitive data to unauthorized access. The types of data include credit cards, tax IDs, Social Security numbers (or other country-level citizen identification data), and authentication/session credentials. Attackers are then able to steal or modify the data to conduct identity theft, financial fraud, and other crimes. Because these data are so sensitive, extra care must be taken to adequately protect them.

- **A7: Missing function-level access control**

  Far too many web applications do little (if anything) beyond an application's presentation layer access control to limit who can access the application's various functions. When the access control is not built into each and every (sensitive) function, attackers can often circumvent the presentation layer access control and invoke functionality that they should not be able to.

- **A8: Cross-site request forgery**

  Although cross-site request forgery (CSRF) might sound similar to cross-site scripting, there are significant differences in how attacks unfold. CSRF vulnerabilities occur, for example, when a web browser receives an image request (e.g., IMG SRC or IFRAME) containing a URL pointing to a site where the user/victim has active authentication credentials. The browser then sends the user's authentication credentials to the referenced site.

  If this image request points to a sensitive site and function, such as a funds transfer page on an online bank where the user is logged in at the time of the attack, the request would appear completely normal to the online bank and the transaction would likely succeed.

  CSRF vulnerabilities are fairly new, but the potential for substantial monetary or privacy compromises is significant. CSRF-laden URLs are trivially embedded on web sites, especially when combined with XSS mechanisms for storing the attacks, as well as spam email messages.

- **A9: Using components with known vulnerabilities**

  All too often, applications are not built (or maintained) with current versions of their various components, including frameworks, libraries, and server software. When otherwise known vulnerabilities creep into an application due to these bad practices, attackers are able to exploit those vulnerabilities and gain various types of access to an application or its data. Further, when these defects involve frameworks and libraries, it is generally the case that the data center operations and/or IT security organizations will not do the updates, because they are considered to be software issues with the applications themselves.

- **A10: Unvalidated redirects and forwards**

  It is commonplace for applications to use redirects and forwards to send their users to other pages (often within the same application domain) for various and sundry reasons. However, failing to validate the address to which a user is being directed can result in users being sent to sites that contain malicious data that can cause harm to the user's computing environment.

So this brief overview of OWASP's most common software security defects is an interesting starting point in understanding application-level problems. It is by no means exhaustive, on the other hand, and it includes only web applications specifically. Still, an examination of the list can raise some interesting insights.

With the arguable exceptions of A8 and A9, every one of the OWASP Top-10 list involves the attacker generating input that results in the application behaving inappropriately. There is a clear message in this fact: Input validation (in the broadest sense) is essential. Input should be validated by both the client application and the server side. Although this might seem redundant, there should be no assumption that the server is being called by a known client. Client-side validation can promote usability and avoid wasting a valid user's time waiting for a server reply from a request with invalid data. The server side must independently validate input as well. This is especially important as more web services are made available to clients other than their originally indented clients. The increased use of "Xyz as a service" and promotion of service reuse across organizations make this vital as well. Adopting a mind-set of defensive coding becomes a critical thing for software developers to learn.

## Wait, It Gets Worse

In the preceding pages, we have tried to show what we believe to be the current insecure predicament of most networks and the applications that run on them. Broadly speaking, security practitioners are divided into two camps (IT security and software security) that don't communicate with each other. The resulting gulf is responsible for many of the security flaws we experience today. It is our contention that the entire model is starting to break down. In fact, it might utterly collapse as movement to the cloud environment continues to fling data and indeed executable code to be run in client contexts out from behind the firewall, new and powerful mobile devices provide increased access to data and systems, and empowered users test system vulnerabilities (whether intentionally or not).

Yes, we see positive trends, and we see improvements in coding technique sand enterprise security practices and appliances; but we think our current way of doing business is heading us over the cliff (see Figure 1.8).

**Figure 1.8**   Where our current way of doing business is taking us.

That is, things can and will get worse if our security practices do not adapt to meet the realities of today's and tomorrow's computing environment. Here is a short list of emerging security-related phenomena. Keeping in mind the history and issues we have covered in this chapter, we hope that a glance at them will suggest to you that there is both trouble and opportunity ahead.

- Cloud and SaaS (Software as a Service)
- Mobile apps and identity management
- Polymorphic malware
- Breakdown of the signature-based approach
- Unified threat model
- Virtualization

- Intelligent agents
- Neural networks

We think that in each case, the new issues raised by these concepts can be ameliorated or even completely addressed by appropriate confluence between developers and enterprise security practitioners. Since the aim of this book is to provide comprehensive practical advice to both camps, and hoping that we have made a good initial case, we will shift gears now to a nuts-and-bolts discussion of some secure application development methodologies we admire.

## Stressing the Positive

It is quite clear from what we've presented thus far in this chapter that we information technologists have made many mistakes in building up the Internet as we know it today. But our intent with this book isn't to dwell on the negative; rather, what we aim to do is to provide some prescriptive and actionable guidance for our readers in the hope that we can collectively dig ourselves out of the hole we're in today.

So let's turn our focus here to the positive.

One of the ways we're going to provide prescriptive guidance is by way of a single fictional and hypothetical story thread that is going to span pretty much the entire book. Our aim is to present this as a sort of a case study, by taking an "insider's view" of a fictional development team and the issues the team members face as they tackle the topics covered in this book.

### Story Background

Our story here involves a small team of software developers who have quite suddenly been thrust into the big leagues, and have a world of learning to do, without the luxury of time.

Our developers, you see, have been successful at building a brand for themselves by way of a small series of mobile apps they've written for Android and Apple iOS devices. Their apps have become quite popular in a relatively small niche field: the medical field.

They launched a small company a year or so ago, and have together written a couple of medical apps that help consumers track their own medical care. The apps do things like log symptoms, record visits to physicians, list prescription drug information (side effects, doses, prescription refills), and so on. In fact, their apps have caught on so well that their little company has suddenly had to wrestle with the stresses and responsibilities of its own success.

Their little software company, which we'll refer to here as Sherman Tank Medical Apps (Scherr-Mantis), LLC, finished its first year of business with a revenue stream that many larger companies would envy—and it is run entirely out of the team members' homes.

But, with a fierce entrepreneurial spirit, our team has decided they want to exploit their own success and grow their little company into a big company—and hopefully get rich along the way. They have already finished the earliest stages of planning their next big thing: a medical app targeted at healthcare providers. They want to build an app that physicians would use in their daily rounds visiting their patients. In this grand vision, physicians would carry around tablet computers and use them to make notes on each patient's progress, prescription changes, and so on.

However, writing a small-scale consumer app is worlds different than writing something that physicians would use with their patients. So, to their credit, our team has decided to court a large investment into their company so that they can team up with some of the "big boys" in the medical world. They envision that the big players would have the necessary connections and such to get their new app out into the professional healthcare sector.

Our team is filled, as you might expect, with all the hubris of youth, combined with a nearly complete lack of experience in industry. Nonetheless, they aren't easily discouraged, and they gleefully start seeking out investors. Fortunately, their track record is adequate to get them the audiences they seek—and perhaps some they hadn't anticipated.

In the early stages of their investment hunting, they find themselves getting noticed by one of the largest medical service companies in existence: Peabody Medical, Inc. The mergers and acquisitions arm of Peabody noticed our team a few months ago, and has actively courted them to consider not an investment, but an acquisition. They lure our team to allow themselves to be acquired by Peabody and get all the corporate support they'll need in order to underwrite their new app and get it out into the vast array of hospitals and such that Peabody currently counts among their client portfolio.

Our abundantly confident team of young developers at Scherr-Mantis is thus thrown into a massive, multibillion-dollar enterprise, where they'll be developing the next great thing for their new employers at Peabody Medical, Inc. They couldn't be happier, or so it would appear at first.

Throughout the book, we'll be following along with their progress and "experiencing" vicariously all the successes, failures, and eye-opening experiences they will encounter.

## The Board Room

It's a late-night board meeting at Peabody Medical, Inc. Contracts have been signed; hands have been shaken; champagne has now been uncorked. The acquisition deal has been sealed; Scherr-Mantis, LLC, is now officially part of Peabody Medical. Our enthusiastic team of young yet naïve Scherr-Mantis developers have seen their dreams come true, or so they think. They are now officially part of the biggest medical software developers in the world.

Among the principal reasons for acquiring Scherr-Mantis is that the Peabody team has been chomping at the bit to get their hands on the "Wandering Medic" (WM) mobile software the Scherr-Mantis team has built. In a few short months, WM has exploded onto the scene and has grabbed a massive market share among medical professionals. The dual iOS/Android app has revolutionized the medical world, with hospitals and patients alike clamoring for more.

At the time of the acquisition, the SM team is immersed in the development of the major 2.0 release of their app, and they are convinced it is going to solidify them as the market leaders. Although Peabody's mobile presence has been at best horrific, they do command a formidable acquisition "war chest," which helped them grab Scherr-Mantis before all the other big players in the space.

Nonetheless, due to the hurried pace that the acquisition demanded, the due-diligence team wasn't able to dive into things at a level of detail they wanted to.

As their exuberance and smiles reach a crescendo, the Chief Technology Officer at Peabody mentions to the (now former) Scherr-Mantis CEO how excited he is to have them among the Peabody team. He tells the CEO, "We need to dive right into your apps and do some security design and code reviews as quickly as possible so that you can see firsthand how we manage our product security cycles here at Peabody."

What the Peabody CTO doesn't know, but is about to learn, is that the Scherr-Mantis team has succeeded to date not by following rigorous processes and procedures, but by the sheer determination and passion of the small development team. Their software and security practices are the epitome of "ad hoc" if ever there was such a thing.

By contrast, what the Scherr-Mantis team is about to learn is that their utter lack of security oversight and process is about to run into its most staunch of foes: the big enterprise. Their "everybody go deep" coding style has served them well for a long time, but no longer. It's not the Peabody way of doing things, and they're about to face the biggest culture shock of their lives. This, despite the fact that the Scherr-Mantis team passionately believes that one of their biggest strengths lies in the very informality of their software development methods.

But not tonight. Tonight is a night for celebration and planning what model Ferrari to buy tomorrow. Tomorrow will take care of itself.

## Summing Up

From the beginnings of the Internet to fresh new mobile apps: What a long strange trip it has been, indeed. But what matters is what we do *now.*

The streams of application development and information security have diverged, even as some of us were watching. Your authors believe that *confluence* is the way the "critical systems" of modern society—communications, transportation, finance, emergency response, for a few—will be made safe and reliable by the community to which our readers belong.

How to start?

We help you kick off your first "confluent" application in Chapter 2, "Project Inception."

> *Sometimes the light's all shining on me*
> *Other times I can barely see*
> *Lately it occurs to me*
> *what a long strange trip it's been*[33]

# Endnotes

1. Internet Crime Complaint Center, "2012 Internet Crime Report," 2012.

2. Ibid.

3. Barry M. Leiner et al., "Brief History of the Internet," The Internet Society, 2011.

4. We're aware that this chronology has a decidedly U.S.-oriented slant. Partly that's because your authors experienced this era in that country, and partly it's because the United States was (in our opinion) a true leader in information and network security in the 1980s. Of course, parallel but slightly later developments were taking place in Europe.

5. J. H. Salzer and M. D. Schroeder, "The Protection of Information in Computer Systems," Proceedings of the IEEE, 63-9, 1975.

6. James P. Anderson, *Computer Security Threat Modeling and Surveillance* (Washington, PA: James P. Anderson Co., 1980), www.securityfocus.com/infocus/1514.

7. National Computer Security Center, Department of Defense Trusted Computer System Evaluation Criteria, Orange Book, DOD 520.28-std, December 1985.

8. In the early days, *network* security primarily came in the form of access control lists ("ACLs") on routers. Most routers can be configured to allow or not allow network traffic based on its source and destination addresses, and the service and protocol being requested. Router ACLs—in effect the earliest network firewalls, although that term wasn't yet used—proved to be inadequate for stopping serious network attacks. Routers could not be trusted to make substantial security decisions, in part because of their inherent statelessness.

9. Dorothy Denning, "An Intrusion Detection Model," Proceedings of the Seventh IEEE Symposium on Security and Privacy, May 1986: 119-131.

10. For information about Haystack see, for example, Rebecca Gurley Bace, *Intrusion Detection* (Indianapolis: Macmillan Technical Publishing, 2000), ISBN: 1-57870-185-6, page 16. For a good contemporary description of DIDS, see S. R. Snapp, S. E. Smaha, T. Grance, and D. M. Teal, "The DIDS (Distributed Intrusion Detection System) Prototype," USENIX, Summer 1992 Technical Conference, San Antonio, USA, June 1992, Berkey, USENIX Association, 227-233.

11. Doug Sheppard, "Beginner's Introduction to Perl," October 16, 2000, retrieved on October 27, 2013, from www.perl.com/pub/2000/10/begperl1.html.

12. Carolyn Duffy Marsan, "Morris Worm Turns 20. Look What It's Done," Network World, October 20, 2008, retrieved on October 27, 2013, from www.networkworld.com/news/2008/103008-morris-worm.html.

13. Clifford Stoll, *The Cuckoo's Egg* (Pocket Publishing, 1990), ISBN: 0-67172-688-9.

14. The best overall discussion of this explosion of federally sponsored security research in this period is probably Rebecca Bace. The systems we are talking about (late 1980s, early 1990s) are discussed on pages 14-24 in her book *Intrusion Detection*.

15. ISOA (Information Security Officer's Assistant) was from Planning Research Corp. of Mclean, Virginia. Clyde Vax Audit was by Clyde Audit. Stalker came from Haystack Laboratories; CMDS (Computer Misuse Detection System), from SAIC (Science Applications International Corporation); and NetRanger, from WheelGroup.

16. "Marcus J. Ranum," retrieved on October 27, 2013, from www.ranum.com/.

17. Tim Berners-Lee with Mark Fischetti, foreword by Michael L. Dertouzos, *Weaving the Web: The Original Design and Ultimate Destiny of the World Wide Web by Its Inventor* (HarperInformation, 2000).

18. Bill Cheswick, "An Evening with Berferd in Which a Cracker Is Lured, Endured, and Studied," 1992, AT&T Bell Laboratories, retrieved on January 2, 2009, from www.cerias. purdue.edu/apps/reports_and_papers/views/1007.

19. "Marcus J. Ranum," retrieved on October 27, 2013, from www.ranum.com/.

20. About NCSA Mosaic, retrieved on October 27, 2013, from www.ncsa.illinois.edu/ Projects/mosaic.html.

21. Barry M. Leiner et al., "Brief History of the Internet," The Internet Society, 2011.

22. The "eight core contributors" of the Apache group were Brian Behlendorf, Roy T. Fielding, Rob Hartill, David Robinson, Cliff Skolnick, Randy Terbrush, Robert S. Thau, and Andrew Wilson. See http://httpd.apache.org/ABOUT_APACHE.html.

23. HTML version 2, a product of the new MIT/W3C Network Working Group, was specified in RFC 1866; see, for example, ftp://ftp.rfc-editor.org/in-notes/rfc1866.txt, retrieved on January 3, 2009. For a good overview of these early events in Web programming, see Roger Clarke's "The Birth of Web Commerce," version 21 of October 2002, Department of Computer Science, Australian National University, www.anu.edu.au/people/Roger.Clarke/II/ WCBirth.html, also retrieved on January 3, 2009.

24. A good short history of Java, from Sun's point of view, is given at http://java.sun.com/ features/1998/05/birthday.html. And yes, we know that the history of Java "open source" licensing is tangled, and we're not going to try to untangle it. The first releases were "free."

25. David Bank, "The Java Saga," *Wired*, Issue 3.12, December 1995, www.wired.com/ wired/archive/3.12/java.saga.html, retrieved on January 3, 2009.

26. Rebecca Bace, *Intrusion Detection*, Chapter 6 (Sams Publishing, 2000).

27. Gary McGraw and Edward Felton, *Java Security: Hostile Applets, Holes, and Antidotes* (New York: John Wiley & Sons, 1996).

28. Gordon "Fyodor" Lyon, *Nmap Network Scanning: The Official Nmap Project Guide to Network Discovery and Security Scanning* (Insecure, 2009).

29. See the SNORT FAQ on the Documents section of the SNORT home page at http://www.snort.org.

30. "Tenable Network Security," retrieved on October 27, 2013, from www.tenable.com/ nessus-15/.

31. Gary McGraw, "Software Security: The Trinity of Trouble," blog post February 26, 2006, https://freedom-to-tinker.com/blog/gem/software-security-trinity-trouble/, retrieved on October 27, 2013.

32. Your authors credit the Microsoft Security Development Lifecycle ("SDL") as bringing the possibility of secure development as a matter of disciplined process into broad acceptance in the community of application coders.

33. From "Truckin'," by the Grateful Dead. Words by Robert Hunter.

# 2 Project Inception

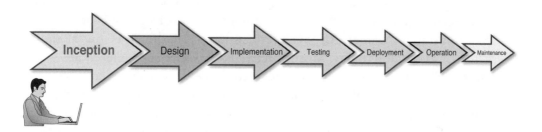

What phase of a project plays the largest role in its eventual success or failure? Various answers to this question are defensible, but we think the pivotal moment often occurs early on.

Take a look at this list of the six phases of an engineering project, as one of us first learned them decades ago (source unknown):

1. Enthusiasm
2. Disillusionment
3. Panic
4. Search for the guilty
5. Punishment of the innocent
6. Praise and honors for the nonparticipants

Your authors have participated in each of these phases, sometimes voluntarily; and it is our conviction that it is most often at the time of *project inception* that innocence, guilt, and praise are determined. Bad decisions at this point can doom a project.

How can you get SSG projects off to a proper, "confluent" start? We recommend forming a project security team. Do it right away—before, for example, drafting a requirements analysis. (The project security team should do that.)

It is common in today's enterprises to have a Software Security Group (SSG), made up of full-time staff whose job it is to assist software development teams with their security tasks.[1] This is in stark contrast to most IT security organizations whose job it is to set policies, review projects' security, and such—essentially review-based functions. The review-based processes inevitably result in adversarial relationships between developers and security teams. The end users might also be involved and be a third relationship to balance. An SSG, on the other hand, should be on the same "team" as the developers. Most effective SSGs we've encountered are staffed with people with significant software development experience.

But irrespective of how your organization addresses (or names) this need, the project security team should be made up of key stakeholders who represent the business and technology needs of the organization. We justify the use of an SSG here and talk more about the makeup of the team in Chapter 9, "The View from the Center."

To make the case for this kind of security team, we will first sketch the way we think most development projects proceed today. Getting specific about the project team we propose, we'll then describe what it should do, talk about what types of participants you should recruit, and discuss how each can contribute throughout the life of the project. We will address a few practical issues, such as budgeting for the team and the seemingly inevitable internal politics, and then finish by addressing specific project inception challenges for small businesses or individual developers.

We are aware, of course, that many of our readers already employ mixed project review teams as part of a mature application development model. If that's your case, we applaud you—and invite you to read on to see our version, derived from our "confluence" theme.

## Without a Formal Software Security Process— The Norm Today

The most common product development scenario observed by the authors at numerous software shops does very little to facilitate collaboration between product development and enterprise security.

In most large companies we have worked with, for example, the product development organization operates largely independent from the corporate Information Technology (IT) and Information Security (IS) folks. Developers own and control the creation of applications, from the gathering of requirements straight through to release. They then hand off the app to the network technologists, who operate and defend the deployment environment (see Figure 2.1).

**Figure 2.1** Working in silos with handoff.

This rigid separation often causes misunderstanding and animosity between development teams and the IT and IS practitioners. It's our analysis that this tension stems as much from a lack of awareness of each other's activities and expectations as it does from a clash of missions. It is often exacerbated, we observe, by differences between the two groups in focus, education, and even worldview. (Security practitioners are paid to worry, after all, to defend an often-nebulous status quo, and to better the unknown future state—all the while advocating for more resources to do the job properly; developers are generally encouraged to focus on concrete milestones and project deliverables.)

## The Development Team View Today

We're not suggesting that the modern corporate programmer works in isolation. Yet from the point of view of the enterprise security personnel, it can appear that way. Let's take a look at a common development scenario.

For the development team in most large enterprises, the requirements-gathering process involves significant interaction with representatives from various stakeholder groups, including business owners, end users, and finance officers. A series of interviews (and spirited discussions of priority and cost) will lead to a set of requirements for the product specifications.

Collected in this manner, requirements will reflect both business logic (e.g., selling a book) and nonfunctional needs (think performance, downtime, and external integrations) of the interview participants. Will security requirements be automatically taken into consideration, or even made a priority? Well, we can say that we have seen it happen; but, generally, business owners care about business processes and operate as if those processes can be considered distinctly from security issues. They often—perhaps rightfully so—assume that security concerns will be "handled" by the security folks. But when security is discussed in terms of business risk language, it becomes apparent that it should be "handled" by the business owners as well.

However, if those esteemed colleagues are not included in the pool of stakeholders (and, as a result, are excluded from the requirements-gathering phase), how likely is it that security concerns will receive expert attention at project inception? Backfilling security enforcement points into an application becomes more and more expensive as the application continues down the software development life cycle.

Does that mean that security issues will never be addressed? No, not exactly. We have seen, as you probably have, many new applications "thrown over the fence" for deployment with no advance warning to enterprise security. Not so much these days, though; a decade of disaster headlines (and red-faced CEO press conferences) has had an effect. What we are stressing here is the need for corporate security involvement in gathering requirements, and even before: at every step and (stretch to achieve this) at every interview. Security is not a product, and cannot be added after the fact!

If you are part of the development world, the sense of this might elude you. Suppose you care a lot about security, and show it by taking the time to interview those experts available to you. What are you going to hear?

The focus of the security folks is likely to be protecting the company's infrastructure from external or internal threats, so their attention will be drawn to the effect your new application will have on the security of the company's infrastructure as a whole. Their requirements, then, will be mostly aimed at achieving or maintaining compliance with applicable security policies. (They might even, after hearing what you want to do, draft up some new ones! Remember, they are there to help.)

Requirements from security, added in separately, will likely differ substantially from the ones collected from other departments. They will tend to place significant restrictions on what the product can do and how it can operate. When security restrictions are formulated in isolation from (even if in parallel with) the definition of requirements from the business units, the opportunity for conflict is heightened. (Hey, is this why you avoid them?)

The real fun starts when the product leaves the development department door and is handed over to the IT department for deployment into a production environment. We should note that deployment might well be done in cooperation with various organizational entities, which could include IT security, business owners, and so on. Either way, this is where the idealized "skunk works" world of product specifications and development meets the harsh reality of a secured operational environment. And many times, this change of environment turns up new issues. Some features might be coded with incorrect assumptions ("What, are you saying I can't have root privileges?"). Others might not have been not tested under real-world security environments ("Why would anybody need to turn on that Security Manager, anyway?"). All in all, it's uncommon for this "write it here, run it there" approach *not* to lead to broken or improperly functioning features in secured environments.

Even after the development team addresses initial bug reports or other complaints from the security side of the shop, the software, if developed in a security vacuum, will likely still be far from security-compliant. Lack of security awareness in the software development and support teams frequently results in incomplete fixes.

It is not uncommon in a "second pass," for instance, to see a buffer overflow bug closed by checking only for an overly long specific string "*AAA...AAA*" specified by the security reviewer, but not for a similarly long random string (say, "*bbb...bbb*"). We have also seen developers who are earnestly trying to close a security hole fail to make changes in an identical code branch only ten lines apart.

Is your company one of those places where security gets a first-look predeployment review? Where the developers then take a whack at a fix, and then resubmit it to the security types? The resulting back and forth is likely to be highly frustrating for both security operations and development teams, as what are essentially the same issues appear over and over again and the product goes through multiple iterations until either it reaches an acceptable condition or the developers run out of time, money, or patience. (This situation leads to the reputation of many security staffs for saying no. Adopting a proactive stance allows members of the security team to enable business processes and instead say, "Yes, you can do that, and we will help you do it securely!")

## The Security Operations Team View Today

The situation on the security side of the house is equally frustrating. More often than not, still today, security operations folks do not get to see the software or provide any input until it has been released and handed over for deployment. How can it then interface into existing security infrastructure, such as identity management, authorization, logging/auditing, networks, security zones.... At that point, making any substantial changes is either impossible (technically, financially, or politically) or rife with difficulties. Instead of baked-in security mechanisms, which substantially reduce the natural emergence in complex systems of security vulnerabilities, the inevitable design shortcomings must be addressed through environmental controls, retrofits, and other compromises.

Product specifications developed without representation from Information Technology (IT) and/or Information Security (IS) departments tend to have similar weaknesses. Often, they do not distinguish clearly between configuration and runtime modes, lumping all activities and data into one continuous set. Code used for development and testing purposes has been left in for "application support convenience." They can require user names (and even passwords) to be embedded in the software, and rely on encryption keys that are stored in plain text in easily accessible files on the same server the app runs on. Just as often, inadequate attention to file access issues results in excessive runtime permissions being required granted for the database and for application users, or unneeded data and accounts left in the product configuration.

If you hand off an application with these attributes, already set in stone, to security people, the version they hand back will include various hacks, tricks, and retrofits, such as network partitioning, firewalls, operating system access control, and so on.[2] All these will be the security team's best attempt to jam a loose lid onto the mass of steaming vulnerabilities endemic to the app—at least, those that can be anticipated. (They might not tell the developers that, but we know what they are thinking; see Figure 2.2.)

The timing of the review, though, is not the only problem. Even if the software product is developed in-house, and its development team is within reach of the IT folks (at least theoretically), *and* the security teams are brought in before deployment, they often are not provided sufficient information and documentation about its design and operation.

**Figure 2.2** Jamming a loose lid on steaming vulnerabilities.

*Any* separate security review, whether it takes place before or during design—or, even worse, when the app is poised for deployment—is unlikely to yield a successfully deep analysis in which the security staff would dream up doomsday scenarios, even if good, up-to-date documentation is provided. Why? It's often a matter of comprehension. As we have previously noted, in the shops we deal with today, most members of IT security departments have operational backgrounds, and little experience in programming at all. This fact, coupled with the usual absence of a representative from the development department in the reviews, means there is no one in the room to explain at a detailed level what the various elements of the application are actually trying to do, and how they interact to do it. This lack of technical information presents a steep barrier to an analysis of risks and possible remediation.

Worse still, IT departments often allocate only one day—perhaps two days—for separate security reviews in their planning, providing neither sufficient time nor resources for any substantial risk analysis efforts. We see this schedule all too often, even for important engagements.

As a result of all of these factors, architectural reviews and conclusions by IT security teams are frequently based exclusively on lessons gleaned from network assessments by automated scanners and studying user and installation guides. Such an approach can identify, for example, open ports. They might uncover many or most obvious bugs, such as buffer overflows. (Wait, does the security team have access to *all* the source code? Really?) Some design flaws, as well, may be unearthed (implicit trust relationships, perhaps, or opportunities for man-in-the-middle attacks). Realistically, however, many non-obvious security issues, especially of the architectural nature (race conditions that create opportunities for file substitution or credential spoofing, for example) will be missed during such assessments— whether for software development or COTS integration projects.

### The Common Result Today

The outcome, too often, is a shallow approach to providing security-related fixes consisting of only the things that the security team can control. Reliance on environmental remedies (perimeter protection, whether by the network or by an individual machine's operating system) often results in avoiding development of proper fixes for security issues. We have seen shops, for example, respond to a security issue by adapting the network infrastructure to facilitate quicker patching (!) rather than paying for costly root cause analysis (a problem-solving method to identify the source of problems) and reimplementation.

Relying on shallow analysis and layered-on-afterward solutions means that your shop will inevitably deploy and preserve software in a security-deficient state. Such faulty products, like a hidden unexploded shell under the thin layer of infrastructural sand, represent a continuous risk to the enterprise, its customers, and its stockholders (if any) for years to come.

Remember, your software will be attacked by villains "from the future," even if it runs for only a decade. The bad guys will have techniques, processing power, and tools for finding weaknesses that are far advanced from what you can test with today. If the security of your applications is important to you, go for help.

## Out-of-Control Layered Security

Over the years, we have seen many applications fall prey to this kind of layered and superficial security. Here's a scenario that seems all too familiar:

- A customer-facing application is developed under contract, and then deployed onto a DMZ network.
- Months go by and a new attack method is disclosed on various Internet groups.
- During a periodic network security scan, the customer-facing application is determined to be susceptible to the latest attack method.

- The contractors who originally built the application are no longer available, and their replacements want a fortune to retool the application "from the ground up."
- Rather than paying this high price, the company running the application decides to deploy a web application firewall that will specifically detect and block this new form of attack.
- The web application firewall (WAF) can be deployed in either of two configurations: (1) It learns the application's behavior on every screen/page, including all data input and so on. In this mode, every input field is positively validated by the WAF, and anything not validated is considered unsafe. (2) The WAF is deployed more like a web application IDS—meaning, it looks for signatures of known web application attacks. The second option is cheaper and easier to deploy, but it is not as rigorous and is limited to the attack signatures it knows about.
- The new WAF is deployed in the second mode, and its signature of attacks is added to the ever-growing list of things the IT security team must maintain.
- Months again go by, and a new attack is again discovered. Only this time, the WAF fails to detect it, so the application again fails a security scan.
- The company's new CISO decides to deploy an additional IDS to detect this new category of attack, since the WAF vendor wasn't quick enough to respond to the latest threat.
- Now, both the WAF and the IDS need to be maintained by the IT security team, but they are from different vendors and have substantially different tools and processes for performing updates.
- Next, the company decides to deploy a security information event management (SIEM) product so that these multiple security products can be managed and maintained via a single "dashboard" view.
- And so on.... The end result is that a hugely complex security network of heterogeneous products are all watching over a single legacy application that has little chance of receiving updates. Meanwhile, the cost of properly maintaining the application itself is likely to be less than the various security products deployed, and the resulting application patches could actually fix the problem(s) instead of merely detecting that they're being exploited.

## The Case for a Project Security Team

Our basic argument for a project security team is that a formal process that takes a systems risk management approach will help to close the gap between product development teams and enterprise security practitioners. Further, including all relevant stakeholders early in the process means that developers, business unit principals, and security operations staff members can work together to design systems that simultaneously address key functional and operational requirements and allow for comprehensive "baked in" security mechanisms. The result will be fewer vulnerabilities in the software and in the workflow.

Key stakeholders from the enterprise security groups (including the incident response team) can provide attack profiles, threat models, and enterprise stance weaknesses, as well as analyze key assets and critical systems. End users will often provide vital insight (whether or not they realize it) on operational vulnerabilities. But to get the full benefit of the "flowing together" of these security insights, every element of the potpourri must be mixed in at the beginning.

In general, security policies, created and maintained by the security operations people, have minimal effect on people in development and do not translate into security coding guides or testing plans. It is rare that, without additional outside motivation, developers would think while coding (or, better, during design time) about how to avoid a buffer overflow; Quality Assurance (QA) engineers would include negative testing for cross-site request forgery (CSRF) into their test plans; or product management would willingly spend scarce development resources on creation of an intelligent fuzzing tool to test the robustness of network-exposed interfaces and custom protocols. Prophylactic activities such as these are often perceived by development and testing staff as obstacles to the successful product release, and ignored whenever possible.

Members of these organizations, able and well trained in modern software development techniques as they might be, can hardly be expected to find their way to sophisticated or even apt and elegant security solutions without a helping hand. The solution we advocate promotes the cross-communication your applications need for a decent chance at real-world security.

# Tasks for the Project Security Team

Exactly what does the security team do? We'll outline here the key facets of the project that the security team should review. We should note too that the BSIMM study details many tasks that would be relevant for a project security team to tackle. Most tasks will benefit from the mix of minds we've been advocating, though there are a few that are best left in the hands of specialists. We'll point these out as we come to them; and when we do, think about who in your organization has the right skills to execute them.

## General Scope Review

The team will have to tackle a few general questions about the scope of the project before getting too deep into security issues as such. The answers will affect how you define security requirements for the project a little later. Here are a few of those questions.

### 1. What Are the Primary Business Goals of the System?

It is rare for *security* to be the primary goal of the system; it's usually secondary at best, ensuring that the primary business goals are met, even when the system is under attack.

The main point might be to sell books, or to track shipments, or to generate financial reports. In the case of the Wandering Medic app, the business is enabling users to manage their healthcare records through their mobile device. Knowing this helps us understand what events would be considered attacks. You need to know what you are trying to prevent and how it can be observed in the first place.

It also helps the team make trade-offs. If you can relate every security decision in the project to a business goal, it's easier for the team to make good trade-offs. Security features are more compelling—and less likely to be squeezed out at crunch time—if you can explain how they support the primary business goals of the application.

### 2. Where in the Maintenance Life Cycle Is the Project?

Not all development projects start with a clean slate. When you are just beginning, it is important to get a clear understanding of what in the project is open to change, and what is relatively immutable. This can also help you understand what kinds of project risks you should be concerned about, and guide security trade-offs throughout the project. When budgets and/or deadlines slip, security is often the first to be compromised.

Here's a set of quick tips for the team to keep in mind, depending on the life cycle stage of the project (see Figure 2.3). We provide much more detailed advice in the chapters that follow, which, we remind you, cover the topics of design, implementation, testing, deployment and integration, operations, maintenance, and regulatory concerns and other constraints.

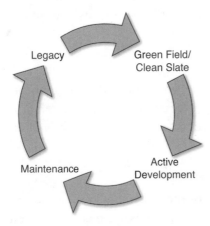

**Figure 2.3**  The maintenance life cycle.

### Greenfield/Clean Slate

This is a brand-new system; you have no code and have a very fluid architecture. No other systems depend on it (because it is new). You are free to make architectural changes and refactor mercilessly. You have the opportunity to include security considerations from the very beginning, in all parts of the design. Life is sweet!

In many ways, this is an ideal situation from a security point of view. You have the opportunity to design in a good security model from the beginning. But you also should be aware that large changes to the system that might affect the security model might come later. A flexible structure is key.

### Active Development

You have a working implementation running in production, but are still making significant changes. You have a well-defined architecture, and external systems are beginning to depend on it. You are still writing new code, adding new features, and integrating with new systems. Making changes at the code level to improve security is possible, but changing the architecture would be costly and risky and would have to be considered carefully.

If users have been included in the development process, adjustments at this stage are made even more difficult. Because they are focused on business rather than system goals, do not necessarily understand the technical issues, and are often impatient with the pace of development, even the most well-intentioned users can be frustrated with complexity and slow progress. Keep them informed.

### Maintenance

The system is stable in production and is not under active development, but you still occasionally go in to fix bugs or security issues. Making major changes to the architecture occurs only at major revisions and is typically out of the question, and all code changes carry a serious risk of regression—especially if you don't have good testing or code control.

### Legacy

Legacy systems can be very difficult to change. The designers have often moved on to other jobs, and you might not even have the source code any more. Deep changes to the system are impractical; most changes you apply at this point are bandages designed to keep the system running until it can be replaced. However, you might still be able to address security issues by retrofitting some defensive measure into the mix—putting a web application firewall (WAF) in front of it, say, or changing the way it's configured.

### *3. What External Constraints or Regulatory Regimes Might Apply?*

It is becoming rare today to find an application that does not need to operate under some set of constraints (see Figure 2.4) in addition to the main business requirement. Your project security team needs to be aware of such restrictions on the first day it begins its work.

**Figures 2.4**　Sample logos from external/regulatory agencies.

For example, the U.S. Federal Trade Commission (FTC) protects consumer transactions and promotes fair and open competition. Your application might need to conform to the Payment Card Industry (PCI) standard, which relates to purchases involving credit cards, debit cards, and other similar mobile transaction instruments. If your shop performs work as a contractor for the United States federal government, your systems might need to conform to the Federal Information Security Management Act (FISMA), and in the European Union, you will need to follow guidelines established by the European Union Agency for Network and Information Security (ENISA).

Publicly held companies are subject to their own set of regulations, which vary, of course, from country to country. In the United States, such an enterprise probably reports periodically to the Securities and Exchange Commission (SEC), and your security team will probably need to take into account the Sarbanes-Oxley Act of 2002.

In addition to these and other external restrictions, your application will of course need to conform to the security policies unique to your business.

Although the authors cannot provide you with legal advice concerning what regulations you must follow or how specifically to adhere to them, we can and do urge you to find someone who can, and add that person to your security project team right away.

Whatever the result of these deliberations, document your answers. Even if you don't have a large team or an external reviewer, clearly documenting initial assumptions (and, for that matter, your threat model—set of possible attacks) can help you find issues yourself. Even if you never read the documents again, the act of producing them can help clarify your thinking and allow others to review.

We've made a start here on the general scope of the project as it relates to information security. It's time to get more specific.

## Security Requirements Review

Most systems will have a few explicit security requirements, typically covering things like authentication, authorization, input validation, or securing communications. These requirements are often driven by organization-wide security policies, and in a large organization, they might not differ much between applications. An internal security specialist might be more familiar with these policies and be in a better position to apply them to your project than developers or business requirements analysts. The specialist might also be able help you identify and seamlessly integrate commercial security packages (authentication libraries, say) that have been licensed enterprise-wide, perhaps even mandated (unknown to you) for your use.

Explicit security requirements are not the only way that security goals interact with requirements analysis. Sometimes, the basic functional requirements of the system involve behavior with security implications, even when they aren't describing traditional security features like encryption or authentication.

For example, a purchase-ordering system might have a particular business process that has to be followed. If a user had knowledge of those business processes, he could "game" the system by manipulating data. For example, the Wandering Medic (WM) app might provide free shipping on prescription refills of more than a 120-day supply, but the app fails to check for changes in the supply amount after shipping costs have been calculated. Changing an order after the review process has begun would result in a violation of the policy, and should be treated as a security breach.

Finding ways that the system can be misused through its own functionality requires a different mind-set—thinking about what the system is *not* supposed to do. It can be helpful to have a security specialist review the functional requirements of the system to try to identify such potential misuses, and make sure that the system's requirements state what should or shouldn't be allowed. This can be particularly helpful to security testers down the line; it might not be obvious to them what results within the system would be considered attacks if the requirements don't specify this or how important it is.

**Security Architecture Review**

The overall architecture of the system must also be reviewed with an eye to security. The degree of review required probably depends on the size and type of the project. A maintenance project that doesn't include any architectural changes might not need an architectural review, whereas an integration project connecting disparate systems together almost certainly does. The architectural review ideally should include architects other than the people who originally designed the system, because the originators might make the same assumptions (even "mistakes") during the review as they did during the original design, and miss security issues as a result. Some mistakes could be subtle, and others could have inadvertently come about because of technology evolution or deployment decisions.

Although system designers must be prepared to make key administrative decisions early in the development process, it is improbable that all design elements can be addressed at the project inception. We typically use a bootstrapping approach whereby the identification and resolution of simpler processes early on will lay the foundation for increasingly complex decisions later in the project life cycle.

**Code Review**

Most projects would also benefit from a comprehensive code review. Given the limitation of time and resources for code reviews, they often focus on three areas: user input, component interface, and basic assumptions in the system design. Using an automated tool, such as Fortify's SCA or IBM's AppScan Source Edition, can help identify common security problems before the code reaches testing, or goes into production. On some teams, there might be a developer with experience using static analysis tools, and it can be valuable to have someone on the team who knows both the code and the security tools well. In larger organizations, there might be a security team that specializes in using these tools and knows how to tune them effectively to your code.

Security-sensitive parts of the implementation, such as authentication and authorization checks, or encryption, should at minimum be reviewed by a security expert with experience with the particular application programming interface (API) that will be used. These parts of the code are often particularly sensitive; a small mistake here can compromise the security of the entire system. And they are also difficult to get right. Depending on the complexity of these parts of the system, it might even be beneficial to get help from someone on the security team to help build these parts of the code. And whenever possible, it's best to reuse a well-reviewed and tested implementation, rather than writing your own. (When it comes to encryption algorithms, especially, we really mean it: Don't try this at home. We don't.)

## Security Testing

*Security* testing requires skills that most *functional* testers do not have. Whereas functional testers focus on making sure the system does all the things the software is supposed to do from a business standpoint, the job of a security tester is to verify that the software does not also do additional things that it is *not* supposed to do—even through misuse or abuse of the software. Developers and functional testers alike all have assumptions on how the system is supposed to be used. We can hear the voices of developers saying, "The end user would never enter 'blah blah blah.'" "True," says the security tester, "but an attacker might!" Security testers use detailed knowledge of languages used in the system's implementation, such as SQL or JavaScript, which functional testers don't normally need to know. They also tend to try to access the system from outside of its usual user interface, such as accessing hidden parameters or URLs (universal resource locators) in a web application, or through intercepting or modifying network traffic. Testing such matters requires detailed knowledge and special tools.

## Deployment and Operations Planning

Most systems are deployed, administered, and monitored by a different team than the one that builds them. When designing a new system, we should think about how it will be configured and deployed in practice—and who will be doing that. It is not enough to design a system that merely can be deployed securely; we also need to make sure that it actually will be deployed securely, and this requires that the development team and the deployment/administration team are thinking about the system the same way. If these teams are not in communication, it is quite possible that the security features that the development team thinks are a great idea might turn out to be a nuisance to the system administrators or the end users. As a result, these features might some day be disabled in a misplaced effort to enhance usability. We have firsthand evidence of customer support people "helping" customers by telling them how to turn off warning messages and bypass security checkpoints. For example, many application developers and deployment teams argue for the firewall to be set to "ANY ANY ANY" so that they do not have to think about the interfaces, or diagnose why something is failing.

To avoid this problem, make sure that representatives of both the development team and the administration team take part in deployment planning. A representative of the end-user group must be involved too. The developers need to know when the security features they are designing are not a good match to the way the system is actually administered in practice, and likewise the administration team needs to understand the purpose and operation of the system's security features if they are to take full advantage of them. (We suggest that this planning be done at the design stage. Hearing that there are "requirements" for 10 different user roles, only to have the administrators use 3 at deployment time because it is "too hard" to manage all 10, is painful and costly for everyone.)

## Putting Together the Project Security Team

The project security team should include a representative from each of the stakeholder groups (see Figure 2.5).

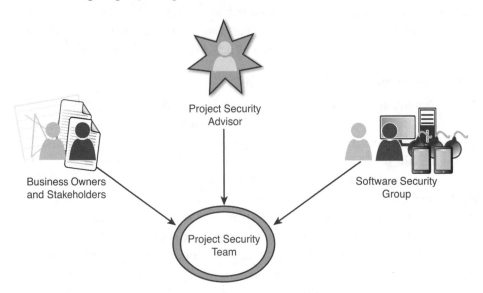

**Figure 2.5**  The project security team.

Even in a small shop, the different perspectives of the groups are vital to avoiding gaps and system vulnerabilities. Do the best you can, even if that is a peer review in which Alice reviews Bob's work, and vice versa.

Of course, given the list of stakeholders, not every member of the team will be a security specialist. Truth is, if they were it's quite possible that no business functionality would ever get written or deployed! A group of security specialists might focus too much on potential attacks and not enough on the primary business goals of the system.[3]

The primary focus of most people on the team will not be security, but something else. It might be testing, configuration management, requirements gathering, coding, or usability. The majority of the security analysis will be provided by a team member that specializes in it, or by an external security advisor. But that does not mean that security is solely the job of the security analyst.

It might be tempting for team members to assume that they can just focus on implementing the features the business asked for, and leave security to the security team. But really, today, is that the way we handle any other key aspect of the system? We don't say that preventing bugs from getting into production is the testing team's job, and therefore developers don't need to worry about avoiding bugs. Instead, every team member has some role in preventing bugs: Requirements analysts strive to prevent bugs by writing clear and unambiguous specifications; architects try to avoid bugs by breaking the system into self-contained, implementable modules with simple interfaces; and developers avoid bugs by writing readable and testable code and maintaining unit tests.

Likewise, although a security advisor might specialize in finding security issues, all team members have an important role in securing the system. It is not something that can be relegated to a third party or done as an afterthought. Security is not a product. Whether it's database design, algorithmic selection, or security solutions, a mix of informed and engaged minds produces the best result when a complex system is being built. Remember: The defender must get it right every time, but the attacker needs to get lucky only once!

## Roles to Cover on the Security Team

We will describe now the roles and responsibilities we see as essential to a successful project security team. We suggest, as you read through, that you try to identify a person (or persons) in your organization to fill each role. (We know that, in smaller organizations, the team members might have to double or triple up to get all the functions covered.)

### The Project Security Advisor

Each project should have a security advisor[4]—sometimes known as the security architect. This person, an experienced security professional, is indispensable, serving as the first point of contact for security issues and questions throughout the project. The advisor provides a virtual checklist, suggests methods and techniques, and helps the team follow the security process for each project, varying methods according to the level of risk.

For example, if the security team wants to know what kind of security testing would be appropriate at various stages of the application's development and deployment, the advisor will work this out and explain. The same individual (it's best for most purposes if the same person acts as advisor throughout) will later be engaged in reviewing the design of the project, as well as giving pointers and suggestions at other stages.

This is not necessarily a full-time job; each adviser might have multiple projects ongoing at one time.

### Software Security Group (SSG)

Another key source of technical expertise in information security, if your enterprise has one, is the Software Security Group—sometimes known as the security operations team. This group, external to the project but internal to the company, should be engaged with the project security team on its first day and, in some capacity, throughout the life of the application.

The role of the SSG is to provide guidance to the team specific to the company's security policies, usages, resources, and even licenses. Which tool should you use to check for buffer overflow, or other implementation-time bugs? Is there an existing, approved API for user authentication? If the app will be running internally and needs a certificate authority, what is available, and how should you make use of it? These are the sorts of technical questions your local SSG should be engaged to answer.

### Identifying the Stakeholders

When we think of the stakeholders of a system, you usually think first of the end users, and perhaps the business owner. After all, these are the people you are building the system for in the first place—and they are generally the people who decide whether the project is a success or a failure.

But there are many other people in the enterprise who will interact with or be affected by the software, both directly and indirectly (see Figure 2.6). In many cases, the way that they interact with the system will have security implications. As we have said often now, key stakeholders from across the enterprise—from the IT security group, to the developers, to the business owners and the end users—must all be engaged, right at the beginning of the process and on to the end. Identifying these individual stakeholders of the security implementation process helps to ensure that all perspectives are incorporated at project inception.

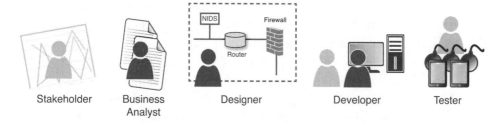

Stakeholder   Business   Designer   Developer   Tester
              Analyst

**Figure 2.6**  Stakeholders.

The following sections highlight these stakeholder groups—who they are, their typical background, and why they are important. As we go along, we will, in some cases, take time to explore how the particular group interfaces with the team, and also to sketch possible challenges and how to overcome them.

### Senior Executives

- *Who are they?* Although leaders are not always directly involved with the daily activities of the project, identifying a champion is invaluable to the success of the project. The leader of your security initiative should be a high-placed executive. Depending on the structure and size of the organization, the executive can be located anywhere in the C-suite, including the Chief Information Officer (CIO), Chief Security Officer (CSO), Chief Information Security Officer (CISO), Chief Technical Officer (CTO), Chief Operating Officer (COO), Chief Marketing Officer (CMO), Chief Human Capital Officer (CHCO), and the Chief Risk Management Officer (CRO).

- *What is their typical background?* They have significant knowledge and experience in their role (e.g., security, finance) and often have great insight regarding the enterprise and the external operational environment.

- *Why are they important?* Every project needs a champion, and *all* projects are security projects. The right senior-level champion can ensure that sufficient resources are available for the project and manage operational processes. Perhaps most important, the senior executive can insulate the security operation from political barriers, providing both cover and ammunition when necessary.

- *Possible challenges and how to overcome them.* Senior executives are busy running their part of the enterprise. It can be difficult to get their attention. And although they thoroughly understand their area (e.g., finance), it can also be difficult to "educate" them on security issues—this is true even when they are convinced of the importance of security, and that is not a given! Your possible champion is driven by his or her bottom line. So link the impact of insecurity to their primary concern—brand image for the CMO, product sales for the CFO, workforce recruitment and retention for the CHCO—you get the idea.

### Project Managers

- *Who are they?* Project managers are involved with the daily project operations. They are the point person and have eyes on all aspects of the project. They coordinate personnel, resources, and operational processes.

- *What is their typical background?* The level of knowledge your project manager might have about security will vary, as will their knowledge of the business. If you are lucky, the project manager will have knowledge (at least at a basic level) of both. And if you can afford it, you will want a certified project manager (e.g., a certified Project Management Professional, or PMP) or at least an individual with significant knowledge and experience managing projects of a similar size and scope.

- *Why are they important?* With so many moving parts, especially when you are pulling together people and resources from across the enterprise, you need to identify one person who is responsible for the ultimate project outcome—one person to go to the champion when resources are needed, one person to take the heat when deadlines are missed, one person to share the glory when the project is successful!

- *Possible challenges and how to overcome them.* Project managers will encounter resistance—overt and covert efforts to sabotage the project. As a result, your project manager should be politically astute and able to work with various personalities. They also should have "thick skin." Resistance is often not personal, but it sure can feel like it sometimes.

### Administrative Users

- *Who are they?* Administrative users are those employees who have special use privileges. These users often access the system using different administrative interfaces than the end users do, often with a higher level of privilege to control and monitor system use. For example, they might be responsible for managing user accounts and roles in the system, setting and implementing policies for how the system will operate, or configuring data for end users (e.g., prices and product descriptions). Database administrators, human resource and accounts payable managers, and office administrators exemplify roles in this category.

- *What is their typical background?* Users in this category typically have in-depth education and knowledge in their area of expertise—finance, human resources, database administration—and probably some level of sensitivity for system security. You cannot, however, count on their having an in-depth understanding of security vulnerabilities. These users want to get the job done and will push for system security measures to fit in with their operational needs, not the other way around.

- *Why are they important?* These users tend to be highly trusted, and have access to files and systems most others do not. We do not normally think of them as threats (and it can often be hard to convince the organization that they might be). However, because the functionality they have access to is sensitive, and its corruption, compromise, or unavailability could have important business consequences, administrative user errors (whether intentional or by mistake) can be costly—and could leave the system in a vulnerable state.

- *Possible challenges and how to overcome them.* Administrative users are highly respected and often quite powerful within the organization.

They can be formidable adversaries to the security project (all in the name of business, of course!), so it is critical to get them onboard with your project early. As with the senior executives, you want to illustrate how security impacts their bottom line.

### End Users

- *Who are they?* In some cases, the end users are the business users, but here we are specifically highlighting downstream users who are not necessarily employees of the organization—customers, business partners, guest users, and, in some cases, attackers. Not all end users have good intent.

- *What is their typical background?* They don't have one. End users are inherently eclectic.

- *Why are they important?* Your users operate day in and day out on the front line of security. More than any other group, they are often the target of security attacks—whether social engineering through a phone call, say, or a phishing email. In addition, and with certainty, some segment of your end users will try to exploit vulnerabilities (known or newly discovered) to their advantage. As a group, they thus represent both the weakest link in your multiple layered defenses, and the front line of your defense.

- *Possible challenges and how to overcome them.* First, end users are usually focused on the job they have to do—the purpose of your software. They typically do not consider or really understand the potential security risks (immediate exposure or down-the-line impact) of what they do (setting a file for universal access, for example). So accidents will happen. Second, if your security measures put up too many barriers to their task, you run the risk of their instituting a workaround that puts the system in a worse security position than it would be without the measures you put in place. You must always keep in mind the usability of every defense you adopt. Third, not all end users have good intent. Some will try to exploit your software for personal gain. Others will work toward causing greater harm. To overcome these challenges, work hard to enlist their aid, provide instruction on proper use, issue security updates as vulnerabilities are identified, and expect the unexpected.

## Help Desk and End-User Support Staff

- *Who are they?* Help desk staff interact directly with end users to help diagnose and resolve problems on their behalf. Large applications might have dedicated call centers, with large teams and with special software to help script and manage calls. For smaller systems (especially internal ones), it might be much less formal; the support staff might even be the developers.

- *What is their typical background?* The background of users in this category will vary widely depending on the size of the organization. In small shops, developers might double as support staff for the end users. In this case, the staff members will likely have a highly technical background. In large organizations with large call center operations, help desk personnel might or might not be college educated, and on-the-job-training might be the primary mechanism for developing staff knowledge.

- *Why are they important?* Like administrative users, these users typically have a higher level of privilege, and use the system through special interfaces. They might have the ability to view (or correct, or cancel) end-user transactions—and possibly even issue refunds to customers (or criminal cohorts!). When troubleshooting, they might have the ability to impersonate end users in order to diagnose problems with their profiles. They might have scripts or troubleshooting guides to follow—which effectively become part of the system itself, in the case that they encode important security decisions (such as what form of identification is acceptable before a password can be reset).

- *Possible challenges and how to overcome them.* In some cases, particularly for large call centers, support staff might be less trusted than other business users. These jobs might be outsourced to other companies, possibly even to other countries (which might bring in different data protection requirements, and regulatory issues). Because these staff interact directly with end users, often near-anonymously over the phone or Internet chat, they can unwittingly become pawns in social engineering attacks. They might even become attackers; it might be very tempting to collude with an end user to issue an unwarranted refund, for example, or to access customer credit card data through the call center interface. A well-designed system should take these risks into account, through policy enforcement, through logging, or by limiting access to sensitive data on a need-to-know basis.

### Network and System Administrators

- *Who are they?* The title says it all.
- *What is their typical background?* The techies.
- *Why are they important?* Although we don't often think of system administrators as "users" of the system, they have a critical role in maintaining a secure system. There are often special interfaces built specifically for them, though we don't always think of them as such; installation scripts, configuration files, and log messages together form the user interface that these administrators use. Unfortunately, because we don't think of them as interfaces, software for the tech types often isn't consciously "designed" at all. So critical questions that should be openly debated and collectively decided on often are just decided by whoever writes a script or piece of glueware. As an example: Does the installation script leave the system in a secure configuration by default, or are there extra (undocumented) steps the administrator must take, such as changing default passwords? "Design" questions like these document assumptions and dependencies and are frequently decided in a vacuum; and as suggested earlier, the absence of overt decisions about any of these questions leaves room for unintentional design gaps and security vulnerabilities.
- *Possible challenges and how to overcome them.* With special access comes increased risk, and the possession of top operating system privileges opens the door to abuses that other users could never carry off. A significant burden of the application's security architecture and design is to defend the system against those who operate it.

### Security Operations Staff

- *Who are they?* The security operations team monitors the system and responds to security events. In some organizations they also operate the security infrastructure such as firewalls, IDS, and WAFs. In smaller organizations, this might be the system administrator, who might also be the developer. But in larger enterprises, this is often a separate formal team that might answer to the Chief Information Security Officer (CISO) rather than the business owner of any given application.

- *What is their typical background?* They might have little to no knowledge of the applications themselves or their business purpose, and instead largely view their job as putting out fires.

- *Why are they important?* They might be in charge of operating firewalls, monitoring log messages, or responding to alerts issued by applications. Although they might be able to observe traffic to and from the system at the network level, they might not know how to interpret it; for example, they might see a stream of HTTP requests to the application, but without knowing the business context, they might not know what operations those requests actually perform, or what policies might be violated by them. If an attack occurs, they might need to respond quickly, perhaps by updating a firewall rule, by suspending user accounts, or in extreme cases by shutting down the system.

  So, when designing a system with security operations in mind, we should ask: Does the application give them enough information (through logs or alerts) to determine when the system is under attack? (The application might provide them with the raw data, but they still need to know how to interpret those measurements—i.e., what the thresholds for action are.) Do they have appropriate response options, and can they tell when to use which ones? It would be a shame to shut down the entire system for something that isn't even an attack, wouldn't it?

- *Possible challenges and how to overcome them.* The challenges here are similar to those for the network and system administrators.[5] The risks here could be even higher, though, since these people often have the keys to the entire corporate perimeter and the audit infrastructure. If there are any individuals in your enterprise who could compromise all or almost all of your intellectual property and protections in a single day, they are probably in this group. Conversely, if you propose to protect information and systems, you had better engage their assistance and make sure they know what you are relying on them to do.

*Legal Counsel or Privacy Office*

- *Who are they?* In almost every company we have worked with, there is a legal counsel onboard, either on staff or on retainer. Many corporations today also have a Privacy Office.

- *What is their typical background?* These are attorneys. If given a choice, you probably want someone with experience in computer law and personal privacy issues. You might also need, depending on your application, help with copyright law or even a patent attorney.

- *Why are they important?* Based on our experience, we advise you to make good use of whomever your company can make available for legal counsel relating to security. Recruit them for the team. They can tell you—as we, your authors, surely cannot—whether the application under consideration is legal to build in the first place. They will likely have advice about the sorts of data you can collect and store, how that is to be done, and under what circumstances and in what manner you can destroy data. (We could be talking about credit cards or other private information from your customers, or what type of encryption is allowed in certain parts of the European market.) Are your algorithms patentable? If so, how do you preserve your rights? Are you infringing on someone else's patent or copyright? How would you find out, and what should you do after you know?

  There are any number of legal issues that could pertain to your application, and *you do not know what they are.* As we said about devising encryption algorithms, bring in a specialist for this. These areas of the law are changing rapidly, in both the civil and the criminal spheres, and infractions can be costly and can tie up the project; so consult the best, most up-to-date specialist available to you.

- *Possible challenges and how to overcome them.* The legal landscape is continuously evolving. Global activity presents an even greater challenge because your organization might encounter conflicting legal and regulatory directives. Your legal team needs to be able to keep pace with liability issues, privacy concerns, and intellectual property rights in all countries of operation. This can be a full-time job by itself. Encourage your legal team to participate with organizations that monitor new policy and legal decisions in country and around the globe.

### Financial and Regulatory Auditors

- *Who are they?* The system might be audited—either internally or externally—to determine whether it is functioning correctly, as well as (in a security audit) to determine whether a good security plan is in place and has been competently executed. Regulatory regimes, such as Sarbanes-Oxley, or contractual requirements, such as Payment Card Industry (PCI) standards, might apply to the system and might demand particular kinds of logging or auditing. So there could be internal audit teams, external audit teams, or both, depending on your organization's circumstances and the issues under audit.

- *What is their typical background?* Some enterprises, particularly those in the financial sector, are subject to external audits, so these would be conducted by specialists representing the auditing entity. Many shops also conduct internal audits, operated by employees of the company.

- *Why are they important?* There are many reasons to include auditors on the security project team. The best one, from our perspective: If your system flunks an audit, it could get taken offline until brought up to specification, so what you want is to avoid that surprise by building a system that is manifestly conformant to requirements. Particularly for financial systems, it is important to design the system in a way that makes it easy to audit; it can be hard to retrofit a system to do this later. Can we track which user performed a particular transaction, after the request has been relayed from the front-end web server, to a Remote Method Invocation (RMI) service, to a database which is then replicated to several other systems? Bringing the auditors in to help design the system—in whatever manner and to the extent such collaboration is allowed—makes great business sense.

- *Possible challenges and how to overcome them.* If you propose recruiting an auditor for the security team, be prepared for the objection that bringing in an outside inspector with the power (let's say) to shut you down is contrary to common sense. We see the issue as a policy question, and suggest you seek guidance from an executive sponsor on this question.

### Developers

- *Who are they?* The programmers.

- *What is their typical background?* Often, developers have a degree in computer science, although a significant proportion (we don't know the figure) are self-taught.

- *Why are they important?* They're the ones who make the apps.

- *Possible challenges and how to overcome them.* We have experienced two distinct challenges in working on security issues with developers. First, we sometimes have to find a way to spark their interest in security. This can be accomplished by management fiat, but we generally find that what works best is focusing on the concept of "security quality" as an attribute of a fully realized software system. The professional developers we know all care about quality. Second, we sometimes find it hard to get across what can go wrong—that is, just how clever and devious some attacks are. The best answer for this we have found is a series of hands-on demonstrations where the developer can actually watch the exploitation take place, down at a detailed level. No developer wants to be associated with developing a system that was just compromised and in the front-page news.

### Policy (Compliance) and Planning

- *Who are they?* The policy/compliance group includes the individuals who will write critical usage policies that govern end-user behavior for everything from remote access, to the physical security of computing devices. These individuals are responsible for planning security across all aspects of the computing environment—users, applications, processes, and hardware. Remember, though—no good attacker ever cared about the "acceptable use policy"!

- *What is their typical background?* We have seen individuals with a wide variety of backgrounds in this role, from degreed computer scientists to lawyers to technical managers to high-powered corporate executives. There's no pattern we have been able to discern.

- *Why are they important?* This broad range of responsibility for ensuring proper system use is vital to overall system security. Design and use go hand in hand. The best, most secure design is still vulnerable to user error; the policy people can save the day by creating good administrative controls. Partitioning your corporate network is a good defense against engineers breaking into the travel-expenses database with an SQL (Structured Query Language) attack; but don't you also want the malefactor to know that if he's detected trying, he'll be fired?

- *Possible challenges and how to overcome them.* Because policy people come from a wide variety of backgrounds, communicating with them on technical matters can be a challenge. Try to find out which approach works best for the individuals you are working with.

### System Testers

- *Who are they?* The system testers are usually corporate employees and they might be members of a Quality Assurance team.

- *What is their typical background?* Testers, like auditors, come from a wide variety of backgrounds. Some are programmers, others are the product of engineering training, and some have very limited technical experience.

- *Why are they important?* We usually think of testers as part of the project team, rather than as users. However, how we design the system can influence how easy it is to test, and this can have implications for the security posture of the resulting system as well. Testers who work from the user interface often don't see hidden interfaces the system might be exposing—for example, web services that are called AJAX-style by scripting in the browser. It can be helpful to include a representative from the testing team in design discussions to help identify parts of the system that have important security consequences that might be difficult to test, and to help the testers get a better picture of what sorts of security failures they should be looking for.

- *Possible challenges and how to overcome them.* Features intended to make the system more friendly to the end user can cause problems for the tester. For example, client-side input validation in JavaScript might mask the input validation code that exists on the server side, with the result that only the client-side input validation code gets tested effectively. But we could design the system to make it easier on the testers. For example, we could include a deployment option to disable client-side input validation, for the purpose of exposing the server-side input validation to testers (as long as we remember not to deploy it that way in production!).

# Some Final Practical Considerations about Project Security Teams

If, in making the case for project security teams, we have made it sound *easy* to successfully adopt the practice—well, sorry about that! We have seen the effort fail, too. Here is what we learned.

### Budgeting for Project Security Team Activities

Compared to most organizations we see today, if you allocate any budget at all for security review, you are ahead of the game. So our main advice is: Do that.

We are going to share some quick pointers with you on this subject, though. You should first try to get a rough idea of how demanding your application will be with regard to security. Is it more or less run-of-the-mill compared to other applications in your enterprise, and the ways they manipulate resources, store and manipulate information, and authenticate users? Are the assets to be manipulated by this application especially sensitive, or subject to special regulation or legal protection? Will the application rely on a shared infrastructure?

In the end, for budgeting purposes, the best way is probably to find an existing application that does something similar—if one such exists—and find out how much time they invested in security analysis. (Better yet, see whether you can find out how much time they *should* have spent.)

After you have a rough idea of how intense the security work will be, you can come up with the budgeting figure. The number will depend, of course, on whether you are using internal resources or hiring outside consultants, perhaps for some kind of specialized security testing of the prototype. (The strategy of bringing in an external consultant to help with security analysis, by the way, can be an especially good idea for small shops or individuals.)

If you do put money in the project budget for security work, be prepared to defend it. It is often the first pool to be absorbed to account for budget overruns in other areas. Also be prepared for complaints from management (or bystanders) about the security budget. This brings us to our second special topic, company politics and how they affect the security project team.

## Company Politics

If you are the first person to introduce the idea of a project security team into your enterprise, we want to warn you that you might well get resistance, both active and passive.

The most obvious objection to the team is the one we have previously mentioned: some variant of "How will you pay for it?" The best answer we can arm you with is the statistic that fixing a bug after the product has been released costs approximately 30 times as much as fixing it during development.[6]

Another thorny issue you should anticipate has to do with who sits on the project team. One problem we have seen is one in which internal politics mandates that each department must have a "representative" on the team, as if decisions will be made by majority rule. We deprecate this practice. Not only might it have the effect of granting a veto on security measures by the various departments, but the practice also will inevitably lend undue influence to each of the departments in attendance at a given meeting—in many cases, an influence unrelated to the impact on a given department of the potential security practice. Management by (veto) committee usually grinds to a halt with a lack of consensus. Keep to the real stakeholders and identify an overall leader who can break the deadlock when parties disagree.

Finally, we take note of the universal challenge of corporate committees: How do you make sure that the people on the team are the right sort, folks who have the motivation, knowledge, time, and energy to positively affect the outcome? What is to stop one or more departments from sending you some hapless loser to attend meetings? Your authors admit here that we do not know; so we suggest you raise this issue with someone you trust and respect in the enterprise. Get the best advice you can about how to recruit the right talent, and stick with it. Enlist the aid of any executive sponsors you have, and their commitment to quality. Ensuring you get the right individuals on the team is likely to be as important as any decision the team itself might make. Note: Good people are often in short supply, very busy, and in constant demand. So approach with an appeal to a specific expertise.

## The CTO's Launch Meeting

The acquisition parties are all long gone, and now it's time to get serious about business. Almost immediately after arriving at Peabody, the former Scherr-Mantis (SM) executives each got invited to brief the Peabody CTO on their Wandering Medic project and its current development status.

They diligently put together a fancy slide presentation for the CTO to describe the project. Expecting more smiles and hugs, they went into the CTO's conference room to deliver the briefing.

However, it didn't take long for both parties to realize just how big the chasm was that separated their ideals and practices. Although the CTO loved the app itself, he was appalled by just how lax the SM team was in their software approach. From his perspective, after all, the app has to handle hugely private patient data and such. How on earth could the SM team have such a cavalier attitude about their responsibilities to protect that data?

Among the big decisions they need to address is how the app will be deployed. The mobile component of the app is the easy part; that will reside on all the clients' mobile devices. The tougher consideration is on the server. They could, for example, decide to sell WM as a turnkey system in which their server component gets integrated into their clients' data centers, or they could provide the server component themselves in a Software as a Service (SaaS) model. Or they could do both, depending on the size and budget of each client. (For our purposes, we're going to assume they'll be primarily deploying the app's server side as an SaaS subscription service.)

On the other hand, the CTO was wise to recognize the value in the app and its market share—and the amount of money Peabody had spent acquiring them! To summarily demand they follow all the Peabody practices would likely break a good thing. And even if it didn't break a good thing, forcing the team to adopt Peabody's practices would doubtlessly delay the 2.0 release, which would be sure to make the Peabody Board extremely unhappy at the next Board meeting.

So then, how could they proceed with development in a way that would make both groups happy? More than likely, they'd have to choose the approach that angers both teams the least, because that seems more than inevitable at this point.

Time for some compromises.

As a first step, it was agreed that a project security team would be launched immediately, and it would be made up of a smaller (than normal) number of people. The team would include a few key stakeholders from Peabody as well as from the SM group. Two key roles were assigned during this process: (1) The security manager and (2) the security advisor.

The security manager is the person in charge of ensuring that all the security tasks they agree to do are done right, and the results are essentially "signed off." This person, they agreed, would be a representative from the SM development organization, and would first and foremost represent the business needs for this project.

The security advisor would be an internal asset who would provide security guidance to the security manager as well as the rest of the team. This person is essentially a security consultant, almost akin to a golf caddy. It was agreed that the security advisor would come from the Peabody's CTO organization.

Now, although the two companies had officially merged and were one organization, there was still a lot of "us" and "them" among the team. Therefore, some basic ground rules were set. Chief among those ground rules was that the discussions between the security manager and the security advisor would be considered to be confidential, similar to "attorney client" privileged discussions. The two individuals shook hands on this and agreed to meet at least weekly, one-on-one.

Beyond that, the security team's first task was to be agreeing on which security activities were absolutely essential to the project. They would jointly agree on which ones provided the most value, impacted schedule the least, and still protected the Peabody brand appropriately.

Our intrepid SM team left the meeting and went straight to their favorite after-hours meeting location: the local pub. They were all pretty aghast at the day's events. The former CEO pointed out the old joke: Cheap, Fast, Good—pick any two. It seemed that the Peabody executives were forcing them to pick all three.

## Summing Up

Kicking off the project with a complete set of good choices can be a ton of work, and we lament that with you; but *failing* to choose, in our world, is often the same as choosing to fail.[7]

An important part of a good plan, when dealing with a system as complex as modern business software, is to bring lucid and varied minds together as early in the project as possible (see Figure 2.7) so that a strong initial design can be devised. Security retrofitting might fix problems you know of, but adding new layers and information pathways inevitably produces new vulnerabilities. As Charles Perrow said in his book *Normal Accidents* (an analysis of disasters such as Three Mile Island and the Challenger shuttle explosion):

*As systems grow in size and in the number of diverse functions they serve, and are built to function in ever more hostile environments, increasing their ties to other systems, they experience more and more incomprehensible or unexpected interactions. They become more vulnerable to unavoidable system accidents.*[8]

**Figure 2.7**  Team choice.

We carry through this line of thinking in our next chapter, with a description of *confluent design*.

## Endnotes

1. Gary McGraw, "Software [In]security: You Really Need a Software Security Group," InformIT, accessed November 11, 2013, from www.informit.com/articles/article.aspx?p= 1434903.

2. Perhaps structural engineer and author Henry Petroski said it best: "Form follows failure, not function." Henry Petroski, The Evolution of Useful Things (New York: Vintage Books, 1994).

3. "You may take the most gallant sailor, the most intrepid airman, or the most audacious soldier, put them at a table together[md]what do you get? The sum of their fears." Sir Winston Churchill, *as recounted by Harold Macmillan in the latter's memoir, The Blast of War (London: Harper & Row, 1968), page 352.*

4. The concept of the security advisor is prominent in Microsoft's Secure Development Lifecycle, as well as BSIMM. (A good SDL reference concerning project inception is http://msdn. microsoft.com/en-us/library/windows/desktop/cc307412.aspx.)

5. It is an old story. "Sed quis custodiet ipso custodes?" asked the Roman poet Juvenal: "But who watches the watchman?" Juvenal, *Satires* (Satire VI, lines 347-8).

6. Over the years we have seen estimates for this factor range from an improvement of 100 times to "only" (and, oddly, precisely) 6.5 times. For a detailed analysis of the "30 times" figure, comparing the cost of a bug fixed in production to one ruled out at design time, see "Planning report 02-3, The Economic Impacts of Inadequate Infrastructure for Software Testing," prepared by RTI and released by the National Institute of Standards and Technology in 2002, retrieved from www.nist.gov/director/planning/upload/report02-3.pdf on August 4, 2014.

7. "Failing to prepare," said Benjamin Franklin, "is preparing to fail." Or maybe it was Henry Ford. We have not been able to ascribe this aphorism with certainty.

8. Charles Perrow, *Normal Accidents: Living with High-Risk Technologies* (Princeton, NJ: Princeton University Press, 1999).

# 3  Design Activities

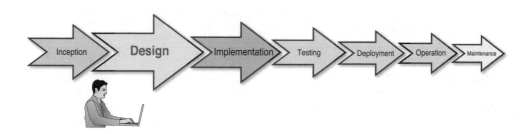

Let's get down to business by diving into some specific things we can accomplish together in our software development efforts. Design is a great starting point. Even for those of you following various agile (or other nonwaterfall) development methodologies, there's always some thought (if not documentation) given to the design aspects of a software project. As such, we're going to take a look at "design" in a general sense and include some aspects that you might or might not consider to be design work per se. These include requirements and specifications. And again, even agile practitioners should find value in these discussions.

But let's start with laying some foundations of what can and should be achieved—from a security standpoint of course—while we're designing our project. We know that a perfectly coded but poorly designed application can end up having egregious security defects. Perhaps more to the point, having an exceptionally clear picture of the application before implementing it, at least fully, can only serve to help. We realize that this concept smacks in the face of some development practices, most notably the family of agile development techniques. At the same time, we also support the notion of prototyping portions of code in order to better develop and understand the design itself. Such prototyping can take many forms, from rudimentary software, to wireframes, to notecard interactions with co-developers.

We discuss here two different categories of things to consider: positive practices to follow, and reviewing an existing design for security defects. Both of these are important to consider, but they're also very different in how we'll approach them.

## Security Tiers

Before we proceed, though, we want to introduce a concept here; we refer to it as *security tiers*. We think it's useful to consider at least three tiers of security *readiness* as defined shortly. Note that we're in no way trying to define a maturity model here; it's simply worthwhile to consider a few security tiers, which will help steer us in the right direction as we proceed. Also, some projects might deem a low tier of security to be quite adequate, even when developed by teams that are highly mature in their software security practices. Thus, these security tiers refer to the state of the end product, not the maturity of the development team per se.

We're also not referring here to identity realms like one might find with single sign-on and other identity management solutions. In those situations, one has to pay close attention to transitive trust models in which an intruder can gain access to a user's session in a low state and use those shared credentials to breach a higher security state.

No, our concept here of security tiers is simply one of readiness within a single system. We believe that the concept is useful particularly at a design level to decide what security solutions to include and how to include them within an application system, whether it be simple or highly complex.

With that in mind, we'll keep the tier definitions to a simple *low, medium,* and *high* here and define them as shown in Table 3.1.

**Table 3.1** Tier Definitions

| Tier | Definition |
|------|------------|
| Low | We think of low level here as meeting a bare minimum set of security standards for secure software. Basically, software written to this level ought to be able to withstand attacks such as those discussed in Chapter 1, but not necessarily contain any more security functionality per se. This is, of course, in addition to meeting its normal functional requirements. |
| Medium | At a medium tier, software not only should be able to withstand attacks, but should also be reporting and alerting security personnel appropriately about the nature of the attacks. (Of course, care must be taken to ensure that the event logs can never be used as a means of attack, such as XSS.) |
| High | At this level, our software can withstand attacks, report problems to security personnel, and be able to programmatically take evasive maneuvers against its attackers. The evasive maneuvers might include simple account locking (with due care to prevent intentional denial of service), user data encryption, recording of intruder information to be used as evidence, and myriad other activities. We think of this tier as a highly desirable state, particularly for enterprise software conducting substantial and valuable business. |

These tiers will serve as a simple but fundamental basis for discussing different things that the development team and the security team can concentrate on during a project's design. Naturally, we'll see them again in subsequent chapters.

It's also worthwhile emphasizing that the low tier is at or above much of today's software in and of itself, because so much of what's running today is unable to withstand even relatively basic attacks.

We should also briefly talk about the rationale for having tiers in the first place. To illustrate our reasoning, let's use a common attack like cross-site scripting (commonly called XSS). For the sake of this discussion, let's assume that our application contains a customer registration form page that prompts the user for his name, street address, email address, and so on. Now, along comes an attacker who attempts to enter some maliciously constructed XSS data into one or more of the fields of our registration form.

If our software has been written to the low tier described previously, it would prevent the XSS data from causing any damage. The <script>

information will be stopped and the user typically be asked to reenter the malformed data. Perhaps this would even happen in the client browser by way of some JavaScript input validation.

However, in an enterprise computing environment, we might want our software to do something more. After all, a street address containing `<script>alert(document.cookie)</script>` (or some far more dangerous scripting nastiness) can only be an attempt to attack our software and not a legitimate street address. Particularly if our application's context is a business processing system, merely stopping an attack is just not adequate.

For a business system, we'd no doubt want to provide some information logging for our security team to look at, perhaps by means of an existing enterprise intrusion detection and monitoring infrastructure. That's where the medium tier comes in. Here, we'd make use of the security monitoring capabilities to provide useful, actionable business data to the security team. We'll discuss what sorts of things should be logged later in this chapter, as well as in Chapter 6, "Deployment and Integration," but for now, suffice it to say that we'd want the security team to have the data they'd need in order to take some appropriate administrative action against the application user.

And in some contexts, we might still want to take this concept further. When we detect a clear attack like the one in this scenario, we might want to have our software itself take some evasive actions. These might include locking the offending user's account, scrubbing the user's account of any privacy information, and so forth.

This scenario helps put in context how and why you might consider designing and writing a particular piece of software for an appropriate security tier. And, more to the point here, it's vital to start thinking about how you'll design these things into your software as early in the process as possible.

A great starting point when you're getting started down this path is to consult with your local IT security team and/or your incident response team. Since they are ultimately the "consumers" of the security components of an application, they absolutely need to be included in this process. For example, the contents of the logging information (tier 2) should be deliberately generated to support the incident response process. The type of information needed by a CSIRT (computer security incident response team) tends to be significantly different than traditional debugging logs, because it must include business-relevant data to find and catch an intruder. The principal purpose of debugging logs, on the other hand, is for developers to find and remove software bugs from a system.

It turns out that many of the decisions we make at this early design stage of a project, irrespective of any software development life cycle (SDLC) methodology we're following, have long-reaching ramifications from a security standpoint. For example, it might seem like a good idea to design and build some input validation all the way out at the application client code—perhaps for simplicity or to unburden the server with these seemingly trivial operations. Even though we know that client-side validation can be trivially bypassed, there are significant usability factors involved that might persuade us to do some of the input validation there—and then validate the data again on the server. For that matter, the server must never presume the client to be free of tampering. Quite the contrary, the design team and hence, the server itself must always assume the client can and will be tampered with. The client side code, after all, resides and executes entirely outside of the server's realm of control.

## Software Development Life Cycle Methodologies

Software Development Life Cycle, or SDLC, methodologies prescribe the way software systems progress from conception to operation stage. There are multiple variations of these methodologies, ranging from very strict and formal waterfall-based models to extremely flexible and loosely organized agile variations. A new acronym, SSDLC (sometimes called sSDLC or SSDLC), has been created to refer to *Secure* SDLC, striving to explain how to transform normal product development life cycle to produce more secure outcome. (We should point out, in passing, that Microsoft calls its SSDLC process the Secure Development Lifecycle (SDL).)

In some business contexts, however, this approach might not be what we want and need. In particular, if a user does attempt to attack our client code, we've by design eliminated our ability to detect the attack and respond appropriately.

On the other hand, if we design the security mechanisms into the core of our software, we stand a significantly better chance of not only detecting an attempted attack, but being able to properly log what has taken place and to potentially take evasive action. We can choose, for example, to lock a user's account if the user has attempted to break our software. (In fact, this response might well even be mandated by the IT security or compliance team.) If that response is programmed in, procedures must be in place to review the triggering actions along with authenticating a user requesting that an account be unlocked. Consider the case when an attacker purposely triggers the locking of the enterprise's CFO's account. The CFO is going to want to get back into the system, but how do you verify that the requester is the CFO when he is yelling at you, and what if the actions were the CFO's and the logs indicate some insider financial manipulation?

All of these things are possible and feasible, but our design decisions can have a tremendous impact on how or whether we go about doing them. For this reason, we need to carefully consider our security design and make consistent architectural decisions that will properly support our business needs later.

## On Confluence

In larger organizations one would expect to find more specialization, which is also true for security folks. Today, in our experience, one often finds IT security practitioners in large shops who elected that specialty early in their careers, and have little or no background in application design and coding. They are likely to be well versed in the latest attacks, and can be experts in setting parameters for firewalls and similar devices, and interpreting the log files. But several fine network security engineers of our acquaintance have no programming skills at all, whereas many others feel they are doing well to cobble together a functional PERL script to manipulate log files. This is the state of the practice today, and one of the drivers behind the need for confluence.

As we've said previously, one of the many key elements of success in addressing security issues properly from the beginning is confluence among the development and security teams. To be sure, many other stakeholders need to be included in the process as well, but none so clearly and comprehensively as these two. The overall process of teams and stakeholders' selection and considerations for doing it are explained in Chapter 2, "Project Inception." The thinking and consideration that should go into designing a business application are clear examples and opportunities of this confluence.

Microsoft's SDL process stresses this concept in a different way. Their cornerstones include both a Software Security Group (SSG) and people in a *security advisor* (SA) role, who act as the primary point of contact for all things security in product development. Note that, organizationally, SAs can belong either to the SSG or to the development organization, but work very closely with the security professionals. As such, they are advocates for the developers, not part of review or audit process that might at times be viewed as an adversarial role. We wholeheartedly support this concept and further believe it to be a vital success factor for developing a secure application system. Existence of such a formal security structure also helps with obtaining a senior management's mandate for following SDL practices and enforcing it consistently at all stages of product life cycle, because grassroots efforts often do not work well with security.

## Key Responsibilities of the SA Role

The key responsibilities of the SA role include the following:

- Acting as a point of contact between the development team and the security team
- Holding SDL-related meetings for the development team
- Holding threat-model and design reviews with the development team
- Educating the development team on threats and best practices
- Analyzing and triaging security-related and privacy-related bugs
- Acting as a security sounding board for the development team
- Advising the development team on enterprise code guidelines, libraries, APIs, etc.
- Preparing the development team for security reviews and assessments
- Interacting with the information security team regarding CSIRT, monitoring, and other processes

We make it a point to describe key collaborative opportunities throughout this book, but perhaps the most important aspect of this exists here during the design process. No matter how rigorously your team engages in design activities, you're more than likely to be successful if you're able to reach out to all the stakeholders and include them as active participants in the design process. Having said that, care should be taken to clearly set roles and responsibilities, in order to prevent a "too many cooks in the kitchen" sort of situation. It is one thing to reach out to a stakeholder and solicit input; that is completely different than handing the helm over to the stakeholder.

In our experience, we've often found design review processes in which various stakeholders are included, but more often than not, the gating functions have been primarily business related and not security related. For example, can the application be developed within budget? Will it be delivered on time? Is the expense justifiable? Although this is all good and essential to do, we feel that security concerns need to also be included as early as possible, and that means including the security stakeholders in the process.

## Requirements

Although many software developers these days eschew the practice of formally gathering and documenting their software requirements, there are many things worth considering at this earliest stage of development. Even if this is done only at an informal or "whiteboard" level, it can significantly help the team in understanding and capturing a project's security needs in addition to its functional needs.

We'll describe these considerations and steps here in several areas: abuse cases, regulatory requirements, and security requirements. Later, we will consider these requirements together with the security tiers we described earlier in the chapter. All these will come together as we discuss the topic of secure designs later in this chapter. Although the overall process is described as a team exercise, the role of the SA is extremely important throughout these activities, because he or she serves as both an anchor and a guiding force for all the participants.

### Abuse Case Analyses

To start with, although abuse case analyses had been used in various ways for some time, McGraw's *Software Security: Building Security In*[1] provides us with one useful description of abuse case analysis. In essence, abuse case analysis looks at the intended functionality of a piece of software and seeks ways in which the software can be misused for evil purposes. As such, it is a review-based process to help us ensure that we're not building something that can be used to cause harm. That said, abuse case analysis can be a powerful means of finding problems with a project before it ever begins.

If the software will likely be misused or abused in a way the owner really does not want to happen, it is a serious problem.

Let's illustrate this with an example. Suppose you're the engineering team leader of your company's customer-facing web presence. One day, the vice president of marketing walks into your office and asks you to add a new feature to the web application: a mechanism for customers to subscribe to a new monthly newsletter the marketing department is launching. Simple enough; you can add a basic web form that asks the customers for their email address and perhaps some other contact data. After you have the information, you simply add the incoming addresses into a database of customers who receive the newsletter. All done? What could go wrong with this scenario? After all, all the functionality that the VP asked for is now complete, right?

Although it's true that this scenario fulfills all the functional requirements, there's a big problem. You probably recognized immediately that anyone could enter a "customer's" information and have her added to the subscription list. That's an abuse case. Heck, someone who really wanted to disrupt us could write a short script that would submit thousands or millions of addresses into our database if we're not careful. That's another abuse case, and one with obvious and really bad consequences. Now, let's take that further, to its logical conclusion.

If we recognize the potential for abuse, we'd want to prevent that from happening, naturally. A first step could be to add a security requirement to the functional requirement that might say something like "only verified email addresses may be added to the subscriber list." It's a good, actionable requirement. Our development team might implement that by sending an email confirmation to each address submitted for inclusion in the subscriber list. Now are we done?

Not so fast. Let's think a bit fiendishly here. If an email confirmation goes to the (intended) subscribers and requires them to verify that they want to be on the list, what could go wrong? Well, there's still an abuse case potential here. The mere act of sending out those confirmation emails could be disruptive. If an attacker bombards our subscription mechanism with fake but carefully chosen email addresses—say, at one of our key business partners—what would happen if our system then sends thousands and thousands of confirmation emails?

So it's not enough to send out a confirmation email; we have to ensure that our application is talking to a human, and not a script. There's another security requirement to consider. We note that CAPTCHAs are routinely used to address this issue. (CAPTCHAs are automated tests used to verify that a user is in fact a human. They usually show a distorted image of a word or phrase that an artificial intelligence would be unable to recognize but the user can read and enter correctly.) Nonetheless, let's add a security requirement such as "subscription requests may be issued only by human users of the system." See where this is going?

It's always best to consider abuses such as the ones we've described here before a system is rolled out into a production environment. But that requires the development team to be able to really think fiendishly, ignoring the mere functional requirements, and to consider how the system can be abused. It has been our experience that this can be a difficult leap for many developers. Security professionals, on the other hand, have been worrying about abuses like this for decades, and thinking fiendishly comes naturally to them. Invite them to participate.

In considering abuse cases, the following are some questions and important areas of concern to consider for each application. These questions are similar to those we'll address while doing a threat model, but let's consider them separately here while we ponder abuse cases.

➤  **How?—Means and Capabilities**

  • Automated versus manual

  In our mailing list scenario given previously, we saw an automated attack against a simple function. Often, designers consider a single use case with blinders on when thinking about how an application might be used. In doing this, they fail to see how the (usually simple) act of automating the functionality can be used to wreak significant havoc on a system, either by simply overwhelming it or by inserting a mountain of garbage data into the application's front end. Never underestimate the determination of a `while true do {}` block.

➤  **Why?—Motivations and Goals**

  • Insider trading

  Automating a user interface into an application is in no way the end of the myriad of ways an attacker can abuse an application.

Consider the human aspects of what an application will be capable of doing, and what sorts of bad things a maliciously minded person might be able to make of those capabilities. Insider trading should be a significant concern, particularly in publicly traded companies. Automation is, after all, a double-edged sword of sorts. We not only are automating a business function, but also might well be inadvertently automating a means for someone to attack a business function.

- **Personal gain**

Similarly, look for avenues of personal gain in an application. Ask whether a user of the application could use the information to "play" the stock market, for example, in a publicly traded company. This can be a significant concern in major business applications in enterprise environments.

- **Information harvesting**

Here, we look for opportunities for an authorized application user to gather—perhaps very slowly over time—information from an application and use that information for bad purposes. A prime example could include a customer database that contains information on celebrity or otherwise VIP customers, such as a patient database in a hospital where the VIP has been treated. That information could be very valuable on the black market or if sold to the media.

- **Espionage**

Although several of these issues overlap significantly, it's useful to consider them separately. Espionage, whether corporate or otherwise, could well be simply a case of information harvesting, but it's still worthy of separate consideration. Consider not just information like the celebrity database, but also company proprietary information and how it could be collected and sold/given to a competitor. What opportunities does the application being analyzed offer up to a user who might be persuaded to do such a thing?

- **Sabotage**

  Even in the best of economic climates, you'll occasionally find disgruntled employees who are bent on damaging a company for all manner of reasons. Their actions might be clear and unambiguously malicious—such as deleting files or destroying records in a company database—but they might also be more subtle and difficult to detect. Consider how a malicious-minded application user might be able to harm the company by sabotaging components in an application.

- **Theft**

  This one is sort of a catchall for things that weren't brought up in the previous ones, but it's worthwhile considering general theft at this point. Credit card account information is a prime candidate here.

Now, it's quite likely a software developer will look at a list like this and throw her arms up in the air in frustration, thinking it's not feasible to brainstorm something like this comprehensively. After all, it is fundamentally an example of negative validation, which we generally seek to avoid at all costs. Although that's true, there's still significant merit in doing abuse case analysis. Of course, the secret to getting it right is to do it collaboratively with some folks who are practiced at this sort of thing—like, say, the information security team.

It is also a good idea to consider separately the likelihood of an attack and the impact of a successful attack. These two things are quite different and bear separate analysis. Impacts can be imagined or brainstormed quite effectively, whereas likelihood can be more deeply analyzed, or even quantified.

Here's how the collaborative approach can work for analyzing abuse cases. After you've gathered a basic understanding of the functional goals of your project, invite a few key folks to take a look at the project and "throw stones" at it. You will want to ensure that all the interested parties are at the meeting; these should include at a minimum the business process owner, the design team, the information security team and/or incident response team, and the regulatory compliance monitoring team.

## Tips on Conducting a Successful Abuse Case Study

To set the stage for considering abuse cases, consider holding a meeting among the key stakeholders: business owner (representative), IT security and/or CSIRT, security architecture, and developers. Before the meeting, be sure to distribute some basic design information about the application being considered. (But still bring copies of these documents to the meeting, just in case anyone "forgot" his copy.) This can be fairly high level at this point, but it must include a list of the business requirements and a graphic visualization of how the application should function, along with some basic narrative descriptions of the application's components and what they do. Data flow diagrams can be useful here as well.

At the meeting, carefully introduce the purpose of the meeting to all the participants. Emphasize that you are only looking for misuse or abuse cases at this time. Your participants will invariably head down the SQLi or XSS path, but steer them back and focus exclusively on how the application's core functionality could be abused.

To catalyze constructive discussion, orally describe the application's functions through its phases: startup, production (including transactions, queries, or whatever else the application does), and how it shuts down. Next describe the normal use cases of each class of application user, emphasizing the types of information each user can access and what functionality she is presented with in the application.
You should be seeking areas of debate at this point. Seek questions like "What's to prevent a user from copying all the customer records off to removable media?" When these questions come up, explore them, and be sure to keep the discussions civil and focused.

At this point, the best way to proceed is to describe the project to the assembled group. Discuss how the system will function and what services it will provide. You should be sure to list any existing security requirements that are already understood. At this point, run through a brainstorming session to collect any and all concerns that come up. The most important thing is to discuss the issues and enable—encourage even—the team to be as harsh as possible.

Take each security concern the group raises to its logical conclusion, and be sure to understand each one in detail. Make a list, for example, of any preconditions that would need to exist for an attack to be successful. So if an attack would need direct access to a server console, make sure that's clearly annotated in the list of issues the group comes up with.

Next, take the list of issues and rigorously consider what security requirements could be added or enhanced to prevent the underlying cause from being exploitable. If an issue is not avoidable, consider security requirements that would enhance the ability to detect an attack if it does take place. A security requirement such as "all access to the application will be logged, with all user actions being recorded and monitored" can be useful, for example, in such situations.

It's also helpful to watch out for some common pitfalls with abuse case analysis. First and foremost, this process must be finite and has a clearly defined stopping point—which should be clearly communicated from the beginning to all participants. Any time you put a bunch of technical-minded folks together in a room, you're never guaranteed the outcome you expect. Engineers have a near-overwhelming inclination to digress in ways you can't begin to fathom. Abuse case analysis is no exception to this. Expect them to discuss low-level technical details such as buffer overflows, cross-site scripting, and a myriad of other things that just aren't relevant at this stage.

To get value out of abuse case analysis, it is absolutely vital to facilitate and guide the brainstorming process carefully but firmly.

### Asset Inventory

We've also found it useful to start at this point to generate an inventory of the sensitive assets the system will need access to. This inventory should include such things as customer records, passwords, and encryption keys, as well as the high-value functions in the application. If applicable, consider prioritizing the inventory in terms of value to the company. Although a large enterprise might have to set up a large corporate project to identify key assets (a customer database, for example), security-conscious folks in smaller places will have their arms around those assets all the time.

In the Microsoft SDL approach,[2] they describe a process called threat modeling. An asset inventory is absolutely vital to doing threat modeling, but it's not the same thing. We're trying to articulate here a very clear understanding of everything of value in our application. In other words, what are the targets an attacker is most likely to go after? If we can build a solid understanding of what the targets are and prioritize them in a relative manner (say, low, medium, and high business value, recognizing that one company's "low" could well be another company's "high" and so forth), then we can also understand what can and should be protected, and how much effort we should put into protecting each.

As we said previously, an application's assets can include important data, but also functions. For example, many applications have an identification and authentication mechanism. Since these are by nature accessible to unknown attackers, they almost always should be included as high-value targets in an asset inventory. That will help us later in allocating the necessary resources for reviewing and testing those modules.

Now, although developing an asset inventory isn't something that can or must be done during a requirements process per se, it's still a good idea to start thinking (and documenting) this as early as possible. Microsoft's SDL process starts this step early as well.

## Regulatory Requirements

Next, we should consider the security-related regulatory requirements that our software is going to have to operate under. In many industries today, our business systems are required to conform to myriad security laws and guidelines. This is particularly true in publicly traded companies as well as certain highly regulated industry sectors such as financial and insurance services, pharmaceutical and healthcare, and public utility companies.

Additionally, companies that operate internationally might have country-specific regulatory and privacy requirements to comply with. Naturally, this can greatly complicate the security requirements process. In some cases, the application itself might need to operate differently based on where the customer, employee, or other user is located.

And especially in these extremely complex environments, it is commonplace these days to find corporate-level compliance officers or at least a compliance monitoring team. Often, the compliance team will organizationally fall under the CIO, COO, Audit, or even General Counsel's office.

Step number one in this part of the design process is to seek out the person or department in charge of compliance monitoring and engage him or her in the process. As a starting point, specifically look for issues such as the following:

- **Data or information that needs to be protected for privacy**

  Many business systems are required to safeguard the privacy of customer data, Social Security numbers, credit card numbers, and so on. These are vital to the security of the application, and the sooner the development team is explicitly aware of the requirements, the better off everyone will be. Find out the specific privacy issues for each data element. In some circumstances, it might also be useful to consider privacy requirements for various markets, even if a product isn't (yet) marketed in some of those markets. Considering those requirements now might well save us substantial grief later, should the company decide to expand into those markets.

- **Data retention requirements**

  Several U.S. Government bureaucracies—and no doubt many others—have stringent requirements on data retention, covering things such things as email and transaction records. It is important to gather all of these requirements and investigate how the application itself can help support them, instead of simply dismissing them to the data center staff to implement. As an example, consider the data retention requirement the Securities and Exchange Commission in the U.S. imposes on broker-dealers. It's called "Rule 17a-4," and it dictates that certain records (trade blotters, order tickets, trade confirmations, and much more) be preserved in nonrewritable and non-erasable format for specified periods. For "communications that relate to the broker-dealer's business as such," the retention requirement is three years.[3] If your app will operate in a regulated environment, we recommend you get expert help to ensure that you facilitate appropriate data retention.

- **Data or processes that require special reporting**

  Many security regulations have explicit requirements for reporting particular types of data access and such. Credit card transactions, for example, might be required to be logged (but not with customer-sensitive information in the logs) under the Payment Card Industry Data Security Standards (PCI-DSS) requirements. There might well also be breach reporting requirements for many applications and the jurisdictions in which they operate.

- **Entity identification or authentication requirements**

  Some sensitive application environments are required to meet minimum standards for strong user and/or entity identification and authentication. PCI-DSS again provides us with ample examples, such as in Requirement 8.3, which says, "Incorporate two-factor authentication for remote access (network-level access originating from outside the network) to the network by employees, administrators, and third parties." Portugal's Digital Signature of Invoices law represents another example of Entity Identification requirement; it attempts, among other things, to bind invoice documents to the software that was used to create it.

- **Access control requirements**

  Sensitive data or functions within an application can require additional access controls for read and/or write access. These are often designated in industry requirements such as PCI-DSS once again. PCI-DSS Requirement 7 states, "Restrict access to cardholder data by business need to know."

- **Encryption requirements**

  In addition to access control, many sensitive data elements need additional privacy and integrity protection using cryptographic controls. PCI-DSS 8.4, for example, tells us, "Render all passwords unreadable during transmission and storage on all system components using strong cryptography." Note here two things: that the requirement covers passwords while both at rest and in transit, and that it leaves open significant options in how to implement the standard, even though it does define "strong cryptography" in the document. It is nonetheless actionable and exactly the sort of security requirement we should be looking for. Further, it is the sort of requirement that can and should evolve with time, as cryptographic algorithms are retired, new practices discovered, and so on.

- **Change-management requirements**

  Many highly regulated industries, such as the pharmaceutical and healthcare sector in the U.S., have rigorous requirements for change management of production business data processing systems. Even though change management is not something that a software developer always has a direct role in, it is still important to be aware of these requirements and to adapt the software practices to fit into them. One exception here regarding change management has to do with source code repositories. Strong access control for both "read only" and "read write" permissions in a source repository should be emphasized, even if only to safeguard things like comments in source code containing sensitive information about a project. The same holds true for a project's bug tracking system.

It would be easy to assume that some of the topics in the preceding list are "someone else's job" and thus outside of the scope of the development team's efforts, but that would be unfortunate. Although some of these topics are in fact someone else's responsibility, in order to be effective, there must be a clear interface between them and the application itself. The more cohesive the bond between these requirements and the development team's efforts, the better the end product will be. Put another way, it should be clear by now that there are many stakeholders in the overall security of a typical business application, and they should all be consulted and included in the planning and implementation.

### Security Requirements

In the preceding section, we discussed regulatory requirements. These tend to be driven by governments, industries, or other standards bodies—but nevertheless external to the company that develops or owns the software. Let's now focus on some internal requirement issues.

From the development team's perspective, the thought process to go through is largely similar: Seek out the appropriate stakeholders and engage them in the process to find out what their security requirements are. The primary difference is the stakeholders themselves. Whereas we looked to the compliance team previously, now we should be looking at the internal information security group directly in this part of the process.

In looking internally for security requirements, there is another place to take a look at as well: internal security standards. Much like their government and industry counterparts, internal standards will often include requirements for such common security mechanisms as authentication, passwords, and encryption. Although they are typically more detail-oriented, quite often they fall short of being truly actionable, but they're still a good place to start looking.

The sorts of things to look for at this point include the following:

- **Identification and authentication requirements**

  Many large corporations have application security policies and guidelines that include identification and authentication. Some go

so far as to designate tiers of sensitivity for applications—
generally three to five levels of security, such as "level 1: customer
data," "level 2: company proprietary information," and "level 3:
public information." Note: These levels are for illustrative purposes.
It is often the case, for example, that customer data covers multiple
data types and corresponding sensitivities. Password and authentication factor guidelines are also commonly found. They'll typically include minimum length, frequency of password changes, and
character set requirements for all passwords and such, along with
any multifactor authentication requirements for the most sensitive
applications. It is not uncommon for a company's internal security
standards or policies to prescribe specific guidelines for proper
credentials storage, specifying certain hashing and/or encryption
algorithms and when those should be applicable. The development
team must follow these guidelines if they exist. If they don't, now is
a good time to define them for this project and those in the future.

- **Event-logging requirements**

  Despite the fact that many enterprise data centers have existing
  architectures in place for centralized event logging, it has been
  our experience that most event logging actually takes place at the
  operating system and web/app-server level. That is, we've rarely
  seen application-level logging that is truly adequate for the incident responders to properly do their jobs. We'll discuss this topic
  in much more detail later, as part of Chapter 6, but for now, let's
  at least ensure that the development team is fully aware of any and
  all event-logging requirements and infrastructures that are in place.
  We say this in the plural because many enterprise environments log
  both operational and security event data, and they often separate
  those two types of logs quite substantially.

- **Disaster recovery and business continuity requirements**

  Most large enterprises do significant disaster recovery and business
  continuity ("DR/BC") planning these days. Although much of this
  has to do with natural disasters such as hurricanes, floods, fires,
  and earthquakes, it is still important to engage in conversation with
  the folks doing this planning. In particular, look for requirements
  around alternative data centers (or hosting services, and so on)
  and other contingency planning in order to understand how your

application will be able to support that type of requirement. The plans often include requirements for rotating to alternative "hot" or "warm" data centers with specific minimum downtime requirements and such. These things are often considered outside the direct scope of the application development process, but it is important to have at least a minimum understanding of the requirements. There might well be, for example, requirements to be able to have an application seamlessly, without downtime, of course, switch to different event logging or other infrastructure servers. These can have a significant impact on how the development team designs and implements many such configuration settings.

- **Incident response requirements**

  Increasingly, corporations have in place incident response teams, either in-house or outsourced. These teams are generally faced with one or more of the following challenges when an incident occurs: diagnose the problem, contain and/or stop the incident, investigate (or support the investigation of) an incident, or perform a damage assessment after an incident has taken place. In pretty much every case, the common denominator and the "lifeblood" of the incident response teams is having a clear and accurate situational awareness of what is going on or what did go on inside the affected business application. This invariably leads to event logging.

  Now, although we've already raised the event-logging requirements previously, incident response requirements can be quite different from ordinary event logging. For example, the incident response team often has a need to capture and store log data and maintain a chain of evidence so that the information will subsequently be useful in a court of law. They also often need to assemble from disparate information sources a clear picture and timeline of what an attacker did (or attempted to do) during an incident, which requires log data to be rather detailed across all the components and layers of a complex business application. This can be a daunting task under the best of circumstances. Timelines can be better reconstructed if components generating log entries have synchronized their times. "System time" policies are becoming even more important as enterprises utilize distributed systems and cloud computing environments spanning multiple time zones, and so on.

As such, it's quite possible that the incident response team will have quite a "wish list" of things they will need from your application when doing their jobs. That wish list is generally borne from experience and operational need when it comes to performing their jobs as rapidly as possible. In reality, their normal mode of operation is to adapt to and to work with the information they have available, but what better time to ensure that they'll have what they need than during the early phases of developing an application?

The best way to do this is to gather a clear understanding of the incident response team's use cases for how they will need to interact with your application during an incident. Meet with them as you would the business owner or user community to find out how they'll use your application.

- **Account management requirements**

  Another commonly set of functional and security requirements can found in account management practices. Corporations often have guidelines and policies for user and employee accounts, as well as for third parties, contractors, consultants, and so on. Employee accounts on enterprise applications might need to be synchronized with employee records in the Human Resources department, for example, to ensure that accounts for departing employees get deactivated when an employee leaves the company. As you might imagine, we've seen many mistakes made in this area over the years. All too many business applications are written in the absence of any means of verifying employment.

  You're likely to find several relevant stakeholders when it comes to account management practices. You might find, for example, that Human Resources can contribute substantially, in addition to the IT Security department for their policies on opening and closing application accounts. But don't stop there. Even the incident response team might be able to contribute with requirements for deactivating accounts during incidents while maintaining their data for forensic analysis or evidentiary purposes.

- **Access control requirements**

  In our experience, access control requirements for applications tend to be rather superficial even in larger corporations. It's not uncommon, for example, to find access control statements that designate user-class and administrator-class users of an application and what they should be allowed or not allowed to do. However, it's not common to find access control requirements that go beyond these simple one or two dimensions.

  That might well be quite adequate for many applications, but it still bears consideration at this early stage. Among other things, it can open up a significant set of possibilities to have more rigorously defined role-based solutions for some more complicated applications.

  With that in mind, the most relevant stakeholder for gathering access control requirements is most often the business process owner—the person who is responsible for the business functionality of the application itself. In talking with the business owner, it's important to listen for language that would lead you to need more stringent access controls than simple user/administrator accesses. Listen, for example, for language like "anyone in accounting should be able to do 'x'," whereas "those in HR should be allowed to only view the information, not change it."

  Irrespective of which departments and stakeholders are considered, a well-designed access control system and policies should be based on the venerable principle of least privilege.

- **Session management requirements**

  Session management is a big issue at a technology level for web-based applications, but it's still relevant for many other application architectures as well. The sorts of things to look for with regard to session management should include timeout periods for inactivity, time-of-day restrictions, location restrictions, failover capabilities, and so forth.

  As with access control requirements, the most likely relevant stakeholder for these issues tends to be the business owner. And the way to approach the topic of session management requirements is to seek use-case scenarios. (These might well already be defined, so be sure to read up on what information has already been gathered.)

At a more technical level, there also might be company standards or guidelines on how to implement session management in an application, particularly if the application is web-based. Enterprise data center environments often make use of either single sign-on or other centralized authentication services and APIs, which are equally important to be aware of and make use of when designing an application.

Hopefully, these standards include security guidelines on such issues as session fixation, safeguarding session cookies, and cookie contents. Great care, too, should be taken in cookie generation. Persistent cookies should be rigorously encrypted, for example. This type of technical session management requirement is not at all likely to come from the business owner, but rather the security team, because these are things that often are discovered during security reviews.

- **Encryption standards**

  Particularly in regulated industries, there are often policies for encrypting sensitive data. Sometimes, these requirements don't come from external regulations, but from the security department directly. At a bare minimum, it is important to find out what these standards are and to conform to them. Most often, the guidelines serve to specify what encryption algorithms are acceptable for particular types of application data. In most cases, they explicitly and strictly ban any attempts to come up with "homemade" cryptographic functions, requiring teams to rely on existing and vetted algorithms and implementations instead. What is often missing in encryption standards and requirements is detailed information on how the entire crypto system should work, such as key generation and management. Those details are typically up to the developer, and great care must be taken in how these things are done.

  These standards are all important, of course, but we should point out that there is still plenty of room to make mistakes. In our experience, far more encryption problems arise from poor key management practices than from selecting algorithms that aren't up to the task—and very few encryption standards even address the topic of how best to do key management.

Password storage is another topic that should be taken up in encryption requirements. It is recommended that password storage standards use a one-way hash function approach that combines the password with other information such as the user account identifier. In this manner the same password used by different accounts will not result in the same password validation value (hash). Being a one-way hash, it should also be computationally expensive to derive the password from the hash value. This helps to minimize the impact if the account and password values are stolen from their storage on a server component.

- **Change-management requirements**

  Most even moderately mature enterprises have documented processes and procedures for handling changes to production applications. For the software developers, the key is to know how best to interact with that process and work within its boundaries. As with disaster recovery and business continuity, these requirements can have an impact on how best to design and implement an application. For example, if an application must maintain login credentials to connect to a database server, it's generally best to keep those credentials in a properties file (of course, protected, as, hopefully, specified in credential management and encryption standards) and never hard-coded in the application's source code. Apart from the security vulnerability introduced by hard-coding login credentials in an application, keeping them in a properties file often makes things easier from a change-management standpoint. This is because changing a properties file on a production system is typically far easier than changing the source code and rebuilding an application. So, as a starting point, the stakeholder to look for on this is generally in either the CIO or the COO environment, or perhaps IT and IT security, depending on who sets the change-management processes in your organization.

- **Patching requirements**

  All software has to be patched periodically. Patching and updates follow very formal processes when external customers are involved, but for internal-only products these rules can be somewhat less rigid, although they need to take into account all of an application's components, from its operating systems through its libraries, frameworks, and others. In any case, the development team should take future patches and possible formal requirements around this process into consideration early in the design phase.

Where things become more complicated is with updating software components that require rebuilding the underlying application software. It is not uncommon for organizations in an enterprise to have an unclear or otherwise unrealistic understanding of which organization is responsible for deploying specific patches. For example, installing operating system patches is generally fairly easy, whereas replacing a software framework requires a complete rebuild of an application. In these cases, the patching is best not left to the IT operation staff.

Also, it is worth noting here in passing that large enterprises are increasingly insisting on security requirements, including patching, in their contract verbiage with software vendors.

As you can see, this list is far more internally focused than the one in the preceding section. It's no less important, however. It's also worth noting that it's more than likely you'll find that no standards exist for many or even all the items in the list just given. In that case, it would be far too easy to dismiss the topic and continue in a "business as usual" mode, but that too would be unfortunate. Instead, we suggest you consider it an opportunity for collaboration between the development team and the security team to put together a meaningful and actionable set of guidelines and requirements to address this list (and more).

### Bringing It All Together

Many of you reading this might well feel overwhelmed at this point. We've just laid out a highly ambitious list of things to consider when gathering the security requirements for a business application. The list is daunting, we agree. However, the news isn't all bad. Let's consider some of the positive aspects of what we've been covering in this section.

For one thing, it's highly likely you won't need to do all of this with every application. There's an economy of scale to be found here. So if, like many organizations, your organization handles multiple business applications, then you can definitely expect to see a reduction in the level of effort with each passing application. Also be cautious of single sign-on environments where a weakness in a relatively low-risk application can result in stealing credentials to compromise a higher-risk application. Either way, the first project that embarks on this path must have executive support because they are more likely to see the return on investment later as other enterprise application projects arise.

Also, remember the notion of having a security advisor working with development teams? Well, here's an opportunity for the security advisor to shine and prove his value to the development effort. The security advisor should, among other things, be expert at all the security requirements an organization needs to conform to, external as well as internal.

At the very least, the organization's security team should be able to provide a significant list of applicable requirements, laws, and guidelines that will need to be followed on an ongoing basis. This list will need to be periodically updated since many of the standards change over time, and the list should include a resource library with searchable documents for each set of requirements.

So although doing this correctly would require a rather significant initial outlay of effort and possibly electronic resources, every application project should be able to benefit from that effort, reducing the per-project costs significantly over time. This, by the way, is a compelling argument for at least some level of centralization of software development infrastructure in an organization.

With that in mind, it has been our experience that the best way of collecting security requirements is via meetings and interviews with the stakeholders. Ideally, this will be done with the project's security advisor on hand, but even if your organization does not have a security advisor, it's still quite achievable. Here are some procedural considerations.

- **Do your homework**

  No matter how eager your stakeholders are to contribute and help, they'll always appreciate it when you spend some time in advance and do some preparation. Start by doing some online research and information gathering about the external and internal regulations you believe are applicable to your application. Download and read the latest version of all of them. If there are preproduction versions of any of these standards in the development pipeline, get those as well. It's quite likely those will become relevant to your application after they're released, so you'll want to be aware of what's coming along, even if they're not currently in their final form.

Make a list of the regulations, standards, laws, and so on, including the internal security policies and guidelines that are applicable to your project.

While reading through all the standards, make a list of questions.

Use this time also to ensure that you deeply understand the business intent of the application. Know what it is intended to do and what it is not intended to do. Ensure that the stakeholders agree to this as well, and understand the pitfalls of mission creep. And be realistic that some mission creep is simply inevitable.

Make a list of all the stakeholders you'll need to talk with. These might be individual people, or perhaps roles or departments (e.g., General Counsel or Compliance Officer).

- **Start with abuse cases and asset inventory**

  Using the most preliminary and basic set of functional requirements for your application, go through an abuse case analysis process for the application as described earlier in this chapter. Some of the issues uncovered in the analysis could well turn out to be addressed in the various security requirements, but it never hurts to spend the time to really understand how your application might be misused after it is deployed. Plus, it's been our experience that understanding the abuse cases helps build your own knowledge of the application and what aspects of it really need to be well protected later.

- **Invite the stakeholders**

  Depending on the nature of your questions and agenda, you might end up doing one-on-one interviews with the various stakeholders, or you might end up inviting them to one meeting. Whichever works best for you, invite all the relevant stakeholders to participate in this stage of the application development process, again being cautious to avoid the "too many cooks in the kitchen" problem.

- **Brainstorm and refine**

  With your stakeholder(s) gathered, ask your questions and dive deeply into the answers. Where answers seem vague, push to make them explicit. You want to seek clear and actionable answers here wherever possible. Toss out topics for discussion that perhaps the stakeholder hadn't considered. You might need to illustrate things via examples and case studies to make them clear. You're also likely to be questioned about the likelihood of something bad happening. Has it happened before? When? And so on.

Gathering the security requirements for an application can seem like a lot of effort indeed. However, getting this step done well will undoubtedly have significant payoffs throughout the development effort, irrespective of the software development methodology your organization follows. And again, we haven't even begun to discuss the security tiers we mentioned early in the chapter yet.

We've placed a lot of emphasis on requirements gathering because mistakes made now can have a multiplying impact later. Neglecting something like a policy on encrypting customer data can result in massive reengineering if we get "surprised" by the requirement after we've designed and built the application. Things get more dynamic and exciting when Agile processes (and variations) are introduced, because they tend to be less planned and more flexible. As the authors have frequently observed, Agile teams skip documentation updates altogether during these so-called springs (literally living by the motto "code is the best documentation"), which creates quite a lot of issues for security analysis. As a result, the security requirements have to be continuously reintroduced and readjusted based on the current project planning—most likely, as a mandatory integral part of weekly sprints.

There's a secondary benefit from going through a rigorous security requirements gathering process early, and it's one we haven't discussed yet. By engaging all the application stakeholders in dialogue long before starting to actually design or develop any code, you're including them in the process rather than asking them to just review and accept your work later. It's rare to find the individual who doesn't appreciate that approach.

## Specifications

If you've done a good job at collecting and synthesizing the security requirements, turning them into specifications—if indeed your process even calls for this step—should be relatively smooth sailing. In essence, the requirements speak to the *what,* and the specifications speak to the *how.* We've seen many examples of the specifications being rolled into the design of an application itself, and many organizations don't bother with articulating a separate set of specifications above and beyond the requirements they've already gathered.

For our context here, we're not going to presume any specific development methodology, but we do want to make sure that our readers understand the benefits that can be gained from documenting the project's specifications.

So let's consider a few examples from our security requirements given previously.

We described a PCI-DSS requirement (8.3) that says, "Incorporate two-factor authentication for remote access (network-level access originating from outside the network) to the network by employees, administrators, and third parties." This is already fairly specific language, but we might fine-tune it for our own application by saying something like, "Use [hardware token] and associated authentication server for authenticating all non-local application logins." We also want to ensure that we have a degree of traceability from our requirements to our specifications. Numbering each, and being consistent with the numbers, can be enormously helpful.

Similarly, we cited another PCI-DSS requirement that says, "Render all passwords unreadable during transmission and storage on all system components using strong cryptography." Here, the specification verbiage, which should be driven by the enterprise's security standards, could become something such as, "User passwords must be transmitted in TLS 1.1 encrypted sockets using (minimum) 128-bit keys and cipher suite [example] and stored on the LDAP server in hashed format using SHA-384 (minimum)." This example, provided here merely for illustrative purposes, clearly shows how a relatively open requirement statement becomes specific to a local environment.

At a minimum, it is worth going through all the security requirements you've collected, and localizing them with specific details on local policies for such things as password lengths and encryption standards.

From a security perspective, we are obviously placing less emphasis on this aspect of the design process. The reason for that is that the core important details typically surface during the requirements phase and not so much in the specifications. That's not to diminish the value of documenting an application's specifications. Quite the contrary, details such as those we've listed here are important, but they also tend to be a fairly direct and simple mapping from the various requirements guidelines and policies.

There is one important exception to this, however: contradictions. Particularly in heavily regulated or complex environments, it's not uncommon to find contradictory guidance in various security requirement sources. One source might, for example, indicate using an AES-128 encryption algorithm, whereas another says Blowfish is adequate.

The rule of thumb to follow here is to go with the higher level of security. But that's not always immediately obvious in all cases, as with the AES versus Blowfish example. In a case like this, it's probably best to seek policy clarification from the IT security organization, or better yet, a professional cryptographer.

## Design and Architecture

Now, with our security requirements and specifications document, it's finally time to start considering the architecture and design of our application—or for our purposes here, the security aspects of the design. If you've been following our advice on collecting requirements, you're likely to find that many of the security details in the design will essentially "write themselves." Okay, that's an exaggeration, but at least many of the architectural security decisions should be made easier from a good collection of security requirements.

These decisions will also be heavily driven by the expectations for security tiers introduced earlier in this chapter—in particular, we're faced with architectural decisions of where to place specific security mechanisms for each security tier. If "tier 1" is your target, the decisions are likely to be quite simple; you can accomplish most of tier 1 within an application's presentation layer, especially server-side, with a relatively small amount of back-end coding being required.

On the other hand, if your target is tier 2 or 3, you'll want to give careful consideration to the security mechanisms you employ, and where they should be placed within your application. Building (essentially) intrusion detection functionality into an application is generally best suited for the business logic layer of an application, but there will still be some security functionality in other areas of the application, from the presentation layer through the data layer.

The important thing is to consider the architectural ramifications carefully, and then implement consistently throughout the application. Mixing and matching architectural components for convenience or familiarity is not a recipe for success.

So it's on to considering the design or architecture of our application. We're big believers in prescriptive guidance of positive practices, rather than (just) reviewing a design for flaws. So we'll start there.

## Prescriptive Design Practices

Perhaps the most important prescriptive practice to follow in designing secure applications is relying on common well-tested infrastructure and reusing already vetted design patterns, but that presents a "chicken and egg" sort of dilemma. By that we mean repeatedly using a set of design components that have proven themselves to be secure. Additionally, it's useful to use design checklists that verify certain positive compliance aspects of design components. Let's consider these things in some detail.

But first, let's briefly take a look at the origins of these practices. Our secure designs should be built on top of sound architectural principles, such as those described by Saltzer and Schroeder in the 1970s.

---

### Saltzer and Schroeder's "The Protection of Information in Computer Systems"

This pivotal work by renowned engineers Jerome Saltzer and Michael Schroeder introduced several data protection principles that are as relevant today as they were when the paper was first written in 1975. These include the following:

- Economy of mechanism
- Fail-safe defaults
- Complete mediation
- Open design
- Separation of privilege
- Least privilege
- Least common mechanism
- Psychological acceptability

Knowingly or otherwise, we make use of all of these design principles in virtually every aspect of our software today. Every person involved in building secure software should be intimately familiar with these principles and how to apply them.

They should also of course incorporate the security requirements and specifications we've spent so much effort in collecting and documenting previously.

---

From there, we should look at various security aspects of our design for construction soundness and turn those into checklists that can then be reused in later projects or verified and validated in the current project. Ideal targets for such checklists should include the following set of focus points:

- **Identification and authentication**

  Things to look for in a strong "I & A" mechanism include con–forming to corporate standards for username and password—minimum length, acceptable character sets, and so on—but extend well beyond that. Software designers should also ensure that all sensitive information is adequately protected while at rest as well as while in transit. They should also ensure appropriate creden-tials management practices, that is, that all passwords are securely hashed and salted, and then stored into a repository. The credential repository itself should conform to any standardized architecture that is in place. Login credentials should also never be exposed in the URL field of a web browser, via a GET method; they should instead be embedded in the HTTP request body as a POST param-eter. For that matter, it is entirely possible that your enterprise already has a standardized identification and authentication, or identity management, architecture, and you'll need to make use of that. That is all well and good, but the preceding criteria should still be considered carefully.

- **Key management**

  Although the topic of key management is substantial, private and symmetric keys, used by an application, require specific handling and have to be adequately protected according to the IT/IS guide-lines. The most frequent solutions here are the use of key stores, file permissions, or specialized hardware tokens for highly protected systems.

- **Access control**

  This one is more problematic to find through a simple checklist process per se, but there are still some things that can be verified. The basic principle to doing access control inside an application is to ask the question of whether a user, an entity, or a process should have access to the data or function it is requesting. That is, all data and function calls should in fact be designed as requests that can be authoritatively answered.

As such, the thing to look for at a design level is a centralized access control mechanism that enforces policy. The policy itself will be set—perhaps dynamically—elsewhere, but internally, there needs to be a means of answering the question of whether a request should be permitted.

What makes this problematic is that every access needs to follow this requesting methodology. We'll discuss this in more detail in Chapter 5, "Testing Activities."

- **Boundaries**

  Every application of even moderate complexity has numerous boundary layers. They can be between components, servers, classes, modules, and so on, but at a design level we generally have a bird's eye view of all of them—at least if we're doing it right. From a security standpoint, boundary layers offer a positive opportunity to verify good practices like input validation and access control.

  Most risk assessment methodologies implicitly map out boundary layers in their threat modeling process by defining security zones (aka trust boundaries). Each zone is then studied for the risks it poses.

  Looking at an application's boundary layers is similar, but generally offers a slightly more data-centric perspective on things.

- **Network connections**

  Network connections, including both physical and VPN, are essentially a single boundary between components, but we list them separately here because they offer different types and levels of security controls. For one thing, in most enterprises, the networks themselves are operated by the IT organization. And further, network-level security controls tend to be outside the direct scope of the application itself, but nonetheless can be useful at independently enforcing some policies.

  For example, a network layer between an application server and a database can enforce permitting only SQL network traffic between the two components. Although the network can't often do much more than that, it does provide us with some useful controls that

help us enforce some of Saltzer and Schroeder's design principles—
namely, compartmentalization, graceful failure, and least privilege
in this case.

- **Component interconnections**

  These are simply another form of boundary layer, but much like the
  network boundaries, separate application components can offer up
  different types of opportunities for security controls.

- **Event logging**

  Event logging is a big topic for application developers, and it is one
  that is almost always not well understood or adequately implemented. The key point that most developers don't get is that the
  customer for event logging should be the IT security or incident
  response team. As such, it's vital to consider their use cases with
  regard to event logging. More often than not, application event
  logging mostly contains debugging information. Although that
  information is useful for debugging purposes, it's not all that's typically needed when responding to security incidents. In addition, the
  security team often needs more business specific logging in order to
  determine the "who, what, where, when, and how" sorts of things
  they need to do.

  From a design checklist standpoint, you should be verifying that the
  security team has provided their log use cases and that those use
  cases will be incorporated into the application's design. For details
  and examples of such use cases, see the discussion in Chapter 6.

- **Session management**

  Most modern platforms and application servers these days provide
  more than adequate tools for building robust session management
  into applications running on them, but mistakes can still happen.
  We'll discuss this further in Chapter 4, "Implementation Activities,"
  but for now, let's ensure that the available infrastructure for doing
  session management will be used for our application.

- **Protection of sensitive data**

  Enterprise applications carry all sorts of sensitive data these days,
  and it's up to the developers to ensure that the sensitive data is
  being properly protected. As with protecting any secret, it's vital

to consider sensitive data at rest and in transit, because each state carries with it a different set of protection mechanisms that should be considered.

- **Data validation**

  Any time our application has to make use of an external service—command-line interface, LDAP directory, SQL database, XML query engine, and so on—we have to ensure that the data being sent to the service is safe, after we've mutually authenticated those components, of course. There are several key concepts in that sentence. First off, we can't assume that a service we're calling is going to adequately protect itself. Second, we have to ensure that the intent of our service request is immutable from change due to whatever data we're sending to the service.

  Essentially, we have to do proper input validation for the current module and output encoding of what will be sent to the service before making the call, and we have to do it in the context of understanding what the next service call is intended to do. That's a pretty tall order, because encoding for a database call will be different from the one for LDAP query, for instance.

---

## Design Checklists

It's a good idea to keep a checklist or two readily available to the design team. These checklists should cover basic topics to ensure they are appropriately represented in various components of a system's design. It is also vital to be cognizant of the fact that checklists cannot capture everything, and can and should evolve over time and quite possibly per application. Still, they can serve as a good starting point for catalyzing thoughts. Sample checklists should include the following:

- Establishing connections
  This checklist should step through all the things one must do in establishing a connection between two application components, such as ensuring mutual authentication and ensuring transport layer protection of data.
- Authenticating users
  This list should point to standard design components for authentication, such as enterprise authentication services and how to invoke them.

- Managing sessions
- Securing data at rest
- Securing data in transit

...and so on. The point is to promote consistent conformance to established design patterns.

Oh, and you'll want to carry many of these checklists forward as coding guidelines (with rigorous annotations) as well. We'll discuss that in the next chapter.

As you might imagine, the earlier list is by no means a comprehensive one, but it does represent a pretty common list of application aspects. For each of these common problems, we should put together a checklist of issues to ensure that we have properly addressed them in our own designs. Plus, since this list of things is pretty common, we can use it as a basis for some design patterns that we'll be making repeated use of.

Now, some of the elements in the list aren't necessarily discrete application components—say, for example, protecting sensitive data—but they are all things we should address as we consider the security aspects of our design.

It's also worth giving careful thought to the feasibility of security aspects of a design. It is a common mistake to overengineer a design and basically attempt to protect everything all the time. The problems with this approach are numerous. For one thing, we're likely to end up with a solution that is too costly for the problem we're trying to solve. It might also be too complicated to be successful, or building it that way might simply take far more time than we have available. For that matter, it is also common to underengineer a design due to tight timelines, budgets, and so on. The key is to find the right balance, as in so many things.

So we have to make compromises, but we have to be able to do so in a principled, businesslike, and repeatable sort of way. That is, we have to have sound justification for the design decisions we make or don't make. That's where a risk management methodology comes in.

Risk management is one of McGraw's three pillars of software security,[4] and it helps us make decisions with confidence. Without a sound way of considering business risks, we're inevitably going to make the wrong decisions by accepting risks we don't understand. That's a big gamble to subject the business to.

We'll discuss threat modeling shortly, but one method that can be useful is to consider an application's most likely *threat profiles*. Think of these as use cases, but from a security perspective: What are the most likely avenues of attack your application absolutely must be able to defend itself against?

For example, we often refer to the "coffee shop attack" when discussing web application security. That is, consider an attacker on an open Wi-Fi network (say, in a coffee shop) using a network sniffing tool to eavesdrop on all the network traffic traversing the Wi-Fi. Now, consider one of your application's users using your application in that same coffee shop. Can your application withstand that level of scrutiny, or does it hemorrhage vital data such as user credentials, session tokens, or sensitive user data?

Similarly, when a mobile application is designed for a smartphone or tablet computer, the most likely risk a user faces is from data left behind on a lost or stolen device. If your application is on that lost/stolen device, what information could an attacker find on the device using forensic tools? Does your mobile application store sensitive data locally on the mobile device?

In designing your security mechanism, keeping a handful of these threat profiles in mind is a healthy thing to do. Of course, the threat profiles need to be specific to your application's architecture, but it's generally not too difficult to find data on attacks against similar architectures.

### Implementation Considerations

There are many aspects of design that directly overlap with implementation. One aspect, in particular, is in designing where to place various security implementations in an application's design. For example, the next chapter discusses input validation extensively. If we were to implement input validation without any regard for our application's design, we would be quite likely to end up with a functioning but unmaintainable mountain of junk.

The reason for this is that it is entirely feasible to build input validation code at just about any layer of abstraction within an application. Further, if input validation is implemented "on the fly," there is a tendency to include such things as regular expressions throughout the code base. This is what can easily result in code that is basically impossible to maintain over time.

So, despite the fact that something like input validation—which essentially does nothing to enhance the functional features of an application—is generally viewed as an implementation detail, it is important to design it carefully into one's security architecture. In the case of input validation code, it should be centralized in implementation and features, as appropriate. If there are multiple distinct functional layers in an application (for example, Web UI, XML processing, LDAP access, and so on), validation can be centralized on a *per-layer* basis—but never scattered around randomly. The same thing goes for access control, which would be quite impossible to slap on after the fact, if it was not properly designed into the product from its conception. And in each of these cases, care should be taken to retain control on the server side of the application, regardless of what validation or access control might be done on the client.

These design considerations can have an enormous impact as well. Again citing the case of input validation, if we implement our input validation at the application's presentation layer, it will largely preclude us from being able to implement tier 2 or tier 3 security features into the application, simply because of the lack of features available to us in the presentation layer.

We'll discuss detailed examples of this in the next chapter, but for now, let's at least be entirely cognizant that our design decisions need to have a firm footing in the reality of our intended implementations.

### Design Review Practices

The common denominator in all development methodologies is to start with a clear understanding of the proposed design of the product. Although we've seen design documents span an enormous spectrum of detail, there is simply no substitute to really knowing and understanding the product's design before proceeding.

Irrespective of your development methodology, you should have a fundamental description of the application and its components. A diagram visualizing all the components is a good starting point (see Figure 3.1). It should include all the physical as well as logical components of the application, at a bare minimum.

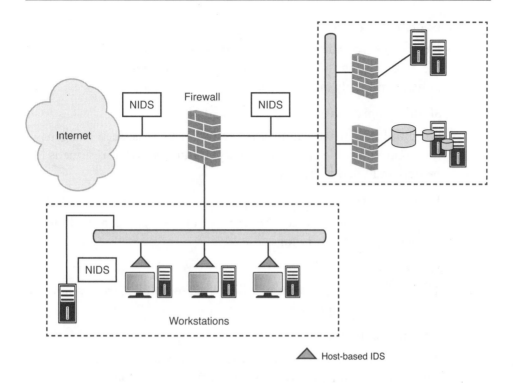

**Figure 3.1** Diagram of a typical enterprise application design, top view.

Other useful things to include in design documentation include the following:

- **Components**

  Each component of an application should be described, at least at a top level. What is it called? What is its primary functionality? What security requirements does it have? Who should access it?

- **Data elements**

  What data does the application handle? What are the sensitivities of the data? Who should be allowed to view the data? Who should be allowed to alter the data?

- **Data interfaces**

  How will data be exchanged through the various components of the application? What network protocols will be used? What format(s) will the data be exchanged in?

- **Bootstrap process**

  How is the overall system instantiated? What security assumptions are made during the bootstrapping? How do the application's components mutually authenticate?

- **Shutdown process**

  On shutdown, what is done with system resources, such as open files, temporary file space, and encryption keys? What residue is left behind and what is cleaned up?

- **Logging process**

  This is the process and components for event logging, to include debugging and security logs.

- **Failure process**

  This includes processes for handling system failures, from relatively simple to catastrophic.

- **Update/patch process**

  This consists of the processes for installing component updates, at various levels and components within the application.

The preceding description is highly simplistic, but at the same time it can seem pretty daunting. If you really take the time to do each of these steps in detail, threat modeling a typical application can be an enormously time-consuming process, which can be time and cost prohibitive for many enterprises. As such, this outline is intended merely to give you an overview of what is involved in the threat modeling process. What's important from our standpoint is how to put any of this into practice.

We've had success at breaking down this threat modeling approach into a more simple process, based on the work of many people in the software security field today.

After you have a clear picture of how the application will work, it's useful to break the design into individual operational security zones, particularly for a distributed application with multiple servers and one or more clients.

Next, for each zone and each element in each zone, articulate (preferably in a table format) each of the following: who, what, how, impact, and mitigation.

- *Who?*

  *Who* can access the zone or element? Not just the registered, authorized users, but who could access the item in general. If it is (say) an application on a mobile device, consider the legitimate user, a user accessing a lost or stolen device, and so on. Try to be reasonably comprehensive in this step. What you're doing is articulating the *threat agents*.

- *What?*

  *What* can each threat agent do to potentially harm the system? Can the threat agents steal a hard drive from a server? Access a table in a SQL database? Masquerade as a legitimate user and get to sensitive data inside the application? And so forth.

- *How?*

  *How* can the threat agents carry out each of the things in the *what* list?

- *Impact?*

  If the attack is successful, what is its impact on the business? What are the direct costs as well as the indirect costs? In what ways is the business's reputation tarnished?

- *Mitigation?*

  For any given attack, what mitigation options are available? How much would they cost (in "low," "medium," and "high" terms if more quantifiable data are not available)?

Assuming you've assembled the right team of design reviewers, it's quite likely this approach will result in some useful and meaningful discussions about the application's design.

You should try to consider as many aspects of the application's design as feasible. These reviews can vary from taking a few hours to taking many days, depending on an application's complexity, and how much detailed analysis is expected.

So it needn't be so difficult to do. And we've certainly found the payoffs to justify the time spent. You might find Cigital's approach to be pretty similar in many ways to the threat modeling process we've just described.

## It's Already Designed

Throughout this chapter—and indeed in much of this book—we have assumed you would be largely working on new projects, rather than assessing or continuing prior work efforts. Well, that can be a rather unrealistic assumption these days. So let's take some time to dive a bit deeper into what sorts of design security activities can be reasonably accomplished even after a system is in production.

One immediate disadvantage we see here is that ex post facto design changes tend to be costly,[5] so you will doubtlessly encounter more than a little initial resistance in trying to make any substantive changes to the design. This is particularly true for projects that are widely deployed and not (just) run from centralized data centers. This means that any design changes that might come out of an ex post facto review need to be rigorously researched and cost-justified in order to be successful. We believe that this inertia is more than likely to result in workarounds and compromises more often than it results in real design changes, which will no doubt present their own challenges over time. Moreover, some fundamental security issues in legacy applications simply cannot be accomplished without complete rewrite of the application. This might happen due to inherently insecure application architectural choices or simply because of underlying platform or language shortcomings—more on that in Chapter 8, "Maintaining Software Securely." But we should still press on.

Another common hurdle to clear is in "simply" finding the design itself. Many software products and systems are built and deployed without any sign of design documentation. Often, the design "documentation" lives in the brains of the people who designed the system in the first place, and quite possibly those people have moved on to other jobs, perhaps in different companies. We feel that documenting a system's design, even if it is done only ex post facto, is in and of itself a huge benefit that will find value over time even if no changes are made by way of a security assessment. Indeed, two of your authors have amassed considerable experience doing just this at a major corporation. A further pitfall of a system that lacks a clearly documented design is that seemingly innocuous changes can often lead to spectacular failures. It is vital for the entire team to have a clear, comprehensive, and deep understanding of the underlying system.

So enough with the impediments; let's look at how to do design review of a deployed system. Here are some general steps to consider, along with some tips and recommendations in accomplishing them.

1. Document the design.

   Start by looking at whatever existing design documentation is available, of course. Depending on your organization's software development process, this could range from nonexistent to voluminous. The important thing is to "get your head around" the design and thoroughly understand what the software is doing. In our experience, this is best accomplished through a combination of documentation, visualization, and human interviews. So start by sitting down, turning off all interruptions, and studying whatever documentation you have. Care should be taken to validate that the derived design accurately depicts the running system.

   Then, if at all possible, seek out the design team and spend some quality time with them and a large whiteboard. Draw the top-level design in the form of the major software elements and dependencies, their functions, communications channels, data, and so on. Next, overlay a state diagram onto that design, and do your best to understand the software's different states of operation, including initialization, steady-state operation, exception modes, shutdown, backup, availability features, and so on. Take this discussion as deep as you're able to. Look, for example, at each component interconnection and ask how it is identified, authenticated, protected, and so on, as well as what network protocols and data types are being passed. Be sure to document any assumptions at this point as well.

   Perhaps most important during this whiteboard exercise, ask questions. Assume nothing. Look for unanticipated failure states. And document all the answers you get. You might well find that your own documentation has details in it that surpass the existing design documentation, such as it might be.

   If you're lucky, much of this will already be in place. But even if that is the case, your priority right now has to be attaining a high degree of understanding of what the documentation says. So even in that fortunate case of having ample documentation, it is still worthwhile to interview the design team and have them explain things in their own words. This will help galvanize your understanding of the system, as well as potentially point out areas of ambiguity and downright errors that might exist in the documentation itself.

2. Perform threat modeling.

   After you are confident that you have a deep and thorough understanding of the documentation, go through the threat modeling process as we've described. You might well have collected ample fodder for this in documenting the design (or studying the extant documentation).

3. Assess the risks and costs.

   Either directly during the threat modeling process vor separately, it's vital to assess the risks and prioritize them.

4. Decide on a remediation strategy.

   The toughest part at this point could well be deciding what the right threshold of risk is for the system you're reviewing. The biggest difference in doing this now versus during the initial product development is that remediation costs are likely to be substantially higher. And not just the direct costs, but the indirect ones. For example, how will deploying a new design inconvenience your customers? How will it affect backward compatibility? The answers to these questions are extremely important.

   The remediation strategy, then, must take all these answers into account, in addition to the normal business impact justifications. For example, a fairly low-impact design defect might well get remediated because its costs are relatively low, whereas a higher impact problem might be delayed until a major release cycle because the costs do not justify the value.

5. Fix the (justified) problems.

   Any issues found that meet your remediation strategy should now be fixed. And, as you might well imagine, it's never just as simple as coding a fix and then checking off the issue as being finished. Since the issue is now, by definition, an important one, it becomes important to dive deeply into the issue.

6. Verify the fixes.

   It's of course not enough to say something is fixed; you have to prove it as well. Especially for security weaknesses, whenever possible you should build test cases that explicitly test for each weakness.

Try also to consider similar classes of weaknesses that might exist elsewhere in the system.

7. Lather, rinse, repeat.

   Essentially, keep iterating through this until you're finished. Mind you, defining that end point isn't easy. What's important is to give each application a level of scrutiny that its value warrants, and to keep at it until that level has been met.

With luck, you won't have unearthed any truly catastrophic design flaws during this process on an application that is already deployed. And if you did, hopefully you found it before your adversaries did. As we said, major design flaws can be hugely costly to fix after an application is deployed.

We should add that it has been our experience that applications already deployed rarely get ex post facto design review scrutiny. That sort of review would usually happen only for the most security-critical software and, even then, usually only if other security flaws have been discovered. Another factor that makes this difficult is when staff is reassigned to work on other projects after any given project has drawn to completion.

## Deployment and Operations Planning

Think it's too early in the game to start considering how the system is going to be deployed and operated? Guess again. We'll come back to this in a lot more detail in Chapter 7, "Operating Software Securely," but for now it is important for us to be sure to understand how our application is going to get deployed and operated. For example, how are our application components going to integrate into the intrusion detection infrastructure in the organization?

### The Design Review

Today is the first meeting of the newly minted Product Security Team (PST) for the ongoing development of version 2.0 of Peabody's Wandering Medic (WM) app. The first step is to decide on some of the basics and what things can reasonably be done, despite the fact that the development team is already well into the implementation of WM 2.0.

It is agreed that a lightweight design review would be the first course of action. The team would use this opportunity to get to know each other, as well as for everyone to thoroughly "get their heads around" the WM 2.0 design itself. After all, the Peabody team had, to date, only seen the WM apps from the outside, and this is their first deep dive into how the system will work.

So the Peabody CTO starts the process by asking the dev team, apparently without a hint of irony, to produce whatever design documentation they currently have. The dev team nervously grins and proclaims their design to be their source code. The code is modular; it is laid out logically; any first-year computer science graduate should be able to look at the code and intuitively understand the flow of operation. The CTO is less than convinced, and he insists on whiteboarding a top-level design flow of the app and all of its components, including both the mobile client components and the server-side components. The dev team is quite frustrated, but because they really want to see the new merger succeed, they agree.

It takes the dev team and CTO staff a good solid four hours of discussions and whiteboard sketching to put together their visualization of the WM 2.0 design. The whiteboard, although quite cluttered and ugly, now contains the first design view of WM 2.0 (see Figure 3.2). It has been a frustrating process, but not without value.

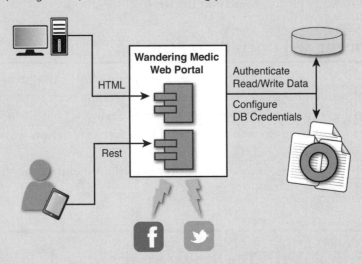

**Figure 3.2**   The architecture of the Wandering Medic portal.

Most of the frustrations have been because the dev team had differing opinions about how some components of the system would work in the final 2.0 product. The discussions have been lively and heated, but the good news is that the dev team itself has been able to solidify their own understanding of the system they're building. In fact, they even reluctantly agree that the mere process of writing their design—such as it is—on the whiteboard has helped them. They stop short of saying that the four hours in the conference room were better than four hours of coding, though.

Still, drawing the design is only the first step in the design review. The team takes a break until morning, when they'll do a quick design review using a threat modeling approach.

Freshly rested, our PST returns to the conference room to start the second phase of their process, the threat model.

With the design drafted, the CTO suggests dividing it into security zones as a starting point. The functional zones are easy: mobile zone, middleware/controller zone, database zone, authenticator zone. As a starting point, these delineations help the team consider them one at a time.

The first step is now to consider all the threat agents (people, mostly) who have access—legitimate and otherwise—across each zone. To get things rolling, the CTO suggests starting with the mobile zone. Then they will brainstorm all the threat agents they can come up with and then consider each in light of the following details. They must be sure to clearly set the rules for the brainstorming session in advance.

- Doctors

Clearly, the primary users of the app are the doctors. They have legitimate access to the devices and the app itself. What could motivate a doctor to attack the system? (1) Financial gain—a doctor might look through patient records to brainstorm "legitimate" medical procedures the patient should receive. Far-fetched, but this is a brainstorming exercise.... (2) Privacy violation—a doctor might want to read the records of a VIP patient, out of curiosity, or to give/sell the info. (3) Competition—a doctor might want to read another doctor's patient information to find out how the other doctor is treating a specific ailment. (4) Coverup—a doctor could attempt to remove or alter information to cover up mistakes. The team continues this brainstorming to come up with as many things as they can that could motivate a doctor to attack.

Now, for each of these potential attacks, the team considers how (technologically) skilled the doctor would need to be in order to be able to succeed.

- Nurses

Although the primary app users are the doctors, without a doubt nurses will also need to use the app. However, they might well have different motivations for (potentially similar) attacks. (1) Embarrassment—a nurse might enter false data to make a doctor look bad. (The team considers that attack case to be more likely than the other way around.) (2) Many of the same attack cases the team identified for doctors also exist for nurses.

- IT technicians

Certainly, the hospital's own IT staff would have to have access to each mobile device. While discussing this, the team briefly considers the case of "BYOD" (bring your own device) situations. The debate on this topic gets quite heated, with the developers primarily saying that they absolutely want to support BYOD situations. In the end, however, the Peabody CTO prevails and says that a medical enterprise environment will never allow patient data on a BYOD device, so they dismiss that case. Secretly, the CTO hopes that decision doesn't come back to haunt them later.... So what would motivate the hospital's own technicians to attack a system? (1) Sabotage—the techs are disgruntled because of continued budget cutbacks, and they want to teach the big hospital conglomerate a lesson. (2) Sabotage—the techs might want to build a Trojan horse into the app deployment so that the app fails if/when a technician is laid off. (3) Financial gain—the techs know about VIP patients in the hospital, and they could use access to the app to look up private details and then sell that information externally. (4) And again, this list continues. The skills required to do an attack, however, are far more prevalent in our IT technicians than in the doctors and nurses.

- Patients

From time to time, it is quite conceivable that a patient will have access to a doctor or nurse's mobile device. In those situations, what might motivate a patient to attack the app? (1) Alter records—a patient might change his own record to show more/less severe ailments. Perhaps this is financially motivated, to attempt to be charged less for a medical service. (2) Drugs—a patient could try to use a device to add or alter prescriptions, for various reasons. (3) Privacy violation—a patient might attempt to look up someone else's medical records.

Of course, patients' technology skills will span a broad spectrum, so it's best to assume that the patient is very technically astute.

- Doctors' families

Unless the hospital has a policy of not allowing staff to take mobile devices home, the team has to consider what the families could do. Here it might be a good idea to consider some actual attack cases as well as inadvertent attack cases. (1) Games—perhaps it's cliche[as], but it still bears consideration. What happens if/when a doctor's family members try to install games (or other nonsanctioned apps) on a hospital-owned mobile device?

Table 3.2 provides the final summary of potential threat agents that the PST team has come up with after an exhausting deliberation, as well as their potential motivations and expected technical skill levels.

**Table 3.2** Threat Agents

| Threat Agent | Motivation | Technical Skills |
|---|---|---|
| Doctors | Financial gain<br>Privacy violation<br>Competition<br>Coverup | Low |
| Nurses | Embarrassing doctor<br>Financial gain<br>Privacy violation<br>Coverup | Low |
| IT Technicians | Sabotaging hospital<br>Sabotaging application<br>Privacy violation | High |
| Patients | Alter records<br>Financial gain<br>Drug access<br>Privacy violation | High |
| Doctors' families | Using third-party apps<br>Privacy violation<br>Embarrassing doctor | Low |
| Thieves of mobile device | Privacy violation<br>Sabotaging hospital | High |
| Device tech support | Privacy violation<br>Sabotaging hospital<br>Sabotaging application | High |

Next, keeping its scope to the mobile zone, the team considers all the following factors. When carrying out this step, the team continues its brainstorming approach. One technique to facilitate this is to use a large whiteboard and construct a matrix (see Table 3.3) with each of the following column headings:

- Target

Here, the team considers all the targets within the mobile zone. The targets can be technical, data, or process based. For this app, the team considers its primary targets to be patient data (including PII, prescriptions, diagnoses, etc.), medical staff accounts, and encryption keys from back-end applications.

- Vulnerability

To consider all the weakness states of these targets, the team must deeply understand the app and how it functions. In particular, they need to consider all the circumstances where the target data is stored on a mobile device, whether in nonvolatile storage, in volatile storage, or in transit to/from the device.

- Attack

To brainstorm the potential attacks, we need to deeply understand the application's architecture—and force some vital decisions—and understand how things will be implemented. For the team's first shot at doing a threat model, they agree to hold off on several of the technology decisions and then revisit them later. For example, one attack they consider is to gain access to any local data stores via their SQLite (or whatever database the implementation team uses) files, which can be trivially done on iOS or Android versions of their app. They also consider carefully whether the access is read-only or read/write.

In fact, many of the issues the team will consider at this point will slowly be updated as the development process continues.

- Impact

There are two types of impacts any vulnerability will have: technical and business. Whereas the development team understandably concentrates on the technical side of this activity, business stakeholders become worried about business impact, so they very strongly push the team to include business considerations in the impact analysis.

- Remediation

This is where the technical world really clashes with the business reality. If the vulnerability remediation requires completely rearchitecting the solution, management gets quite impatient. This is where the impact analysis is really utilized, because the team and business folks will have to evaluate the *risks* of additional costs and delays incurred while fixing security issues versus not doing it and potentially being hit with breaches, data losses, and similar niceties. None of which Peabody wants to happen, of course—and neither does its CTO want to reimplement the portal.

**Table 3.3** Matrix

| Target | Vulnerability | Attack | Impact | Remediation |
|---|---|---|---|---|
| Patient's data | Stored on device<br>Stored on SD<br>Transmitted in clear | | | |
| Encryption keys | Stored on device<br>Transmitted in clear | | | |
| Staff accounts | Stored on device | | | |

## Summing Up

Whatever your application, and no matter what security tier you think it falls into, taking the time to think it through to the end before you start coding is essential. There is a reason many of the masters of chess and the Oriental board game Go train themselves to sit on their hands when considering their next move. Contemplation, even with a move clock ticking, pays off.

Perhaps you use a formal development life cycle. Maybe you've formed a project security team, or will just kick around ideas with friends. (Or will you, lacking a collaborator, explain your technical problems to an empty chair? It has worked for us.) Whatever your process, we hope the structure and tips in this chapter ease the "take it apart; good, now put it back together" thinking essential to "confluent" design.

Ready, set, go! It's Implementation time.

## Endnotes

1. Gary McGraw, *Software Security: Building Security In* (Boston: Addison Wesley Professional, 2006).

2. Michael Howard and Steve Lipner, *The Security Development Lifecycle* (Redmond, Washington: Microsoft Press, 2006).

3. For details, see "SEC Interpretation, Electronic Storage of Broker-Dealer Records," Securities and Exchange Commission, www.sec.gov/rules/interp/34-47806.htm.

4. McGraw, 2006.

5. Barry Boehm, *Software Engineering Economics* (Upper Saddle River: Prentice Hall, 1981).

# 4 Implementation Activities

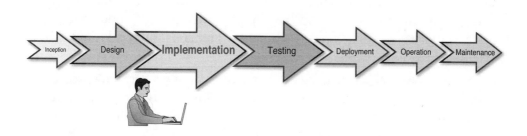

Inception › Design › Implementation › Testing › Deployment › Operation › Maintenance

**W**e come at last to a discussion of security at implementation time. We will focus particularly on the good that can be done if information security teams and software development teams collaborate at this stage. In many ways, security in implementation is easier to talk about than for design and planning activities. Measuring success in this stage is certainly easier, given the quality of automatic coder checkers available today. Is that why many security teams focus entirely on implementation? Or is it because (in our experience) so many security bugs originate in this phase of development? Whatever the reason, development gets more than its share of attention in most security reviews—and now we've arrived there. Let's talk about how we can draw together wisdom from two disparate disciplines to make our code as strong as it needs to be.

## Confluence

What role is there for security practitioners in development? You might be thinking that coding falls solidly in the domain of the programmer, and that security folks coming from outside of the development organization (SSG, IT Security, Information Security) can contribute little. That's a common and even traditional notion with which we soundly disagree. One of our aims with this chapter is to demonstrate the value a good security team (particularly SSG) can bring to bear during coding.

Consider source-code analysis tools, powerful in the hands of knowledgeable programmers. They call out several types of coding errors. But in our experience they still require substantial human analysis to be truly effective; in analyzing a coding security mistake, it is vital to comprehend the code context of the bug in order to identify potential attacks it makes possible. Static code analysis remains today a knowledge-intensive task.

An appropriately staffed SSG organization can most certainly provide significant value here. We have often seen developers look at a bug list from a static analysis tool and not be able to articulate a clear exploit scenario an attacker could use to penetrate the system. A knowledgeable security engineer might not grasp all the nuances of the code deficiency, but usually would have a better knowledge of target environments the application will run in and be able to describe a realistic exploit scenario in substantial detail. Together with a senior developer who knows the code inside out, they will form a very powerful team to efficiently eradicate security issues from application code.

We spotlight this and other types of collaboration in this chapter, as we step through several facets of modern code development.

## Stress the Positive and Strike the Balance

In analyzing software security topics, there is a natural tendency to focus on the mistakes that people have made over the years. Indeed, studying and learning from real-world mistakes—ours as well as others'—is a vital practice that the technology community as a whole has been woefully inept at. If we recognize that particular frequently observed ways of implementation almost always lead to security weaknesses, such practices should be called out in big bold letters—"DO NOT DO IT!"

However, just imposing restrictions is not nearly sufficient. After all, product teams need to deliver, and if given no help, they will either be forced to ignore the guidance, or fail to meet the schedule—and neither outcome is desirable to the company. In practical terms, it is insufficient to simply state, "never store cleartext credentials"; the guidance should also explain how to handle them properly.

Therefore, it's also important to look at positive practices, and positive coding examples and practices in particular. Instead of just providing a list of obstacles to avoid (as in the previous example), which can be frustrating for those of us who like to build things, positive coding guidelines ("properly salt and hash credentials") can actually help developers write good code by providing solutions. To be useful for developers, however, even the positive guidelines should be detailed (specify acceptable algorithms, modes, number of iterations, etc.) and should be accompanied by compliant coding examples for most popular frameworks used within the company (see Figure 4.1).

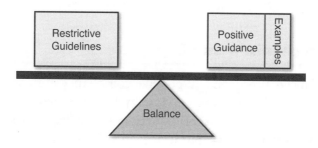

**Figure 4.1** Strike the balance.

We'll cite several examples of doing just that, such as OWASP's Enterprise Security API (ESAPI). But the point for now is that positive practices should be a focus in our coding efforts, custom tailored to suit our working environment. Of course, these positive coding guidelines, detailed recommendations, and examples have to be reviewed and maintained on an ongoing basis to remain relevant in the rapidly evolving technological landscape.

With positive guidelines for security and coding style in place, code reviews become easier as well, since you're no longer (just) looking for coding mistakes, but rather verifying positive compliance with defined coding standards. We find validating positive compliance easier and less prone to error than trying to find bugs in code. Such a positive compliance way of approaching secure code is, to be frank, rare; but it is exceptionally powerful, and well worth the effort.

We recommend that your developers collaborate with the enterprise security staff to identify and clearly understand the threats and attacks your environment is likely to face. Questions that could be addressed this way might be, for instance, "Should we be protected against potential XSS attacks by internal employees?" or, "Do we have to ensure confidentiality of employees' personal data against access by the company's IT staff?" From that clear understanding, you will be able to develop a set of balanced coding guidelines, consisting of a healthy mix of detailed positive and negative instructions (accompanied by working examples), designed to defend against the anticipated threats and assist with development of fortified applications.

After balanced coding guidelines have been established, you can turn your attention to the interesting stuff: the business logic in your software.

## Security Mechanisms and Controls

So with a balanced approach and positive compliance in mind, let's consider some of the most common, essential, and security-relevant software mechanisms that enterprise-level software needs to address. This list is not comprehensive, but it does include a range of fundamental building blocks.

### Network Connections

In today's wildly networked world, it is vital to establish network sockets securely and with confidence. After all, it is the network connection that so much of an application's business data is typically going to be riding. And the most common network security mechanism available today, to both web and non-web applications, is the secure socket layer (SSL). SSL provides us with a range of valuable features, from protecting the confidentiality of our sensitive information to verifying its integrity. Additionally, SSL can effectively be used to provide a high degree of mutual authentication for client-to-server and server-to-server communications for all sorts of services.

Certain important practices should be followed in implementing sound SSL sessions. Most of them should be decided upfront, during the design stage, and configured during deployment. (For additional details, see Chapter 3, "Design Activities," and Chapter 6, "Deployment and Integration.")

For example, the question of whether to use one-way or mutual SSL authentication (i.e., to require SSL certificates at either or both ends of the network socket) is an important one to ask during design. Another such fundamental question is, "Will the application set up its own private Certificate Authority or rely on commercial or enterprise certificates?" Of course, any such certificates, whether created by a private or external Certificate Authority, would be subject to the organization's certificate policy. This policy should prevent using outdated algorithms and short keys, among other things, and security folks from SSG would be in the best position to advise developers about requirements in this area.

With server-to-server connections, requiring certificates is relatively painless, but when connecting to lightweight clients, certificates can become unwieldy and difficult to manage. Correspondingly, proper implementation of mutual authentication involves a highly tedious, but necessary, process of setting up SSL trust and certificate exchange (automatic or manual) among all SSL communication endpoints during installation. Ideally, applications should rely on configurable platform services for this task whenever possible. If, however, this highly recommended practice is not followed for some reason, implementers are also responsible for the nontrivial task of hooking into the SSL handshake process to incorporate certificate authentication and access control mechanisms.

```
import java.io.InputStreamReader;
import java.io.Reader;
import java.net.URL;
import java.net.URLConnection;

import javax.net.ssl.HostnameVerifier;
import javax.net.ssl.HttpsURLConnection;
import javax.net.ssl.SSLContext;
import javax.net.ssl.SSLSession;
import javax.net.ssl.TrustManager;
import javax.net.ssl.X509TrustManager;
import java.security.cert.CertificateException;
import java.security.cert.X509Certificate;

/*
 * The Ch4SSL class implements functionality of both
 * java.security.cert.X509Certificate
 * and javax.net.ssl.HostnameVerifier.
```

```
 */
public class Ch4SSL implements X509TrustManager, HostnameVerifier  {
  // Start X509TrustManager methods

  /*
   * Sample Trust Manager simply delegates by default to the specified one.
   * Change its isClientTrusted() and/or isServerTrusted() methods to
   * customize trust decisions.
   * Multiple trust verification strategies can be implemented by applying
   * special rules to passed certificates.
   * For example, one may customize verification of hostnames, validity,
   * chain, etc, based on X509Certificate fields such as
   * getSubjectDN(), getSigAlgName(), getNotAfter(), getIssuerDN()
   */
  private X509TrustManager defTM = null;

  public Ch4SSL(final X509TrustManager defaultTM) { this.defTM = defaultTM; }

  /*
   * Delegate to the default Trust Manager to verify client's identity
   * based on the presented certificates.
   * Modify this method to do any special handling or replace default
   * client verification logic.
   */
  public void checkClientTrusted(X509Certificate[] chain, String authType)
➥ throws CertificateException {
   printCerts(chain, "Client-" + authType);
   if (this.defTM != null) { this.defTM.checkClientTrusted(chain, authType); }
  }

  /*
   * Delegate to the default Trust Manager to verify server's identity
   * based on the presented certificates.
   * Modify this method to do any special handling or replace default
   * server verification logic.
   * If failed, may want to present a dialog box to the client asking
   * whether to proceed with connection.
   */
  public void checkServerTrusted(X509Certificate[] chain, String authType)
➥ throws CertificateException {
    printCerts(chain, "Server-" + authType);
    if (this.defTM != null) { this.defTM.checkServerTrusted(chain, authType); }
  }
```

```
  /*
   * Delegate to the default Trust Manager to verify server's identity
   * based on the presented certificates.
   */
  public X509Certificate[] getAcceptedIssuers() { return (this.defTM != null
➥ ? this.defTM.getAcceptedIssuers() : null); }

  private void printCerts(X509Certificate[] chain, String authType) {
    System.out.println("Certs length: " + chain.length + ", authType: " +
➥ authType);
    for (int c = 0; c < chain.length; c++) {
      X509Certificate cert = chain[c];
      System.out.println(" Printing certificate " + (c + 1) + ":");
      System.out.println("  Subject DN: " + cert.getSubjectDN());
      System.out.println("  Signature Algorithm: " + cert.getSigAlgName());
      System.out.println("  Valid from: " + cert.getNotBefore());
      System.out.println("  Valid until: " + cert.getNotAfter());
      System.out.println("  Issuer: " + cert.getIssuerDN());
    }
  }
  // End X509TrustManager methods

  // Start HostnameVerifier methods

  /*
   * Example HostnameVerifier by default trusts all specified hosts.
   * It gets called if the URL's hostname and the server's
   * identification hostname mismatch.
   * Change its verify() method to customize trust decisions based on
   * SSLSession parameters and specified hostname.
   */
  public boolean verify(String hostname, SSLSession session) {
    System.out.println("Trusting host: " + hostname);
    return true;
  }

  // End HostnameVerifier methods
}
```

## Identification and Authentication

Whether a human user, a server, or another process is connecting to your code, it is vital to properly identify and authenticate (I & A) the connecting entity. We will look next at some of the commonly used options. Anything less would expose the software to a myriad of attacks (including, for example, a man-in-the-middle, or MITM, attack).

SSL can be very useful here, as explained previously. If your situation is a server-to-server connection, the SSL certificates can provide a solid basis for identification and authentication. This should be pretty much the standard for B2B (or service-to-service) types of applications, in which services communicate in the back end and do not require user interaction.

If your application instead uses a client-to-server connection, the situation is a little different. The most common client-to-server I & A in widespread use today remains the username/password combination. Although username/password has been used for years and years, it still has its place. Unfortunately, simple implementation mistakes still often occur.

The basic process flow for a username/password I & A is shown in Figure 4.2.

## Traditional Authentication Flow

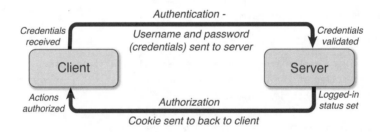

**Figure 4.2**   Traditional implementation flow.

The most common defect in an I & A mechanism is the compromising of the confidentiality of the username and/or password while the login request is in transit. The second most common mistake is the compromising of the confidentiality of either or both of these credentials while the data is at rest. We have lost count of the number of times we have found passwords either coded directly into an application—in plain text, not obfuscated—or just stored on disk.

Unfortunately, many developers simply do not realize that protection of usernames, although not as critical as passwords, is still very important.

If an application returns the "helpful" message "account XYZ is locked out" after a few random password guesses, it has just revealed the XYZ username to a would-be attacker.

For somebody dealing with security all the time, such points might seem too obvious and not worth reiterating, but they would have a potential to trip non-security-minded developers. It is therefore advisable to perform a periodic "reality check," engaging someone who is knowledgeable in both disciplines and can look at security advice provided to developers with a critical eye.

Remember that it is also necessary to encrypt the network communications as well as to protect the passwords while they are stored away in the authentication server's data store. For the former, we usually turn to SSL, as described previously, and for the latter, it depends on the intended usage. When dealing with client passwords, a cryptographically secure hash algorithm with random salt is usually used for protecting the confidentiality of the plain-text password. On the other hand, credentials, used for authenticating service-to-service connections, have to be stored in secure stores using reversible encryption. (We will talk more about the corresponding chores of key and credentials management later in this chapter.) Remember, you are setting the security of your application and its assets to the level at which you protect the place you store the application passwords!

In Chapter 3, we highlighted the necessity of integrating with common I & A mechanisms and following applicable standards. Here we just note in passing that, in coding an I & A mechanism, it is often necessary that the developers interface with one or more enterprise services, because many enterprise environments have built centralized I & A infrastructures. Within an enterprise, authentication among its services is usually addressed by some type of internal single sign-on (SSO) mechanism. This would be different from the externally facing services (if they exist), which would, most likely, rely on OAuth protocol to integrate with external providers. This separation into external and internal authentication domains is shown in Figure 4.3.

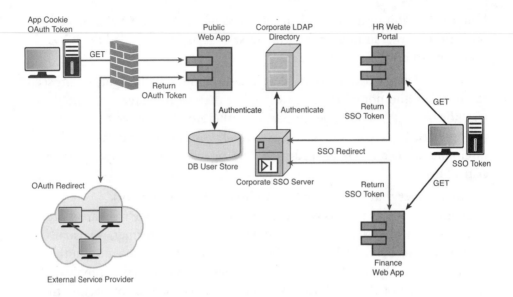

**Figure 4.3**  Internal and external I & A integrations.


## Session Management

For networked applications—especially web applications—session
management is a vital concern to be addressed with due care and caution.
Often, the application server provides the basic tools necessary to do
session management effectively. But it is up to the developer to use those
tools properly. In our experience, mistakes here abound.

One very common implementation error is to inadvertently disclose
session credentials while they are in transit. Of course, we can again turn
to SSL for encrypting our network connections. The latest versions of most
browsers and application servers have added explicit support for a special
"Secure" cookie attribute, which instructs the browser to send such cookies
only over an SSL-protected connection.

Unfortunately, the situation isn't necessarily that simple, because
attacks can be targeted against the session management mechanism itself.
Many web applications, for example, enable users to use the application
for a while before fully authenticating and encrypting the sensitive portion
of the login session. (This often occurs on web retail sites, for example,
where customers can fill up their shopping carts, and then authenticate and
encrypt to enter their payment and shipping information.)

This practice presents a session management challenge: Since the unencrypted part of the session is generally handled without any network encryption, the session credential and identification ("remember me") cookie is exposed. The safe practice here is for the developer to invalidate any active session tokens before allowing the encrypted and authenticated portion of the session to continue. Alternatively, instead of invalidating the existing tokens, developers can add a special "secure authenticated" token, returned only in the protected context. This is the approach used in many mainstream web application servers (such as Weblogic) that handle login cookies on behalf of the deployed web applications.

Another potential problem facing the application developers is *session fixation,* in which the attacker attempts to lure unsuspecting users into using a specifically crafted session of his choice. The answer to this problem is regeneration of a user session upon a successful login. After successful user authentication, any existing session information from the unauthenticated session should be copied over to a newly created session with a different session ID. The old session is then invalidated—for example, using the HttpSession.invalidate() method—and the new session is attached to the request. This approach is illustrated in the code fragment presented next.

```java
public void newLoginSession (HttpServletRequest request) {
  // Obtain the current session or create a new one
  HttpSession s1 = request.getSession();

  // Iterate over and copy session's attributes
  Map<String,Object> attrs = new  ConcurrentHashMap<String,Object>();
  Enumeration names = s1.getAttributeNames();

  //Use HttpSession.getAttribute(name) to obtain attribute values
      ...

  // Invalidate an existing session, if any ...
  s1.invalidate();
  // Force ID regeneration by creating a new session
  HttpSession s2 = request.getSession();

  // Copy attributes into the new session
  // Use HttpSession.setAttribute(name,value) to add attributes
      ...
}
```

The mainstream application servers usually take care of this task automatically. However, developers must remain vigilant and take the protective steps described previously if they choose to perform logins programmatically.

The previous session protection steps constitute very minimal, passive defense, mandatory for all web applications. However, in the spirit of confluence, application developers should also try to actively detect attempted attacks to create security alerts and perform blocking actions (discussed in more detail in Chapter 7, "Operating Software Securely"). For example, to combat session fixation attacks, an application could maintain a list of recently invalidated sessions and check for login attempts into those sessions. Or if application users should log in only from a single computer or device, the application could implement device pinning or restrictions.

### Access Control

Access control—sometimes referred to as authorization—is often neglected or poorly implemented in software. At its core it is simple. All access control comes down to asking and answering one basic question: Is the calling entity permitted to do what is being requested?

Simple, yes; yet access control might be the one single security attribute that is most often done wrong. One common reason: a flawed architectural assumption, particularly with regard to web applications, that a simple presentation layer access control is sufficient. In fact, these can often be trivially bypassed. Bypassing naïve access control implementation becomes even more trivial when there is a thick client application, which tries to assume authorization control responsibilities and connects to a "hidden" interface opened by the server-side application specifically for this client. Such hidden interfaces are usually easily discoverable using simple network scanning techniques, leaving the server application wide open to access from the network.

Sound access control requires a set of access control mechanisms that are well thought out and consistently implemented throughout the application's architecture. These should include the presentation layer, of course, but then should extend through the controller and/or business logic layer, as well as the data layer.

As you might expect, implementation specifics will vary quite substantially, but they should always effectively deal with the "Who gets access?" question. Additionally, the actual implementation here should conform to your organization's enterprise architecture.

Unfortunately, authorization responsibilities tend to be distributed across many layers and applications (see Figure 4.4). Most enterprise-grade systems incorporate some level (more or less sophisticated) of access control capabilities (usually in the form of RBAC), which are adjustable by the application's administrators. Infrastructure components, on the other hand, belong to the IT domain and enforce access control restrictions according to the resources they are aware of and work with. For example, web authentication servers, such as SiteMinder, will have a coarse-grained layer of authorization policies based on HTTP resources (i.e., URLs). Application servers, such as Weblogic, enforce policies based on the underlying JEE constructs: JMS queues, servlets, JSPs, EJB methods, and so forth. The resulting picture is not pretty, not to mention the management burden and potential access control gaps!

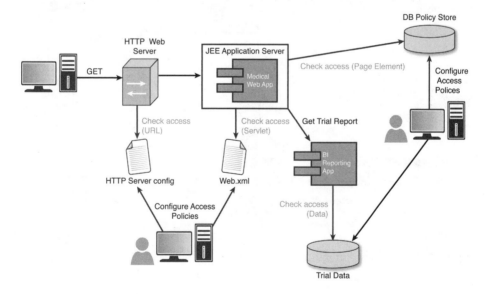

**Figure 4.4** Decentralized authorization.

Many enterprise environments include centralized access control mechanisms, or at least common architectures for doing access control. In most cases, it shouldn't be necessary to reinvent that wheel. A centralized access control implementation has a single (logistically speaking) server (called Policy Decision Point, or PDP). The PDP answers the "Who gets access?" question from all layers based on the requester's context and using a resource naming scheme (URL, page elements, table columns, etc.) appropriate for the requesting layer. Based on the PDP's response, the integrated agent (called Policy Enforcement Point, or PEP), will grant or deny access to the requested resource.

Ideally, the same server will also take care of mapping the user to roles appropriate for the resource the user is trying to access. Not only does such a centralized policy server provide for uniting different infrastructure pieces into a cohesive picture, but its role-mapping capabilities will also tie the role-based policies of enterprise applications into the overall access control setup. This more sane view of the world is depicted in Figure 4.5.

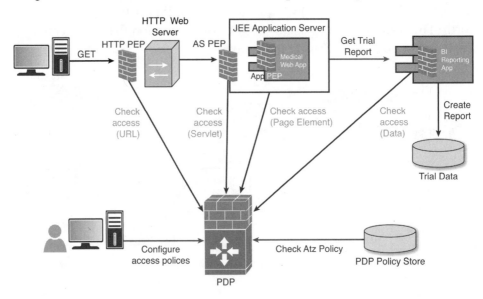

**Figure 4.5**   Authorization using PDP and PEP.

## Event Logging

Event logging is a huge topic and an aspect that is all too often poorly executed in live code. One misconception that is quite common, based on our experience, is that logging is an extension of the debugging process. In other words, all the debug traps and such that we put in our code while we're writing it, we merely change to log calls in our production code.

The fundamental misconception with this approach is that the event logging is being written for an audience of software developers. It is a dangerous misconception, which can lead to leaking vital security or private data in production systems. (Hey, what's wrong with logging those entire incoming messages?) Can we kill that idea, at least for production enterprise software? That is, technical support people and, sometimes, developers do need these technical details to resolve reported issues (provided that sensitive data does not get logged, of course.) However, your authors believe that the primary audience that you need to address in your event logging (from the security viewpoint) is the security team, often the computer security incident response team (CSIRT) or forensics investigators.

We already introduced this concept in Chapter 3, but it is worth reiterating it here: Start considering the CSIRT to be the audience for your application's event logging, and you'll quickly develop a new view of when to make an entry and what it should say. Of course, you will want to consider how they will use the information, and for what purpose. In our opinion, it should be a mandatory practice during later stages of the development process to require all developers to run their components with only production-level audit logs enabled and trying try to trace back what the application was doing! That would put their audit log information to a real test. Security folks can definitely share their views and experience when it comes to what belongs to these logs. We'll address that topic in more detail when we talk about deployment and operation activities in Chapters 6 and 7.

Having CSIRT folks as consumers of audit log data raises the question of audit log integrity. If there was an attempted intrusion, did the perpetrator attempt to conceal his tracks by modifying audit logs (assuming he was able to obtain access)? Signed and time-stamped entries in the audit logs might be necessary in certain high-security environments, and the development team needs to recognize this requirement early on.

## Protection of Sensitive Data

There are, of course, many times when we need to protect sensitive data in our software. Although we're not going delve into how to use various crypto APIs here, there are just a couple of absolutely key principles that we have to be mindful of. We have to properly protect sensitive information both at rest and in transit. That is just plain old common sense, right? It is, but it is in our experience staggering how often developers neglect one or the other. What's important to realize is that the mechanisms we will employ vary depending on whether the secrets we're protecting are at rest or in transit.

Let's consider first the in-transit case. There are two questions to ask at this point: Must this data really travel at all? If it does, how will it be protected en route?

Consider the data passed around in session cookies. Ideally, cookies should include just the session identifier and should not reveal any sensitive server-side information, such as usernames or roles, to avoid disclosure in case they are intercepted by a third party. If additional information does have to be included, such cookies should be encrypted on the server side and should be completely opaque to the client.

Thinking more generally, almost every modern programming language and platform provides good support for common security features for communication protection, such as SSL encryption, Web Service Security, or special data security attributes. To continue with the earlier cookie example, in addition to Secure, another very useful attribute for cookies is HttpOnly (see Figure 4.6), which serves to protect against cookie stealing in XSS attacks by unauthorized client-side scripts.

| Response Header | Value |
|---|---|
| (Status-Line) | HTTP/1.1 200 OK |
| Alternate-Protocol | 443:quic |
| Cache-Control | private, max-age=0 |
| Content-Encoding | gzip |
| Content-Type | text/html; charset=UTF-8 |
| Date | Fri, 02 May 2014 23:56:54 GMT |
| Expires | Fri, 02 May 2014 23:56:54 GMT |
| Server | GSE |
| Set-Cookie | GAPS=1:rPxG_FYWpUyMOafG2UAmvqLeduytDg:4v9SESHDOPv8mw4o;Path=/;Expires=Sun, 01-May-2016 23:56:54 GMT;Secure;HttpOnly;Priority=High |
| Strict-Transport-Security | max-age=10893354; includeSubDomains |
| X-Content-Type-Options | nosniff |
| X-Frame-Options | DENY |
| X-XSS-Protection | 1; mode=block |
| X-Firefox-Spdy | 3 |

**Figure 4.6** A secure cookie example.

Of course, this protection relies on the availability of proper client implementation, which is not guaranteed. Many popular browser plug-in technologies (for instance, Java Applets) cannot handle HttpOnly cookies properly, forcing applications to abandon this protection mechanism. So the selected solution might not always be available/feasible, requiring upfront research and investigation.

Such platform-level services and features are readily available (via either configuration or public API) to application developers today and should be actively used to combat common attacks. Members of IT/IS teams can be consulted about available configuration options and attacks they are devised to protect against.

Selecting a protection mechanism for sensitive information at rest is harder. There are several choices. Picking the right one depends on the actual architecture of your software itself. Encryption can be performed at multiple levels; we have seen disk encryption, file encryption, and field encryption, all with different trade-offs. For example, many enterprise-grade databases offer a transparent data encryption feature, protecting all stored data against copying directly from the disk and taking care of key management chores. Unfortunately, this mechanism will not guard against unauthorized data viewing at runtime, because data is decrypted upon access and will be served up in the clear. The next level of protection would require field- or attribute-based encryption capability, which would typically be implemented at the application level. When talking about file systems, one will consider using an encrypted file system (an OS-level task) versus encrypting individual files, or fragments of those (as an application responsibility).

User credentials represent a special case of sensitive data. Common security practices recommend storing user credentials in scrambled form, after applying a unique salt and running them through a one-way transformation, such as PBKDF2. However, in those cases in which a password is used to connect to another system, a reversible encryption algorithm must be used, along with a unique initialization vector (IV) for each password entry.

In our experience, sound application of cryptographic techniques tends to come down to *randomness*. Random numbers are used for generation of cryptographic keys and session identifiers, among other attributes. What will happen if generated random numbers are not *entirely* random, but are predictable with a significant degree of confidence? Nothing exciting—for the application, that is.

Now, to actually achieve the desired protection, such random numbers have to be unpredictable, truly random. Yet there is a limited supply of truly random events available to operating systems (most are externally generated), and applications must be sensitive to that. Guess what is going to happen if, upon OS booting, all applications at once start requesting random numbers for all possible uses? The operating system's random pool (so-called entropy pool) is going to become exhausted, and it might either block waiting for replenishing (a very slow process), or switch to generating pseudo-random numbers. Obviously, neither possibility seems appealing, so developers should be very conscious about usage of random numbers in their applications and should review such requests carefully with somebody who is well versed in both security and operating system design.

Either way, you'll need to decide on one or more cryptographic algorithms. If you are lucky, the information security department or some other authority in your organization will already have policies on what encryption and hashing algorithms to use for different tiers of sensitive data. They might also provide implementation guides, and even code samples.

In situations in which no cryptography policy exists, turn to publicly available sources such as the U.S. National Institute of Standards and Technology (NIST). NIST provides guidance to U.S. Government organizations (called Federal Information Processing Standards Publications,[1] or FIPS) on how to encrypt sensitive data, and is an excellent starting point when you're looking for appropriate encryption algorithms.

It is worth noting here that specific recommendations (algorithms, key, IV, and salt lengths) for secure hashing and encryption of credentials are regularly updated with advances in cryptography and sheer computing power. Staying up-to-date with the latest recommendations in this area remains the joint responsibility of development teams and SSG.

One last practical note: It will be a substantial complication if an application has to be updated and redeployed every time a new algorithm recommendation is issued. (This is often the case with large enterprise systems, deployed in production for many years, or even decades.) Developers (with help from SSG consultants) should anticipate this issue, and come up with configuration-driven implementation schemes to allow upgrading algorithms and increasing key lengths without code changes.

## Key Management

Even after you know how you will be encrypting your data in its various forms—algorithm, key length, and so on—a vital decision remains: how to do key management. That is, encryption mechanisms have to use keys or passwords to encrypt their data. *Where* you store those keys and *how you protect* them are two of the most significant implementation decisions you will make. So, congratulations! You have transformed the problem of protecting all the sensitive information *in situ* into one of protecting the keys associated with its storage.

The first question to ask in this case would be, is this application going to need unattended booting? A hint: If it is a Windows Service or a UNIX daemon, the answer is yes.

For those applications that expect to have user interaction during startup, the answer is actually quite straightforward. Do not store the key at all! Instead, they should prompt the user for an administrative password and use a password-based key derivation function (such as PBKDF2, commonly implemented on most modern platforms) to derive the encryption key, using the so-called Password-Based Encryption (PBE) process.

Unfortunately, most enterprise applications fall into the no-startup-interaction category. In practice, that means that they have to obfuscate the key by some more or less advanced method and follow this chain at start-up time to arrive at the actual key. There is, of course, the option of hardware-based protection modules, which can be used to store key material off the hard disk. We like this approach, but we have seldom seen it used to date in business. (We have seen it used predominantly in the government and military sectors.)

In reality, if the application can walk the deobfuscation chain to arrive at the actual encryption key, so can the attacker, if he has full control of the computer. So the real protection in this scenario comes from very tightly controlling file permissions of the file with key material. And, of course, never hard-code such keys in your applications! A unique key should be generated for each new installed instance of an application, and it had better include some management utilities or scripts to periodically rotate such keys.

## Data Input

All data entered into an application should be validated to ensure that it is safely consumable by the application. Here are some broad principles. (What makes this topic so broad is that a modern application can contain a great many different sources for data input. Each one can use a different API for inputting the data.)

First: Positive input validation tends to be a better choice than negative input validation (that is, the whitelisting versus blacklisting approach to validation). That is, assume that all data is dangerous until proven safe. This goes for all input sources. When you're working on the server side, it is best to assume that none of the incoming data has been validated before. This has particular implications for composed systems in the SOA (service-oriented architecture) world, where system designers often fail to realize that each of the interconnected systems usually takes turns acting as a client and as a server.

Of course, different input sources will have different degrees of trustworthiness. The baseline level of trustworthiness must be founded on sound decisions, thoroughly vetted through a threat modeling process and the application of realistic trust boundaries. Ideally, all inputs would always be checked and sanitized equally well; and indeed in certain critical systems (flight control software comes to mind) this is a hard requirement. In practice, however, most application teams, already under strong scheduling pressures, treat it as a soft requirement and select a subset of inputs for verification and sanitization, while considering remaining interfaces trustworthy and not requiring additional validation. False assumptions about trust boundary placement or lack of proper validation of tainted external data can be devastating, as was evidenced by the Heartbleed OpenSSL bug,[2] which was actually a trivial input validation.

That said, the next issue you face, as we discussed in Chapter 3, is where to place the input validation in the application's architecture. The truth is that an application of any significant size will end up having multiple validation layers, each responsible for a particular type of data. As a call proceeds from one application layer to another, each layer should be responsible for its own validation and should not rely on somebody else having done it for them. For instance, the Web UI layer is best suited to check for XSS attacks. Although it might also perform some cleansing of SQL data along the way, authoritative validation of any supplied SQL statements (or their parts) for SQL injection attacks should be performed at the DB interface layer, before statements based on that input are executed.

Let's take a look at two examples of input validation in action. Whereas the field validators are instrumental at stopping attacks, the SQL and XSS validators shown next use a blacklist validation approach. **Note that this shows how such verification should *not* be done, because blacklisting is trivially bypassed in most cases.**

```java
import java.io.Console;
import java.util.regex.Matcher;
import java.util.regex.Pattern;

/* A validation class that uses Java regex to validate input fields and
 * implement a primitive (and easily bypassed!) blacklist filter against
 * XSS and SQL Injection
 */
public class Ch4Validation {

    // Regular expressions for fields validation

    public static String REGEX_EMAIL = "^\\w[-._\\w]*\\w@\\w[-
._\\w]*\\w\\.\\w{2,}$";
    public static String REGEX_DATE = "^\\d{1,2}\\/\\/\\d{1,2}\\/\\/\\d{2,4}$";
    public static String REGEX_24TIME = "^(([0-1][0-9])|([2][0-3])):([0-5][0-
9])(:([0-5][0-9]))?$";

    public static boolean validateFields(String email, String date, String time) {
        System.out.println("Validating fields: " + email + ", " + date + ",
" + time);
        boolean result = email != null && date != null && time != null ?
            result = email.toLowerCase().matches(Ch4Validation.REGEX_EMAIL) &&
            date.toLowerCase().matches(Ch4Validation.REGEX_DATE) &&
            time.toLowerCase().matches(Ch4Validation.REGEX_24TIME) : false;
        return result;
    }

    // Regular expressions for blackbox XSS and SQLi validation
    // Bad idea, as blackbox validation is easily bypassed!

    public static String PATTERN_WEB = "\\b(script)|(<)|(>)|(%3c)|(%3e)\\b";
    public static String PATTERN_SQL =
"\\b(SELECT)|(UPDATE)|(INSERT)|(DELETE)|(GRANT)|(REVOKE)|(UNION)\\b";
```

```
public static boolean checkParameters(String parameters) {
    System.out.println("Basic verification of string: " + parameters);
    boolean result = false;
    if (parameters != null) {
        Pattern patWeb = Pattern.compile(Ch4Validation.PATTERN_WEB,
➥ Pattern.CASE_INSENSITIVE),
            patSql = Pattern.compile(Ch4Validation.PATTERN_SQL,
➥ Pattern.CASE_INSENSITIVE);
        Matcher matWeb = patWeb.matcher(parameters), matSql =
➥ patSql.matcher(parameters);

        result = matWeb.find() || matSql.find();
    }
    return result;
}
}
```

## Data Output

No matter how rigorous and thorough we are with our input validation, it is always safest to assume that some data has found its way into our application without first being validated. This is a simple practicality in today's complex enterprise computing environments.

With that assumption, we then need to ensure that all the data we output from our application is safely consumable in the target client environment. So, for example, if the client software connected to our application is processing XML-formatted data, we need to ensure that any data we send its way is properly formatted and not subject to XML injection and other associated dangerous data attacks.

This practice goes by different names, from output validation to output encoding or escaping. Whatever we decide to name it, the underlying principle remains the same. Format untrustworthy application data so that the original intent of your application's formatting remains unchanged and immune to data injection weaknesses in the specific output context. If you think of the application as a machine for transforming input into output, it's the job of the implementer to make sure that what comes out of the machine strictly conforms to applicable standards, no matter what sort of garbage (to use the historical term) has been passed in and which validation mechanisms have been implemented upstream. Of course, there are environmental controls, such as web application firewalls, to help you weed out this garbage. However, if application implementers could adopt a proactive approach to encoding, in case there's something bad flowing through the network stream, the corresponding layer of your application will be the last stop that will render this data harmless. Frustrating the bad guys can be so rewarding!

Output encoding is very context-dependent and is performed according to the type of consumer that will be processing this data. The end goal, though, is always the same: preventing various types of injection vulnerabilities in different application layers.

Arguably, the most well-known type of injection can happen within the user's browser. It is called Cross-Site Scripting, or XSS. There are multiple places within an HTML page where such XSS can occur: HTML entities and attributes, JavaScript, CSS, and URLs.

Quite understandably, OWASP covers this topic in great length. Its XSS Cheat Sheet[3] makes a great starting point for study of this issue. Further, OWASP's ESAPI library sets a de facto standard for handling output encoding for various contexts. With aids like these available, we find it heartbreaking that some developers continue to ignore this problem.

In the best traditions of open source code development, the best place to see the full list of available ESAPI Codecs (which denote output contexts) would be directly in the source code.[4]

```
// Example of encoding an input parameter for HTML context
String safeHTML =
➡ ESAPI.encoder().encodeForHTML(request.getParameter("myparam"));

// Example of encoding an input parameter for JavaScript context
String safeJS =
➡ ESAPI.encoder().encodeForJavaScript(request.getParameter("myparam"));
```

## Service Connections

Naturally, there are many situations in today's highly connected computing environments in which we need to safely establish connections between servers. These include connections to databases, directory services, file servers, business partner connections, and so on.

From the standpoint of protecting a business application, a service-to-service connection is really no different than any other application interface, and all earlier reviewed considerations are fully applicable. There is one exception to this statement, though, which is important to realize in SOA environments, because there are two distinct identities in play when a call is made between connected services. Indeed, there is a user identity, on whose behalf the call is being made. However, the calling service itself also has an identity, and the recipient must be able to reliably authenticate and authorize this calling service! This fact is often lost on developers, but after we've accepted it, we're able to move forward with making service connections that work reliably. In fact, the entire previous list is fundamentally identical for service connections and for user interfaces. The fact that our service connection might be to a trusted business partner shouldn't relieve us of the responsibility of taking all of these security precautions.

After all, if we make a fundamental mistake in setting up these connections, such as failing to ensure adequate mutual authentication of the systems in question, we open our software to enormous vulnerability exposures. Weak authentication, for example, can quickly result in so-called man-in-the-middle attacks in which an attacker masquerades as a remote server and steals credentials or other sensitive information.

## Code Reuse

Of course, these things alone will not make software secure. However, they do make up some basic building blocks that will be useful throughout the application. For that reason, it's a good idea to have these sorts of building blocks—and some others—sitting around to be used over and over again (see Figure 4.7).

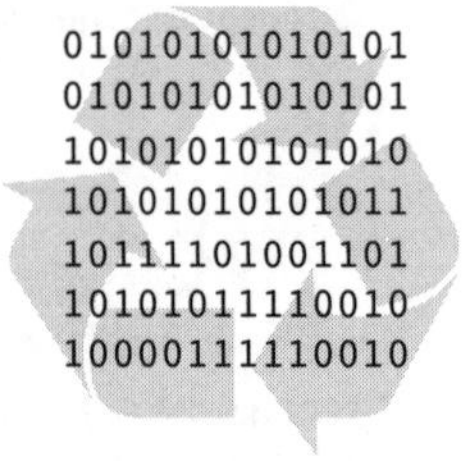

```
01010101010101
01010101010101
10101010101010
10101010101011
10111101001101
10101011110010
10000111110010
```

**Figure 4.7**   Code reuse.

That concept of having a standard set of security mechanisms handy was the basis for launching the Enterprise Security API project over at OWASP. We'll cover that in more detail in the next section, but for now, understand there's real strength in doing things this way. There are a several compelling reasons. Allow us to explain.

## Write Once, Review and Use Many

When it comes to security mechanisms, few people would be surprised that design or implementation flaws can have massive ramifications. Indeed, when security teams do code reviews, they often gravitate to the highest-risk portions of the code, and that often takes them to these security mechanisms.

Security-related code (particularly, it seems to us, cryptographic material) can be complex and notoriously difficult to do right, even for mature security specialists. This tells us that security mechanisms should be designed carefully, implemented pedantically (and rarely), and reviewed and tested rigorously. That, in turn, tells us that developing security mechanisms properly can be costly. However, the costs can quite easily be recouped over time by using the code over and over again, effectively spreading the cost over many projects.

Of course, open source implementations, such as ESAPI or OpenSSL, and publicly reviewed cryptographic algorithms also have their inevitable share of costly bugs! These can become especially devastating when they are discovered in widely used components. The effect of the Heartbleed OpenSSL bug, mentioned earlier in the "Data Input" section, was greatly exacerbated by the extremely broad usage of OpenSSL in Internet-facing systems. It caused widespread misery across many enterprises upon its disclosure.

Nevertheless, open source projects benefit greatly from having many well-trained professionals (both individuals and whole teams sponsored by some of the largest software vendors) poking at them, looking for holes and finding obscure flaws. This approach can turn up bugs that software teams in individual vendors are unlikely to discover. Also, some software bugs will be weeded out eventually just by virtue of undergoing multiple reviews, running the shared security code in so many various products and configurations. This factor again contributes to the security of the most widely used components.

Not all software is suitable for reuse, but we're fortunate that security functions certainly are. Just be sure to always use up-to-date versions of shared components with the latest patches applied!

### Enterprise Integration

Many of the mechanisms we've discussed here ought to exist in the realm of enterprise infrastructure. These include centralized authentication services, crypto key management, and so forth. Many (most?) modern enterprise environments will have existing standardized architectures, libraries, and even products in place to handle these infrastructure services.

And here's where we find another benefit to standardizing our security mechanisms. We should ensure that our security mechanisms properly integrate into those infrastructure components so that our software is conforming to the prevailing enterprise architectures. This topic is covered in greater detail in Chapters 3 and 6.

### Positive Compliance

If we're effective at reusing security functions in our code, there are strong benefits other than the direct cost reductions. One excellent benefit is that our code reviews through security mechanisms become easier because we're not (just) looking for errors in others' code, but verifying positive compliance with corporate code patterns, guidelines, libraries, and so on.

Put another way, it is always easier to prove a positive than a negative; and if you have access to exemplar code that has already passed a review—or, better yet, has been certified to be in compliance with standards relevant to your enterprise, and perhaps its regulators—we recommend you make extraordinary efforts to employ it in your implementation.

This is an enormous benefit to us, as code developers, and we can make good use of it.

## Coding Resources

In the previous text, we examined numerous security mechanisms and discussed some of the issues involved in implementing them. These are excellent examples of common mechanisms that every enterprise software development shop should have in its bag of tricks. But getting started down the path of having a set of enterprise implementations of these things can be more than slightly daunting. To that end, it's a good idea to build off of others' work whenever feasible. To put it another way, "Steal from your friends."[5]

Depending on your circumstances, you might find that adapting an existing library like OWASP's ESAPI or OpenSSL is the right way to go. Alternatively, any one of the reasons we've cited here could be sufficient justification to spend the time to put together an enterprise security API of your own. If you happen to be the first in your enterprise or coterie to pass this way, taking the trouble to package essential elements for convenient reuse not only is a matter of good citizenship and discipline, but also could turn out to be self-serving if you tackle similar issues in the future.

So let's delve a bit deeper into some resources that are available to the enterprise developer.

## OWASP ESAPI

"ESAPI (The OWASP Enterprise Security API) is a free, open source, web application security control library that makes it easier for programmers to write lower-risk applications. The ESAPI libraries are designed to make it easier for programmers to retrofit security into existing applications. The ESAPI libraries also serve as a solid foundation for new development."[6]

Even if none of these ideally fits your organization's needs, the ESAPI is a good starting point to consider in implementing your own security API.

For developers, it is important to understand that ESAPI is more like a toolbox, which provides convenient tools for commonly needed security functions. These tools, or building blocks, referred to as "security controls," address tedious and difficult tasks that pretty much any application team has to deal with—and where most errors tend to happen. The ESAPI toolkit defines the following security controls:

- Authentication
- Access control
- Input validation
- Output encoding/escaping
- Cryptography
- Error handling and logging

- Communication security
- HTTP security
- Security configuration

Or, if you prefer to see it as a picture, take a look at Figure 4.8.

## Architecture Overview

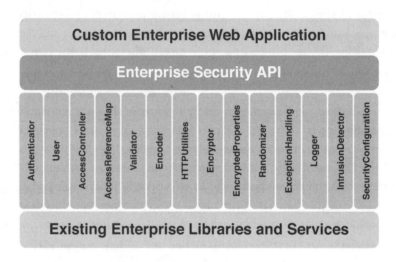

**Figure 4.8**   ESAPI architecture.

As already has been said, these controls were designed to help address the most commonly encountered security tasks. Not surprisingly, they also stack up well against OWASP Top 10 enumeration. It turns out that ESAPI provides at least some services for most of the Top 10 categories. The image in Figure 4.9 demonstrates how ESAPI was matched up against the Top 10 categories at the time when ESAPI was originally conceived and designed back in 2008.[7]

## OWASP Top Ten Coverage

| OWASP Top Ten | OWASP ESAPI |
| --- | --- |
| A1. Cross Site Scripting (XSS) | Validator, Encoder |
| A2. Injection Flaws | Encoder |
| A3. Malicious File Execution | HTTPUtilities (upload) |
| A4. Insecure Direct: Object Reference | AccessReferenceMap |
| A5. Cross Site Request Forgery (CSRF) | User (csrftoken) |
| A6. Leakage and Improper Error Handling | EnterpriseSecurityException, HTTPUtils |
| A7. Broken Authentication and Sessions | Authenticator, User, HTTPUtils |
| A8. Insecure Cryptographic Storage | Encryptor |
| A9. Insecure Communications | HTTPUtilities (secure cookie) |
| A10. Failure to Restrict URL Access | AccessController |

**Figure 4.9**   The ESAPI match for the OWASP Top 10 for 2007.

Although the OWASP Top 10 listing has been repeatedly updated since then,[8] you can check to see that ESAPI is still very relevant for the tasks it originally set out to address.

One of the explicitly stated goals of ESAPI designers was to make retrofitting into existing applications and frameworks painless. At the time of this writing, ESAPI provides an impressive set of reference implementations for many popular languages and platforms, including Java EE, .NET (C#), Classic ASP, PHP, ColdFusion/CFML, Python, JavaScript, C/C++, Objective C, and so on. Additionally, although ESAPI does supply reference implementations for the security controls previously listed for various platforms and languages, it allows easy extensibility via custom implementations of particular controls. For example, this makes it easy to integrate with a centralized enterprise authentication and access control system, or to enforce central policy on data validation.

### Programming Cookbooks

Although we're not huge fans of "cookbook"-style references for learning the principles of developing secure software, they have their place. Using them as a source for primitive routines that will make up the ingredients of an enterprise security library is one such place. Note too that we're not referring to operating system or application platform security cookbooks, such as *Red Hat Enterprise Linux 6 Security Guide.*[9] Although such texts are useful in their own right, they are best used for configuring and running complex software systems, not for writing secure software.

## Implementing Security Tiers

Here we want to return to the notion of security tiers we introduced in the preceding chapter. At a minimum, we want to ensure that all the code we develop is at least compliant with the low-security tier in that it is able to withstand the sorts of attacks we anticipate will hit it in its deployed environment. That's to say the code must be able to *continue to operate* and do the job we are writing it to do.

Where things start to get interesting from our coding perspective is when we progress upward to the medium- or high-security tiers, and that's the real point of this section. We want to address here the "art of the possible," as a former co-worker of ours liked to say.

To begin with, most modern application-level languages have rich feature sets for exception handling. For example, Java has its `try-catch-finally` block, which can be extremely useful for many purposes, including ours. At a very simplistic level, we can construct code blocks around our security-related operations that look something like the following:

```
try {
  // some_security_operation;
} catch security_exception {
  // do_this_instead;
} finally {
  // clean_up_things_after_exception;
}
```

As simple as that example is, it opens a world of possibilities for us. The power of branching our code in various directions based on the outcome of a security operation is the key for enabling us to do interesting things when our code is under attack.

One need not be a programmer to recognize the potential here, and that is the key to where we can find opportunities for confluence between our security and development teams. Traditionally, the security teams were seldom (if ever) consulted during the coding process. But if we include them in the process, we can achieve great results. Of course, the proper way and level of exception handling will differ depending on the technology and the nature of the application. It is impossible to provide guidelines for each and every situation. What is possible, however, and what we aim to do, is to describe how to view exception branching from the security flow standpoint, and then apply this logic to a specific design you (the reader) are dealing with.

Looking at our previous example, we should consider the business owner of our software to be the customer of the entire `try` block. That, after all, is where the business functions will primarily reside in our code. The security team, on the other hand, is another important customer of the `catch` block (besides developers, that is). It is here in the `catch` block where we get to do something when we detect a security issue. Of course, product architects and product managers should take notice, too, and translate their input into specific requirements or even standards, as explained in Chapter 3. Moreover, properly caught and handled exceptions help to deter hackers who are looking for signs of unhandled exceptions as they are trying to find their way into an application.

The `finally` block is important to security as well. This is where we need to clean up unfinished business to make sure that our assumptions aren't violated, even in the event that something goes wrong. (See now why traditional network firewalls, while important, are insufficient for our purposes?)

The `catch` block is where we can codify our security policies, or delegate their processing by calling out to a standard solution via a plug-in. The latter approach is applicable both to exception processing (within the `catch` and `finally` blocks) and to the normal processing flow, where a security-relevant decision has to be made. This kind of adaptive security behavior is further discussed in Chapters 6 and 7. Here, it will suffice to note that such a centralized service will likely be under the auspices of the IS department (either directly or indirectly), and the development team would have to stay in touch with those folks while implementing and testing this feature.

From the product implementation standpoint, such adaptive behavior requires additional integration and introduces greater complexity in design and configuration. It provides two great benefits in return:

- Dynamic reconfiguration of security policies without code changes
- An ability to make security decisions based on real-time situation and history (perhaps, after all, we should reauthenticate that user, based on previous login attempts into his account)

## Code Reviews

Few things are more dreaded by software developers than code reviews (see Figure 4.10).

**Figure 4.10**    The dreaded code review.

Scrupulously reviewing one's own code, for example, is terribly difficult. The static analysis software and other tools will take you part of the way. Make maximal use of them. But be aware that some coding deficiencies can escape even the best automated filters today. As for the manual filters—your eyes, that is—if you were blind to a bug the first time, do you really think you will find it on subsequent passes? We don't have any magic dust that will make that dread go away, but we can offer some practical guidance that might well make things flow more smoothly.

First of all, let's clarify that we're referring to both the traditional manual sort of code reviews and (partially) automated code reviews making use of static code analysis tools. Many software development organizations use manual code reviews to look for functional aspects of the code, as well as conformance to coding guidelines. However, not many software development organizations use code reviews to focus specifically on security problems in the code base.

Although there is nothing wrong with doing functional code reviews, there is also a lot of value that can be found in doing security reviews—or at least including security in existing code review processes.

When done well, manual code reviews can benefit an entire team of developers. There are just a few things to bear in mind.

### Don't Overdo It

Manual code reviews can be intense, tough, and time-consuming. You're expecting your software developers to look over someone else's code and find issues. So keep in mind that there is a strong human tendency to glaze over details after a certain point, as a result of either diminishing returns or waning energies. Be realistic in how you schedule code reviews. Tackle just one or two code modules per review session, for example.

### Navigate Wisely

Since you're limiting the scope of the manual code reviews to small chunks of code, you need to have a deep sense of priorities within the code. Zoom in on the most security-sensitive modules of code and start there. Spend your time wisely. As a starting point, we might suggest looking at the interfaces between modules and components, as well as following data received from external inputs (or, as referred in static code analysis, "tainted data").

### Details

Group code reviews are by nature very detail-oriented. Someone has to lead the discussions, and someone needs to take meticulous notes in order for the effort to pay off.

### Knowledge Sharing

Knowledge sharing is perhaps the single-most-valuable aspect of doing manual code reviews. Whenever developers get together and critique some code, there's bound to be useful knowledge sharing among them.

## Ground Rules

Manual reviews always imply lots of individual interaction. This has to be planned for, and carefully. All review participants should feel free to voice their concerns and questions about any of the code under review, irrespective of ownership. Criticisms should never be personal, but should be about the code itself. When a developer becomes overly defensive about his code, senior participants should be experienced enough to steer the conversation carefully, and in a nonconfrontational way. Similarly, someone in the meeting should be taking notes on each of the issues discussed. Each issue should be tracked thoroughly. In short, everyone should be encouraged to engage and participate in the process, with a common goal of improving the code base. If, in the end, participants view the code review exercise as successful and productive, they are also much more likely to find that it was acceptable, even if it initially caused some heartburn.

## Bug Tracking

Code reviews by themselves are pretty useless if they do not produce any trackable results. These results can be captured in various ways—from formal bug-tracking systems (e.g., Bugzilla[10]) to spreadsheets. The important part is to preserve the location and context of the problem so that developers do not have to double-guess later as to what is the actual issue they are supposed to fix. Also, when handling bugs logged during such reviews, care must be taken to follow all internal procedures for security issues, established by the company's IS department.

## Facilitation

To run group code review meetings in a useful way, someone has to facilitate the meeting properly. The person in the facilitator role, whether formally assigned or not, will have a lot of things to keep track of (mostly technical, and sometimes of a personal nature). As such, he or she should be a senior and broadly respected team member, capable of driving the entire process efficiently and communicating clearly. In individual code reviews, in which developers work tête-à-tête, things tend to be less formalized, but the participants should still carefully track the issues and strive to steer the discussion in productive ways.

If, after all is said and done, you find yourself the last and only security reviewer of your own code, know that we have been there. ("Been there, done that, failed," says one of your authors.) To jog loose bugs you inserted in the first place (or left in, if maintaining code), you will need to force your brain into unfamiliar development territory. If you have the time, try coding up the most security-sensitive program sections two or three ways. (You do know which sections those are, right?) Solving the various small technical issues more than once can have several security advantages. Not only might you discover a safer approach the second or third time around (and, possibly, using another language or programming platform), but we also have found that forcing ourselves to reexamine a "solved" problem can make us aware of threats and potential loopholes we were blind to earlier. It will not hurt, of course, to Do The Right Thing and use this opportunity for extracting the most common and security-sensitive sections into shared components or services in the spirit of code reuse, as was already suggested earlier in this chapter. In a real pinch, try explaining how your code works to an empty chair. Some grizzled veterans who are not afraid of looking foolish swear by this technique; if you find us some day talking to ourselves while coding, that's why.

## A Day in the Life of a Servlet

We will turn our attention now to an extended scenario that illustrates, we think, much about what can go wrong while implementing even simple software. We call this section "A Day in the Life of a Servlet" because (even though it takes place, in our imagination, over several months) it shows events from the point of view of the servlet. No, we don't talk in the first person ("I was born on a laptop on the 4th of July"), but we do showcase the primacy of the software. More important than the business case, overwhelming considerations of time and money, and the private lives of managers is the stuff that actually runs on the iron. Often, it counts not what it's supposed to do, but what it does *not* do. So, okay, what does your software actually do?

### Conception

Here's the hypothetical (but realistic) scenario, one that we have seen play out in live situations more times than we care to recall. Let's put you in the picture. You're the engineering team leader of an enterprise web application that performs some useful business function. One day, your boss tells you that you must implement new functionality. The application's users, say, need to have a way to look up their personal account records—stored in a simple SQL database table—in one easy function. A simple (even *clear*) requirement! You set out to make this work. After scoping out the general shape of how the program will work, you assign one of the junior engineers on the team to implement the change.

The application itself is a lightweight Java EE servlet, built on top of a popular open source application container (let's say it's Apache's Tomcat). Of course (ahem), since the application is going to be used only by company employees, it doesn't go through the same level of rigor that a customer-facing application might. Nonetheless, you want to ensure that things are done right. To build the basic functionality, the developer quickly whips up a standard servlet omelet using his favorite IDE. In this servlet, he looks up necessary information in the back-end database using this simple SQL query:

```
// Read the employee name from the incoming request
String db_query = "select employee from employees where name = " +
➡ webreq.getParameter("employeeName");


...
ResultSet employee = db_stat.executeQuery(db_query);
```

After a quick "look-see," you're satisfied that the new code fulfills the functional requirement. You let the boss know that it's up and running, and then turn your attention back to more important matters. After all, this isn't a revenue-producing app, so going through rigorous quality control and testing doesn't seem necessary. Sounding familiar yet?

### Teething Pains

A short time later, alarmed by new vulnerabilities reports, the IT security team runs detailed vulnerability scanning of applications on the internal network. They send a report to your boss calling out an issue with your app, some kind of "SQL injection vulnerability." Of course, the boss immediately fires off a "fix this now" note to you. What do you do?

Concerned, perhaps, for your job, you go out to the Web and search for information on "SQL injection." There's some useful data out at OWASP about the SQL Injection itself[11] and a helpful prevention checklist,[12] so you forward a few relevant links to your developers and tell them to make sure that the app is free of SQL injection.

Matters can progress in two ways here.

Faced with a penetration report detailing a glaring SQL injection attack, it's not uncommon to see (here's the first scenario) the developers simply extend the earlier presented validation class to implement a "blacklist"-based filter that prevents that specific attack from recurring. Let's play that out: When the testers rerun their tests, sure enough, they can't break back into the application! Everyone considers the situation to be resolved, when in fact your software feels (okay, software probably can't feel yet) as vulnerable as ever.

```
/*
 * Second edition of the validator class that uses blacklist filter to
 * protect against only a specific variation of SQL Injection
 */
public class Ch4ValidationEx {

    ...

    public static String PATTERN_WEB = "\\b(script)|(<)|(>)|(%3c)|(%3e)\\b";

    // An "extended" SQL Injection validation filter
    // that checks only for a specific test case
    public static String PATTERN_SQL_INJ =
➥"\\b(1=1)|(SELECT)|(UPDATE)|(INSERT)|(DELETE)|(GRANT)|(REVOKE)|(UNION) \\b";

    public static boolean checkParametersEx(String parameters) {
        System.out.println("Extended verification of string: " + parameters);
        boolean result = false;
        if (parameters != null) {
            Pattern patWeb = Pattern.compile(Ch4ValidationEx.PATTERN_WEB,
➥ Pattern.CASE_INSENSITIVE),
                    patSql = Pattern.compile(Ch4ValidationEx.PATTERN_SQL_INJ,
➥ Pattern.CASE_INSENSITIVE);
            Matcher matWeb = patWeb.matcher(parameters),
                    matSql = patSql.matcher(parameters);

            result = matWeb.find() || matSql.find();
        }
        return result;
    }
}
```

But we're going to assume that your team is better than that. Let's follow the second scenario: They actually take the time to read the OWASP papers and opt for the recommended way of using the parameterized query solution to the SQL injection problem. So forget that blacklist approach. Instead, their first solution to the problem looks like this:

```
// Utilize a prepared statement to defeat SQL Injection attacks
String db_query = "select employee from employees where name = ?";
PreparedStatement db_stat = db_conn.prepareStatement(db_query);

// Use positional parameters to provide employee name
db_stat.setString(1,webreq.getParameter("employeeName"));
ResultSet employee = db_stat.executeQuery();
```

With the fix in place, the security team reruns the scan. They are satisfied, at least for now.

### Growing Pains

A few months go by. The company's annual penetration testing team (our scenario, our rules) comes in and runs more in-depth tests on the enterprise applications. This time, they find a "cross-site scripting" vulnerability deep inside your application. The regular, run-of-the-mill vulnerability scan had failed to find it, but for the penetration test, the test team spent some time "training" the black box scanner to help it do a better job of mapping out the application's Web UI, and these efforts paid off by finding a new XSS vulnerability in the application.

How is it going with your boss? Now you're back to square one, and back to the OWASP web site to do some studying on just what a cross-site script problem really is. And once again, in fairly short order, you find the relevant papers[13] and have the developers dive back in to fix the problem.[14]

The problem turns out to be in the blacklist validation of the input parameter for employee name (again!), which was echoed back with the records. This time, you instruct the developers to do rigorous positive input validation throughout the application, as well as output escaping to prevent any extant malicious data from doing damage on a client. The developer responsible for fixing it looked at the available resources and chose to use ESAPI for validation and encoding, as shown here:

```
// Encode the employee name from the input for HTML context
String name = ESAPI.encoder().encodeForHTML(
       webreq.getParameter("employeeName"));
```

This basic "whack a mole" process goes on for a while, until you have pretty much covered all the big issues in the OWASP Top-10.[15] But now everyone seems pretty happy that the application is safe and sound.

## Software as Hapless Victim

Unfortunately for you, however, there remains undetected a nasty little access control weakness in your application. One day, a disgruntled employee learns of the weakness. She exploits it, and collects private information on all the company's employees. Later, some of that information—she sold it—is used to steal the identities of a handful of employees. The media picks up the story, causing embarrassment and reputation damage to the company. Your company's top management hires a computer security incident response team (CSIRT) to come investigate the attacks and find out how the attack happened, and who did it. (Got the shakes? We empathize. Even to this point, your authors have been on every side of this story.)

The outside consultants turn out to be quite competent, but there's an obstacle to successful analysis: The application hasn't been properly integrated into the company's enterprise security infrastructure. Even if it "wanted" to, it has no way to tell the doctor where it hurts (or, to switch metaphors, to tell the police where the sucker punch came from.) Thus, when the CSIRT goes looking for logging data, at best they find operating system and low-level application logging that falls far short of providing the answers to the questions of Who, What, Where, When, and How (WWWWH). The access log data they find might well look something like this:

```
192.168.5.11 - - [07/Mar/2014:11:22:51 -0800] "GET
➥ /myapp/Search?t=1458aaaaaaaaaaaaaaaaaaaaaaaaaaaa%<%u0123%u7007%u3290##
➥ HTTP/1.1" 401 13246
192.168.5.11 - - [07/Mar/2014:11:28:45 -0800] "GET
➥ /myapp/ResetPassword?param1=1 HTTP/1.1" 200 12431
192.168.5.11 - - [07/Mar/2014:11:28:53 -0800] "GET /myapp/Webs?param=do
➥ HTTP/1.1" 200 8806
192.168.5.11 - - [07/Mar/2014:11:30:32 -0800] "GET /myapp/Get?topic=home
➥ HTTP/1.1" 401 13246
```

```
Accompanied by these error entries:
[Mon Mar  7 11:23:53 2014] statistics: Can't create file
```

➥ /home/httpd/myapp/data/qsaff.txt - Permission denied
[Mon Mar  7 11:27:37 2014] [info] [client 192.168.5.11] (101)Connection reset
➥ by peer: client stopped connection before send body completed

From this, we see plenty of log data, but take a note of what is *missing:* business information. The problem here is that the logging was written for developers to debug problems with the application, not for a CSIRT to investigate a security incident. To be truly useful to the CSIRT, the developers need to understand that the CSIRT is the consumer of the security logs, and to log information that is useful to the CSIRT process. We'll come back to that later in this chapter and in Chapter 7, where we discuss operational issues.

For now, however, after many hours of collecting and analyzing data, the best the CSIRT can do is to put in place network-level monitoring for any future attacks against the system. But the attacker has already accomplished her objective, and no future attacks are likely to come from this attacker. She got away with it, and she still works for the company.

### Can We Close the Barn Door Now?

Company executives, after reviewing the incident report, launch an initiative to get all business and privacy critical applications up to par with enterprise standards. It's task force time! Before you know it, your boss is back in your office explaining what needs to be done. And now you're faced with challenges that far exceed the initial and simple goal of just developing something that satisfied the functional requirements.

How will you begin your new work? Well, let's consider the task of the incident responders now. In our scenario, their task is to discern what took place on a system they probably aren't very familiar with, and they are supposed to do that simply by looking into the available data. Let's discard the Hollywood notion of computer forensics and consider what information the CSIRT would really have to work with.

On a typical server like the one we've described here, there would be various system logs that record logins, logouts, messages being transferred, URLs requested, and so on. More often than not, there would be little if any logging by the application itself. If they're lucky, the SQL database will be logging connections and SQL queries, but that won't tell the CSIRT who was logged in to the application. Since most middleware logs in to the back-end database via a single canonical username and password, all SQL transactions appear to come from that user profile, from the perspective of the SQL server.

What's missing, for starters, is *application-level event logging.* Many enterprise applications like the one we've described here don't do any appreciable event logging. Of those that do, all too many simply log the most basic of events—application logins, logouts, catastrophic exceptions, and so on. These logs, as we've said, are typically written for the developers, not for the CSIRT.

Compare that against what the CSIRT is trying to do: answer the questions of who attacked the system, what was stolen/altered/deleted (or just accessed), where the attacker originated, when the attack took place, and how the attacker performed the attack. We should know who was logged in to the system, but how would the CSIRT even know when the attack took place? Based on external reports, they might be able to narrow that down to a range of weeks, days, or even hours, but what if multiple people were logged in when the attack took place? What if there were several steps involved, at different times and places? How can they tell for certain who the attacker was or how the attack was carried out?

To answer these questions, the application would need to log not just more information, but fundamentally different information *which would facilitate the piecing together of an entire sequence of events.* Really, to be useful, this type of logging (remember the WWWWH questions?) should be planned well in advance, during design stage, as explained in Chapter 3. Of course, this planning should also cover vital third-party components used in the application (whether commercial or open source), either by controlling its logging granularity (if possible), or by wrapping its entrance/exit calls with application-specific logging calls.

### How to Raise a Well-Behaved Servlet

To see how this debacle might have been avoided, let's return to our servlet example and consider two different logging cases: when we detect an attack, and a normal business operation.

For the first case, let's consider a malicious data injection attack such as XSS or SQL injection. You've built a solid positive input validation mechanism. You block everything except provably good data from entering your application. How does that impact what your app logs? In this case, we used an ESAPI validator to allow only valid data to pass. That was not enough, was it? Unfortunately, our validator was missing logic for handling exceptions and logging failures.

So instead, let's bring that validator back into the business logic in your middleware, see when the validator fails, and branch accordingly. But is it sufficient to simply branch, log the "attack," and lock out the attacker? What if input validation is done on a user's real name, and you're allowing only uppercase and lowercase characters (e.g., [A-Za-z])? Now, what if someone named O'Shaunessy tries to use our application? Okay, we can allow the single-quote character. Now what if someone accidentally types "O,Shaunessy"? The perceived attack might be a simple case of stupid fingers. You certainly wouldn't want to jump to conclusions.

### Doing the Right Thing Can Be Hard

Positive input validation is both a good thing and a hindrance in a way. You block anything that is deemed unsafe, but in order to take appropriate steps, you now have to do a different type of input parsing. It is necessary to examine the actual data that was entered and identify whether it was an attack or a simple user error. That requires a bit of careful thought and consideration.

There are several factors working against the implementer striving to do the right thing. For example, there is canonicalization. For example, an XSS attack could well contain the string "<script>". That string can be expressed in many different ways. Trivially, it can be "<scRIPt>" or "<ScripT>", just to name a couple. When dealing with case-insensitive data, one may, of course, convert all inputs to uppercase and try matching to permissible string constants or regular expressions. However, counting Unicode and other encoding schemes, we can encode "<script>" in 1,677,721,600,000,000 ways.[16] Seriously. That means that naive black box attempts will likely fail. But it doesn't mean you should just give up.

When we insert IDS branching for flagging potential attacks, we have made a first step toward our stated goals. (Clearly, that methodology isn't scalable; we'll come back to that topic.) Next, however, consider what is being logged. Does the application directly log the attack we've identified here? After all, it is trivially easy to use a logging mechanism like Log4j to send the data to an enterprise logging facility.

Say, just how is that data going to be consumed, anyway? Could the code be unwittingly passing some dangerous data to our security team, only to have them fall prey to the attack? (We've cleaned up after *that* mistake more than once.) Could that team even be the primary target of a sophisticated attack designed to exploit a poorly written application? Clearly, these are not career-enhancing scenarios.

No, you have to log the attack—recalling the "Who, What, Where, When, and How" questions—and ensure that the attack data is rendered harmless for the investigators.

Wait, wait—if you alter the attack, how does that impact our ability to use that as evidence when we call in law enforcement?

As we've sketched, the situation quickly becomes quite complex. We will continue this discussion with further considerations and details in Chapter 7, when we talk about post-deployment operations.

## The Code Review

Our Product Security Team (PST) is starting to feel pretty good about how things are going. Even the newly acquired development team agrees that there was value in going through the design review. After all, they learned things about their own system that they really hadn't properly considered before.

So, with that positive experience in mind, they set out to do something that many developers get nightmares over: the code review. And not just any code review, but a security review before their new corporate overlords. The core team had done informal peer reviews of code blocks from time to time, but usually just for functional reasons like trying to find a particularly elusive bug. Security reviews had been something they'd heard about but had never really tried. Actually, for them it is just another manifestation of bureaucracy running amok in a large company.

They start by doing a basic code inventory of sorts, and quickly determine that their code base is in the order of 50,000 lines of code (LOC) on the mobile devices and 100,000 LOC on the server side.

And now they also come to a technology hurdle: Their app is being implemented in both Android and iOS versions. That means that they have code (predominantly) in Objective C and Java. How best should they handle reviewing these two largely different technologies?

Right off, technical problems abound:

- The Peabody software security group has substantial experience using two different static code analysis tools, but neither is able to handle ObjC.

- The static analysis tools they have for ObjC aren't security tools per se. Rather, they are tools for finding common quality issues, such as memory leaks.

- Neither the existing Peabody developers nor the new team has any significant code guidelines or examples in either Java (for Android) or ObjC. This means that their scanning will be starting from scratch in every sense.

Starting from scratch analyzing (and then remediating) tens of thousands of lines of code is going to be an enormous undertaking! Somewhat discouraged at the realization of what lies ahead, the team is distraught. Nonetheless, they are not willing to admit defeat, so they hold a meeting to discuss the problems and attempt to find some middle ground solutions.

The meeting starts with the team recounting for the Peabody CTO their seemingly endless list of "insurmountable" problems and difficulties.

After long and careful consideration, the CTO agrees that they'll strike a compromise for now. The short-term plan is as follows. They'll address the biggest issues in the OWASP Mobile Top 10 Risks document (insecure local storage and insecure communications) via positive code examples that they'll verify through their code reviews. The code patterns will be jointly written by the dev teams of "both" companies.

They agree, however, to launch a longer-term plan that will include a rich library of code patterns for common security mechanisms. They'll also contact all the static code analysis product vendors and find out their road maps for iOS and Android support. Where products exist, they will test-pilot them for possible inclusion in their code reviews.

So they designate a small dev team to develop a handful of code patterns for securing local data storage on both platforms and to perform strong network communications. This seemingly trivial task turns out to be a little less trivial, because there are a myriad of issues to address on both platforms, and no solutions seem to be perfect enough for either group.

The process, which they figured they could rip through in a couple of hours, ends up taking them a few days. Nonetheless, when they finish, they return to the laborious process of the code review, this time with a vastly limited scope in mind.

In the abbreviated code review for this project, the team finds several issues that need to be cleaned up in both their Android and their iOS implementations, so they again dive into the coding. This time, however, with their previous research on the code patterns complete, they're far more confident, and the code fixes end up being fairly straightforward.

At the end of the code reviews, they call it a qualified success. They're pleased that they did indeed find and fix (prior to delivery!) issues with both local data storage and secure communications. At the same time, they recognize that they still have much work ahead to build a robust code review process.

Our former Scherr-Mantis team is privately humbled by it all. Despite their earlier trepidation about taking on a secure development process, finding all those defects in their code has made believers out of them.

## Summing Up

The implementation phase of your project might be where a "confluent" approach makes the most noticeable difference. From source-code analysis to enterprise integration, if the developers in your shop are not working together with enterprise security experts to implement a collaborative design, you're ceding an advantage to attackers—as well as your competition.

That said, there are a lot of ways to code up any solution. We tried to shine a light on some possible approaches with our examples, but of course there's only one way to find out whether your stuff works the way your project team designed it. Can you employ the principle of confluence in your test methods? That is the focus of our next chapter.

## Endnotes

1. These highly useful documents are available online at http://csrc.nist.gov/publications/PubsFIPS.html.

2. For a good overview of the 2014 Heartbleed vulnerability in OpenSSL, as well as related and subsequent issues, see http://heartbleed.com/.

3. https://www.owasp.org/index.php/XSS_%28Cross_Site_Scripting%29_Prevention_Cheat_Sheet#Output_Encoding_Rules_Summary.

4. http://code.google.com/p/owasp-esapi-java/source/browse/trunk/src/?r=1869#src%2Fmain%2Fjava%2Forg%2Fowasp%2Fesapi%2Fcodecs.

5. The slogan of the Digital Equipment Corporation User Group Library in the 1980s.

6. www.owasp.org/index.php/Category:OWASP_Enterprise_Security_API.

7. http://owasp-esapi-java.googlecode.com/svn/trunk_doc/latest/org/owasp/esapi/doc-files/OWASPTopTen.jpg.

8. The current version is OWASP Top 10 2013, https://www.owasp.org/index.php/Category:OWASP_Top_Ten_Project#tab=OWASP_Top_10_for_2013.

9. https://access.redhat.com/site/documentation/en-US/Red_Hat_Enterprise_Linux/6/pdf/Security_Guide/Red_Hat_Enterprise_Linux-6-Security_Guide-en-US.pdf.

10. https://bugzilla.mozilla.org/.

11. https://www.owasp.org/index.php/SQL_Injection.

12. https://www.owasp.org/index.php/SQL_Injection_Prevention_Cheat_Sheet.

13. https://www.owasp.org/index.php/XSS.

14. https://www.owasp.org/index.php/XSS_(Cross_Site_Scripting)_Prevention_Cheat_Sheet.

15. https://www.owasp.org/index.php/Top_10_2013-Top_10.

16. "OWASP Enterprise Security API (ESAPI) Project," Dave Wichers, AppSec EU09, www.owasp.org/images/1/11/AppSecEU09Poland_ESAPI.pptx.

# 5  Testing Activities

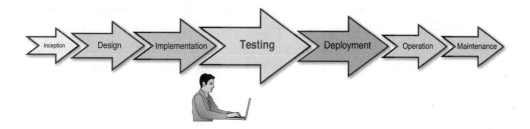

Inception | Design | Implementation | **Testing** | Deployment | Operation | Maintenance

**W**here does testing belong in the secure life cycle? Can the security of an application be ensured by exhaustive testing of all possible inputs and endpoints—by "testing security in"—without properly caring for it in the preceding phases of product development? We hope the answer is clear by now: absolutely not! Neither do security activities cease after the testing phase. What is special, then, about this phase of software development?

If you happen to have skipped the previous chapters, please do go back and read them first. Proper testing relies on information collected in earlier stages! It will be used, too, to influence those stages themselves, in case of iterative development. Security testing is no exception: Quality Assurance engineers need to know what to test, and how to test for security. They must be aware of decisions made during the requirements and design phases.

Of course, this book is not about security testing itself (there are plenty of materials on this topic already available), but about *confluence* and its effect on software development. How does this concept affect security testing? In many ways, large and small, from setting up realistic deployment environments, to exchanging expertise with security tools, to jointly reviewing testing plans for gaps.

We begin this exploration by posing a few questions to highlight advantages of the confluence-driven development approach.

## A Few Questions about Security Testing

In this section we delve into some fundamental issues regarding security testing. We've seen far too many organizations that fail to build robust security testing programs, so let's start by looking at the big picture.

### Where to Start?

As a testing team, we now have an application that, let us assume, has gone through a security vetting process during design and implementation phases. In addition to a gazillion lines of code that make up the application modules we are about to test, those phases should have produced additional artifacts that will help us determine *what* to test. Optimally, a quality assurance (QA) representative will have participated in several requirements-gathering and design meetings, making sure that the technical documentation includes necessary information for creating comprehensive security testing plans. Typical documents might include those discussed in the subsections that follow.

### Architectural Diagram(s)

As shown in Figure 5.1, a good architectural diagram shows important components, exposed interfaces, and the connections among them.

### Data Diagram(s)

Data diagrams complement architectural ones to reflect flow, handling, and storage of sensitive data. As Figure 5.2 suggests, such data might include various credentials and protected information, including financial (such as banking account), personal (a Social Security number), or health data.

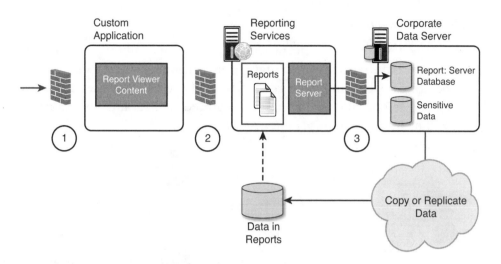

**Figure 5.1**   A sample architectural diagram.

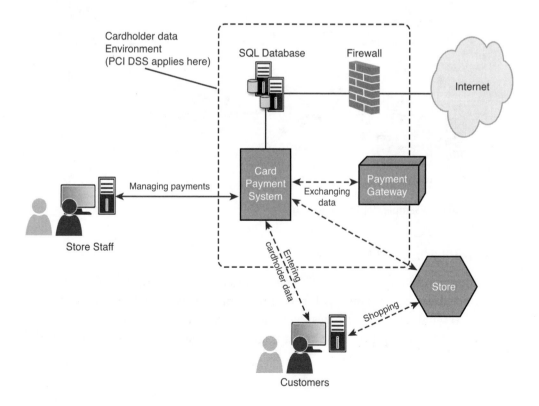

**Figure 5.2**   A sample data diagram.

*Deployment Diagram(s)*

Early in the development cycle, product requirements will specify an exact set of supported environment configurations, including specific versions of the operating system, and other key software elements, databases, directory servers, and so on. These requirements, captured as diagrams (see Figure 5.3), will be invaluable for planning QA activities.

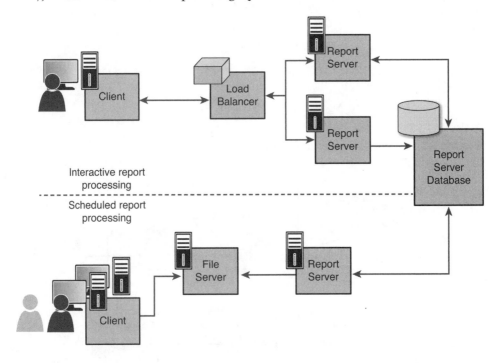

**Figure 5.3**   A sample deployment diagram.

*Supported Functional Use Cases*

A fundamental component of testing specification is a good set of supported use cases. These will reveal not only the expected functionality, but also what application's designers do *not* expect it to handle. Use cases provide the starting point for creating possible attack scenarios for security testing.

*Hardening Guide*

What does the development team recommend, at this stage, about how customers should set up the product in the most secure state? (We hope this guidance will not differ too much from the default installation!)

If the QA team has all these documents on their hands, they have an ample opportunity to define and develop their security testing approach during the implementation phase. (Unless, of course, we are dealing with Agile processes, which call for a very different dynamic of interteam interactions and where these documents might remain in flux until the very end of development process. In our experience, this dynamic usually does not go very well with security planning.)

## What Testing?

But wait—what exactly is meant by the catchy phrase "security testing"? Let's consider. A common mistake we see today, when it comes to security testing, is to do nothing more than a penetration test (often, externally contracted). Big Fail.

Don't mistake us. Penetration testing (or "pentesting" as it is commonly called) has its place. (Hint: It's better as a periodic activity after deployment.) And more and more, we are seeing contracts written that require pentesting as part of the SDLC, just like regression testing (that's a given at your shop, right?). But it falls far short of being an adequate security assurance practice and cannot replace regular security testing. Ever tried using a laser pointer to lighten up a spacious dark room? That is what pentesting will do with your product: provide a narrow and detailed view of a tiny point on a far end of the room, while failing to reveal a calamitous mess in the dark corners next to you. To extend the metaphor, we'll point out that sometimes what is really needed to illuminate hard issues is a lamp the size of a Hollywood searchlight. Pentesters can only go so far. Sometimes they stop out of fear of breaking your app (or, if external, your web site). Often, they stop because they found a fatal bug that crashes the app. But you want all the bugs, right? For that, context is king.

About pentesting and its limitations, we like what McGraw and Migues[1] say in their analysis of BSIMM statistics. They argue that the importance of security testing activities significantly increases with the age and maturity of security assurance programs. Here's the money quote:

*Perhaps the most interesting observation here is that effort in Penetration Testing starts out very high in young initiatives just getting started and decreases dramatically as software security initiatives get older. This makes intuitive sense since Penetration Testing is a great way to determine that you do, indeed, have a software security problem of your own. The problem is that Penetration Testing does little to solve the software security problem—that takes other activities.*

In this chapter, we illuminate the world outside of pentesting to provide a more comprehensive view of security testing activity. We recommend the use of various testing teams, engaged with the project at different points of its life cycle and with differing goals. The cost in time and resources of this ideal scheme will be substantial—as are, in our experience, the security quality rewards.

### Regular QA

The regular QA teams' main goal is to confirm that functional requirements are met. Testing is aimed at verifying that the application behavior matches the prescribed one as closely as possible. The primary outcome of their work will be functional bugs against the product development team. There's a secondary outcome: tools and processes that can be used against future versions of the product, making sure that the bugs that were caught and fixed in this release remain fixed. In the best case this means a full harness of regression tests.

### Security QA

The security QA teams are primarily interested in finding gaps in security planning, so most of their activities are devoted to boundary conditions and determining broken assumptions. The primary outcome of their work will be security bugs for the product development team to remediate.

### Pentesting Team

Pentesting teams also try to identify security gaps, but, unlike QA, they usually have neither access nor time to develop an exhaustive set of security tests, concentrating instead on selected areas—sort of searching for needles in a haystack. The primary outcome of their work will typically be management reports containing details of security findings.

### Informational Security (IS) Testing Team

Technical members of IS organizations typically come from network administration and operational background, so their efforts are typically concentrated on environment testing, mostly in the form of running various OS and network scans and reviewing deployment models. Typically, these teams become engaged either for systems already in production, or in preproduction state, so any security findings tend to be immediately reported up the management chain, especially if they threaten to delay product launch or normal operation.

Do you see the impact of confluence in this combination? Although most development teams would more or less have a good grasp of the first three categories of security testing, the activities of IS testers are typically terra incognita for them, since developers are rarely confronted with deployment issues in their products. In fact, many members of enterprise development teams will have only a vague idea about the ways their products are deployed and operated in the real environment. (In your company it's different? Celebrate!)

Members of the IS teams, on the other hand, typically do not have a good grasp of development processes, looking at the software strictly as black boxes with network-bound ports and certain data I/O operations. This chasm is manifest to people in implementation consulting roles, those poor souls who spend months at the production sites trying to put the systems into production. Good implementation engineers will be able to provide great feedback to the team managers willing to listen to their advice. In this capacity, they straddle development and operational worlds, and their participation in the product design and testing processes should be highly encouraged in all teams.

Since the idea of Security Quality Assurance engineers will be new to most readers, we'll dig down a bit here. Who are these SQA folks, and how do they differ in what they do from traditional QA?

Regular QA testers perform functional testing to *confirm* that certain modules or interfaces operate exactly as expected and specified. Security QA personnel, on the other hand, attempt exactly the opposite! Given a product's build and functional specifications with use cases developed during the design phase, they will try to define a set of tests covering interactions outside of the expected use cases. That is, the main purpose of their testing consists in violating design and implementation assumptions (all together, one at a time, or certain subsets of those) according to their liking and experience. They seek to determine whether software can hold its ground.

Security QA folks can come with different forms and backgrounds. They can be just security-minded members of the regular QA team, or a dedicated team with special security training. What makes them part of QA, however—and distinguishes them from pentesters—is close involvement in the release process, access to product documentation and developers, and management reporting structure.

That last point about management reporting structures is very important. Integrated management involvement ensures proper connection of the Security QA personnel into the software development life cycle (SDLC). And psychologically—well, if you've ever had the opportunity to contrast a security problem report communicated by a colleague with one mailed in from an external, faceless, contextless pseudo-attacker, you'll appreciate the distinction. Developers sure do.

We have one remaining point to make here about the nature of security testing you will be doing, and it arises from the many-faceted background of your authors. Note well: The security testing requirements of applications developed *for internal deployment* are going to be substantially different from those developed by software vendors *for selling to outside customers*. We've done both. This book concentrates mainly on the case of internal development.

The key difference between developing for internal and external targets consists, in our experience, in the involvement of the Information Security team in testing. We have only rarely seen that done for commercial products (alas!). Since most of the IS personnel will have network or operations security background, they will not be looking at the software design diagrams; rather, they will be deploying network and OS scanners against the deployed application instances! The primary targets of these tests would be environment settings, open ports, proper patches, permissions, and so on. There are overlapping items of interest, of course—for example, secure communication channels, credentials and key storage, file permissions in the installed components—but those IS guys bring a defender's eye to the testing process that is rarely engaged in commercial product development.

## How Much?

Software testers of all kinds would often be happy with testing software more or less forever, because they can never be certain of its real behavior after it has been put into production. Unfortunately, when planning security testing, one has to also realize the painful (for some of us) fact that no amount of the most rigorous testing will ever be able to ensure absolute security. Why so?

The most obvious problem here is that there is simply no way to predict what types of inventive attacks will appear next. Software built 15 years ago did not protect against XSS or CSRF. These attacks had not been invented yet, and there were no test cases that could detect them. When applications undergo security testing today, the best we can hope for is to execute a more or less complete set of tests for issues that we know about. But when a new attack type is discovered tomorrow, made public at the next security conference, and publicized by the media, it will be the job of Security QA to update its test suites to check for this new attack vector as well when a new software release comes around.

A second issue: Security bugs are very often the product of programmers' sloppiness and corner-cutting practices to get new releases out the door. Okay, we'll say it for them, with sympathy: "Who cares about what security says; we need to get the release out by the date set by the senior management!" With bonuses and performance reviews on the line, nobody can really blame them. Deadline considerations like this have burdened the software we all use with bad bugs that are unexpected, are difficult to detect, and lurk unnoticed in applications for many years and through multiple releases, becoming buried under layers and layers of new code.

Finally, there is the issue of plain economic cost. The longer you test, the more resources will be spent and the later the product will be released. Clearly, testing forever isn't the answer, but then what is? The answer comes from a deep understanding of risk. To know what to test, how to test it, and how rigorously to run the testing, one simply must know the business value of a piece of software. We often refer to this as the "so-what factor." Software with a substantial "so what" deserves more intense testing than software without. That stands to reason, but how do we best answer the very real question of how much we should test? Perhaps as much as the testing itself, this question gets to the core of what is important in security testing.

**When to Stop?**

Depending on whom you talk to, the answer can range from "never" (a contracted pentester) to "now" (an engineering manager of the development team). Really, there are many ways to look at this question, and many reasons to consider. Let's play a little game of multiple choice:

The team should actually stop testing _____.

1. Only when the software has zero security bugs

2. Immediately!!!

3. When release criteria are met

4. When senior management says so

Even without being deeply familiar with the details of the software testing process, anybody who has taken multiple-choice tests before knows that several answers on the list will look plain wrong, and the real choice is really between a couple more realistic ones. Looking at the options given previously, we will recognize that the first option is merely wishful thinking, but hardly a realistic expectation in real-life development. Unfortunately, all released software has bugs, whether or not we like it. It is just a matter of how obvious those bugs are and how serious their potential consequences are.

Number two on the list represents the deeply concealed wish of many project managers, which in our experience tends to surface as the planned product release date moves closer. However, if development process is properly organized (and especially if the Security QA and the Release Manager do not report to the same senior manager as the development team), the SQA folks should act as gatekeepers of a sort to ensure that important testing is not circumvented and sacrificed to the "Release Date Deity."

Looking again at our little quiz question, we consider that the third answer is the right one.

In an organization that takes security assurance seriously, the release process includes an explicit set of security readiness criteria. Examples could be "No open bugs with a CVSS score greater than 4.0" or "No open XSS or CSRF bugs." Note also that it is at this juncture in the testing process where the central security team can step into the spotlight, both as the authors and as the enforcers of those security readiness criteria. Security

QA folks will be very busy discovering and filing the bugs (as well as, one hopes, interacting with development to explain the details). But SQA's actions should be closely aligned with the standards issued by the corporate security team. Otherwise, development and release management teams will be confused. More than the usual chaos might ensue as a result of conflicting guidance on priorities and readiness criteria. Your result could be project delays, or product releases of substandard quality—or, in the worst case, both at the same time. Yes, we've seen it.

Okay, you passed the quiz. But our fourth option deserves discussion, too. Stopping when senior management says so should not be discounted, although in saying this we might offend our friends who are software security purists. We have seen dialogue between the corporate security team and senior management remarkably like the following:

**Security:** *"But this software has 23 open security bugs of High Priority—it just cannot go out like that!"*

**Exec:** *"We have an awfully important industry event coming up; all our major competitors will have products based on XYZ (mobile, Cloud, etc.) technology there. We must be there as well!"*

**Security:** *"But this will be publicly reported!"*

**Exec:** *"It is about the market presence; I personally commit to fixing these issues before this release is picked up by the first customer."*

**Security:** *"Okay, whatever."*

Guess what? Security assurance (of which security testing is an internal part) does not exist in isolation; this is something that many pure technocrats fail to comprehend. Continuing with our hypothetical example, suppose that the security guys have their way and the application is released a year late, with all known security bugs fixed. But when product management brings it to the following trade show, will they discover that their competitors have already closed deals with the most important players in this market, leaving this perfected software to compete for table scraps? Good judgment, they say, comes from experience; and experience comes from bad judgment. We caution you to profit from the prior bad judgment of your authors, and not delay product release to the bitter end.

Overall, this decision (Hamlet, if he were a project manager, would declare, "To release or not to release?") is a complicated balancing act between competing business interests. It is closely linked to the "so what?"

factor explained earlier in this chapter. If releasing with known security defects will actually hurt the business less than not releasing the software, well, somebody must be bringing in revenue to pay the high salaries of those security professionals and developers!

In such situations, the senior folks in the security group must be able to put on their business hats. They cannot afford to remain pure "security techies," pick all the fights, and attempt to block everything—not if they keep the company's business success in mind.

## Tools of the Trade

Now that we've answered the questions "who" and "when," our next logical query is "how." While researchers spend vast amounts of time manually analyzing theoretical properties of communication protocols and resistance of encryption ciphers to brute-forcing attacks, these methods are not suitable for the majority of security testers out there. These worthies in fact seldom have time to analyze deep characteristics of a particular piece of code at all. Their tasks are usually restricted to finding ways to break applications by throwing large quantities of bad data at them. Security testing tools are really indispensable at this stage, because in skilled hands they allow testers to quickly produce a useful number of test cases and permutations.

Before we start with traditional security testing tools, let's talk for a second about source-code scanning. Should it be considered part of Security QA's arsenal? Our answer is a resolute "No!" This "No" is not to the usage of source-code scanning technique itself, but to its usage in QA organization. Source scanning techniques were already covered in Chapter 4, "Implementation Activities," so here we will just briefly outline why it should *not* be part of the QA process.

### Lack of Coding Skills

Let's face it. QA and developers have different training, and, more often than not, QA members are trained not to untangle application's source code but to interpret the functional requirements and run massive numbers of tests against the product in the shortest amount of time possible. Therefore, when a source scanning tool will start complaining about unvalidated parameters in the array XYZ, QA testers might not be able to properly judge whether it is a false positive about array variable XYZ itself, or a real issue with an unvalidated element "k" within that array (XYZ[k]). As a result, they will be tempted to just log all reported issues as bugs, adding to the strains on the already stressed (can we assume that?) development teams.

## Lack of Proper Context

The same report might turn out to be a false positive or a true positive, depending on the context of the code in question. If a variable is assigned a value from a custom cleansing function, but the tool is not aware of it, it will be reported as an unvalidated parameter. Only somebody with good knowledge of the code and product's architecture will be able to figure this out, and fine-tune the tool to properly treat this and similar occurrences. The person who can do this will likely be part of the development, and not the QA team. It is unlikely that a QA tester will know the internal API for validation and encoding, again resulting in a bulk of false positives, entered as security bugs against the development team.

## Timing

Finally, by the time QA teams typically get their hands on the product, it is way too late for executing such analysis. We are talking about the final phases of the development cycle here, when developers are very rushed to complete their tasks, and would be least inclined to spend any significant time helping QA to sift through the initial source scans and fine-tune source-code scanners.

So if testers of all shades do not (or should not) run source-code scanners, what do they actually run?

The answer depends on which security testing team you are dealing with: product QA, IT, or IS. We will talk about that in a minute. However, they all have one thing in common: They all use so-called *dynamic* tools, designed to run against executing applications. This is different from the toolset executed during the development phase, where it would be either code scanners (as explained previously), or a more or less complete set of unit tests.

A Security QA team, depending on its sophistication, experience, and staffing level, will likely run a mixture of (a) point-and-shoot fuzzing tools, such as HP's WebInspect or IBM's AppScan (to name a few) and (b) home-grown utilities, designed to test proprietary protocols or interfaces. Many members of Security QA teams have some programming experience (often in languages such as Perl or Python), sufficient to put together a few homegrown tools given a specification document or a sample data feed. Such utilities can be readily developed using open-source fuzzing frameworks, or added as extension plug-ins to existing tools.

This approach is commonly known as *grey box,* in which details of the protocols and interfaces are well known and one tries to inject faults by making intentional modifications to the input data. This is where Security QA can have a clear edge over all other testing teams. Since they deal closely with development teams and know the products' internals, they can build testing utilities for specific cases, and not just rely on "over the counter" ones. Going further, they can fine-tune their commercial testing tools for specific products. Other powerful weapons in Security QA's arsenal are manual and semiautomated tools (example: Burp Suite Professional), which enable you to intercept, analyze, and modify data samples to include invalid or intentionally malicious data to test an application's defenses. Such tools are highly customizable and can be used instead of, or in addition to, homegrown security testing utilities.

The picture is quite different with IT security. You will be hard-pressed to find people with development experience here, since most of its members will have primarily operational backgrounds. Perl experience might be present as well, but you'll tend to find that less commonly, and to a less sophisticated degree, as with QA. However, never underestimate the power of those command-line scripts! An experienced script developer can be invaluable when it comes to rapid testing or automating testing tasks, which is a must when dealing with large product deployments. On the other hand, IT personnel will usually lack knowledge of product internals, and will often have a variety of products and versions to test in very limited time, so they will be severely limited in what they can do to customize their testing environments. As a result, one will likely find here a few common testing tools (again, WebInspect, AppScan, and/or some open-source ones) running in their default configurations. These tools can be coupled with network, OS, and compliance scanners, such as Qualys, to check for open ports, improper OS configurations, and so on. All these tools and utilities can be automated and glued together with scripts to run against a great variety of hosts and applications, with results fed into enterprise processing centers. These can then be aggregated and displayed on nice-looking status dashboards as pie charts, graphs, and so on, if the effort is justified.

Finally, tools of IS security teams would be reflective of specificity of their tasks. If IT security sometimes acts like a police squad, then IS folks tend to operate like FBI. Correspondingly, along with the common tools, such as application scanners mentioned earlier, they would bring in Intrusion Detection Systems and forensic tools. Where and how can Security QA and IT/IS security testing teams benefit from mutual cooperation? Actually, as it turns out, such opportunities abound.

First, and most obvious: When IT and IS teams get to start testing product staging (and production!) deployments, they mostly do it blindly. Even internally developed applications are treated as black boxes by those teams! The reason, as we have explained, is the wall properly existing between development teams and IT/IS security departments. This is coupled with the peculiarities of IT testing realities: very compressed timeframes (days, not weeks, as in development) and constantly changing product landscapes. These factors inhibit thoughtful exploration of details. And even when deep analysis is attempted, internal technical documents are often not available. Have you seen the situation in which there is no access to representatives from development teams?

A logical first step to right this situation would be making representatives of development teams (maybe even members of the Security QA organization) available for internal deployments to advise IT teams about a product's features and interfaces. The best opportunity for that would be before and during IT Architectural Reviews. (Do not confuse those with the Architectural Reviews performed by development teams and covered in Chapter 3, "Design Activities"! The IT ones concentrate on deployment, hosts, and physical connections.) However, it is invaluable for IT reviewers to know which interfaces and protocols are exposed, what their default states are, and where one should go to change those settings. Some of these might be covered somewhere in publicly available documentation; but, as we commented earlier, compressed IT project schedules foresee only quick scanning of technical documentation, not in-depth studying.

The benefits of such participation are mutual, for both members of the development teams and Security QA.

For developers, it is often an eye-opening experience (not always a pleasant one) to see how their products are tested in real environments. Since development teams are usually quite far removed from actual deployment, the products are sometimes not built with this task in mind, making configuration tasks very awkward and unintuitive. This "ivory tower" factor can be doubly potent when it comes to security processes. How many times have we all seen products that can be deployed only using Administrator accounts, in Windows, or as root on Unix? Quite often, the main reason is a simple lack of knowledge in development teams as to how to work with programs without elevated privileges. Worse yet, although an application might be required to work under plain user accounts, some of its features might in the end turn out to be broken, because it never occurred to the developers to try running their code without privileges!

On top of this comes the IS security team (or a contracted consultant) with their security policy requirements and checklists. Here, development teams might suddenly realize that file permissions are not what they had expected, or were accustomed to. Verbose logs, containing all types of interesting data, are viewed as a curse rather than a blessing in this environment. Worse still, a developer-only bypass login mechanism will be treated not as a helpful debug feature for production support, but as a deployment-blocking high-severity security issue. If these requirements are uncovered only during testing by IT/IS teams, the entire product deployment is in for either significant (immediate) trouble, or a ton of environment-based workarounds (deferred trouble).

All in all, IS security folks would welcome participation of development representatives when they set up their IDS and forensic tools. In the ideal world, as products go through the preproduction testing, the hand-off process from the development team would include the set of audit records and alerts that IS department will receive from the product and configure in their utilities. When these features are implemented properly, IS folks have a chance to test deployment environments in a proactive, rather than purely reactive, way. Chapter 7, "Operating Software Securely," is going to address this process in greater detail.

## Security Bug Life Cycle

No matter how hard and extensively an application is tested, bugs will still be there; it is just a question of how many and when they will be discovered. This also applies to security bugs, as explained earlier in this chapter. What really matters, though, is who discovers the bug, when they discovered it, and how it will be fixed. Figure 5.4 illustrates the security bug life cycle.

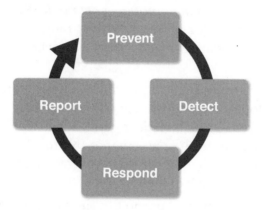

**Figure 5.4** The security bug life cycle.

The easiest bugs to address, of course, would be either those discovered during development time or, better, those discovered during source-code scans performed at check-in.[2] For example, a submission containing code that fails to sanitize input parameters accepted from a JSP page will be rejected at the scan gate. At that point the developers will be forced to "do the right thing." At least, that's the theory. In practice, since source-code scanning tools often incur unreasonable performance and resource impacts, large products often resort to periodic nightly scans (weekly, perhaps), rather than attempting a full scan at check-in time. The outcome of analyzing the results of these code scans will then be filed as security bugs against the development team.

The proper placement of source-code scanning activities is often debated. Some argue that the scans should be owned by a centralized security team, or even a QA organization, which are responsible for executing the scans before release. However, it is the firm conviction of your authors that source-code scanning for security bugs must be performed as frequently as realistically manageable and as close to the developers actually writing the code as possible. (We provide more details on this topic in Chapter 4.)

Similarly, when a product's Security QA detects a potential security issue from running its testing tools, they will file a security bug report against the development team. Another potential source of internal security bugs would be the Risk Analysis exercise, performed during the design phase. Although the items identified at that stage tend to be larger in scope (for example, *"add validation of incoming data in RESTful services"*) and cover entire features (or, rather, the lack of those features), they still represent security issues and will most likely be tracked internally as security bugs.

Such bugs often result from corner cutting during a product's infancy, when small development teams work against the clock to get the 1.0 release out the door. As products mature, their problems, as with people, can grow into chronic diseases, difficult or even impossible to address at an advanced stage. That is why Risk Analysis activities, covered in Chapter 3, constitute such an important milestone of the S(ecure) SDLC.

In all three cases mentioned previously, since bugs were discovered during the application development cycle, they will be triaged by the product's Engineering Management during development, as well as by the Product and Release Management as part of release readiness reviews. Depending on the bugs' severity and scope, they might or might not be fixed in the current release. In the latter case, the bugs will become candidates for the next patch, minor release, or major release, depending on the agreements negotiated between the product team and the security oversight folks.

Figure 5.5. illustrates how things *should* work. In practice, there is an economic complication. Security fixes do not add any new functional features, and will not help to bring in additional revenue. So unless they have strong backing all the way to the very top of the company, security teams often face an uphill battle trying to force development teams to address long-standing security issues in the upcoming releases, because it all comes at the expense of functional features. In those unfortunate cases, the parties sometimes just talk past each other with no discernible effect on security quality.

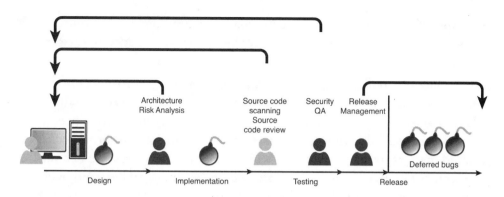

**Figure 5.5**  S(ecure) SDLC.

Complications worsen in the case of older products, as requests to fix internally reported security issues run into especially stubborn resistance from the development teams. Anybody who has been around software security for a while has certainly heard, "But this code has been this way for many years; why should we change it now?" Only when the software becomes exposed in the spotlight, and researchers and hackers really start beating on it, are the hidden "gems" suddenly revealed, much to the chagrin or amusement of development teams. The reasons for such a burst of attention are various: acquisition of a much smaller niche company by a high-profile industry vendor with deep pockets, perhaps, or an announced sale of the product to important customers, such as banks or critical infrastructure operators. In either case, suddenly there is a directly linked monetary reward for finding the hidden skeletons in the product's code closet.

We can't leave this topic behind without discussing the impact of *external* security bug reports, after product release. Those can come either from customers or from security researchers or ethical hackers. Maybe it shouldn't be the case, but we are here to tell you that in our experience, externally reported bugs are often dealt with in a substantially different way from internally reported ones. The threat of imminent external disclosure, with all the associated headaches for a vendor, can be a powerful motivating force for accelerating a fix. Of course, this is mostly applicable to software vendors, in which researchers can obtain access to the software for offline analysis. However, such reports are possible even with an internal enterprise software (when used in an SaaS model, provided to partners, etc.), if bug information is leaked by a former employee, for example. We've also seen the case in which a determined hacker finds a way to penetrate at least some of the protective barriers embedded in the service offering.

As Figure 5.6 illustrates, an external report with the prospect of imminent disclosure is when the countdown starts, because time really plays against the software vendor. Customers usually can be convinced to wait, for a reasonable time, and generally are not inclined to bring security-related matters to broad daylight. Many prefer to apply pressure behind the scenes. However, there is no such leverage with researchers and hackers, who earn money and publicity by loudly lambasting large corporations, Robin Hood–style.

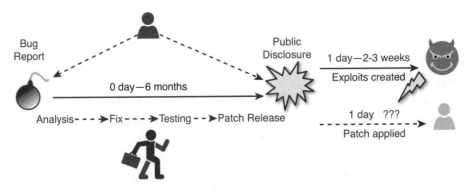

**Figure 5.6**   The countdown begins with a bug report.

Some of those folks might even choose to report the issue immediately, resulting in a zero-day security issue and a PR disaster for the company. To be fair, many disclosers these days follow responsible procedures, often providing months-long notice to a vendor. Although a six-month timeframe might seem like a long time, the reality is quite different when one thinks about all the typical testing and deployment processes involved with patching large product installations, multiple versions and product platforms, and so forth. And after information about a vulnerability becomes public, companies can expect to see exploits published within a matter of weeks, sometime even days! (Examples abound, but consider one that arose as we were writing this chapter: the Apache Struts vulnerability CVE-2013-2251,[3] which had an exploit attempted the very next day after the announcement, and a Metasploit module available in less than two weeks.[4])

After the clock starts ticking, the team is on the hook to implement and test the fix within a very short timeframe, since it will now have to be production-ready by the time the bug is publicly disclosed. To make things more exciting, often enough there is a long-standing product issue behind this bug, which has been neglected for years despite all the nudging of those boring security nerds. And this is where the real "fun" begins, with finger-pointing, blame assignment, and all other typical attributes of a dysfunctional process.

The corporate security team often ends up smack in the middle of all these hurried activities, because it has to interact with external researchers on one hand, work with the same team—who perhaps had been loathe to deal with the issue earlier—on another hand, and, in many cases, also coordinate the entire process of preparing the out-of-cycle security patch for delivery.

## The Security Testing

At last, our dev team is feeling pretty confident about what they'll be doing. After all, they've done security testing of their previous app releases. Right? Well, sort of. When the team meeting convenes to discuss plans for security testing of the new release, they're asked to describe the testing they've done in the past. That's when things begin to go pear-shaped.

They proudly say that their product releases are all "penetration tested" by an independent testing team. That's great, the CTO says.

And then they start to dig deeper. Just what did the penetration test entail? Well, they paid a consultant to try to break the security of the app, just as a "hacker" might.

What processes did the test team follow? What aspects of the apps were tested? Can we see the reports? What defects were fixed? And so the questioning goes, for a long, painful amount of time.

Clearly, the dev team's confidence is not supported by facts. They again find themselves on the defensive.

Being familiar with the indicators already, the CTO suggests that the team again find some compromises to get through the current dev cycle, with an eye toward improving things in the future.

So considering the most common security testing methods (penetration testing, dynamic validation, fuzzing, and risk-based testing), combined with the OWASP top 10 mobile risks list, they decide on a checklist approach to their testing.

The testing they agree to looks roughly like this:

- Static validation testing
  - Start by examining the sandboxed areas for programmatic data at rest, looking for unprotected sensitive data.
  - Then, look outside the sandboxed areas for nonprogrammatic (e.g., cached) data that contains application-sensitive information.
- Dynamic validation testing
  - Look for any sensitive data (e.g., login credentials, session tokens, patient data, and other "PII") that is unprotected in transit.
  - Ensure that the SSL certificate verification is adequate.
- Penetration testing
  - Perform client-side data injection (fuzzing "light") on data fields, verifying that strong input validation is in place.
  - Also do server-side data injection.
  - Lastly, perform server-side output testing to ensure that untrusted data is being contextually escaped before being output.
  - Validate that the session token behavior is random and consistent with server-side best practices.
  - Perform additional penetration testing similar to a web app test, primarily on the server interface(s).

Although this is a fairly simple list, it gives the team a basic set of things they can test for. It certainly goes beyond what a traditional penetration test (in our experience) is likely to discover.

So, after a bit of clarifying definitions, the team sets out to do some security testing. They set up a test bed environment for both iOS and Android platforms. They gather a few tools they'll be using in their tests. In short, they prepare and test their test bed, and start practicing the testing they'll be doing on the live apps.

Most of the tools they'll be using are either freely or quite inexpensively available. Tools for examining file systems on mobile devices, such as iExplorer on iOS, are easily found. Similarly, they turn to network proxy tools like Burp Suite, network protocol analyzers like Wireshark, and debuggers for doing their dynamic validation.

The next step is for the entire test team to get spun up on how to use all the test tools. For that, they task one of the senior team members (with the help of an intern) to do a deep dive and then do a couple of internal training sessions for everyone else who'll be doing the testing.

The toughest part is finding tools to do the input fuzzing. For most of those, they end up building their own. After all, they have the code that builds the various views (iOS) and activities (Android); all they need is a test rig that will bombard those inputs with some carefully chosen garbage.

The toughest part is actually coming up with the various test scenarios (and input data) they'll be hitting the attack surface with. For that, they turn to online dictionaries of data for SQL injection, cross-site scripting, and so forth.

Additionally, they take an inventory of all the app's inputs—its attack surface. From that, they generate a set of regular expressions describing the data they expect as input for all cases. In their fuzz testing, they start with generating data from these regular expressions, but they extend that. For example, if an input field is expecting an integer, they use regexes for integers, but also for floating-point numbers, strings, and more. Next, in the fuzzing, they build test scenarios that span all the combinations and permutations they can come up with for each and every data field.

Of course, all of this seems like a tremendous amount of effort to our team. There is good news, however: The effort is "front loaded." They spend plenty of time designing the tests and building the tools, especially the fuzzers, but then they're able to "fire and forget" (for the most part). And they know that they can keep using and reusing much of the test rigging they've built.

Perhaps the most difficult part of the fuzz testing isn't constructing the test inputs, but observing the results so that they know when the software fails. After all, fuzzing a target helps only if you know when and how it fails. In the test rigging, they carefully watch for exceptions to be thrown, return codes, and such.

And so the security testing proceeds.

## Summing Up

The security testing phase is a pivotal moment in the product development life cycle. It is at the end of this stage, after all checklists have been signed off and all release readiness reviews completed, that the product actually sees the real world. The product, which had existed so far only in the heads of its architects and managers—and scattered on developers' computers as a bunch of disparate components—finally comes together and runs as a functional and operational entity.

Similarly, various corporate groups are focused here as well, including developers and designers, security architects, Quality Assurance with its tools and test suits, and the IT security folks who have begun drawing their deployment and testing plans. For most systems, the testing phase is the first and last time these groups will all, simultaneously, be engaged.

By now, the reader will realize that the authors strongly argue against this "normal" state of affairs. Hey, let's try to hold these teams together! They should continue cooperating going forward, during the deployment, operation, and maintenance phases, the topics of our next few chapters. Onward!

## Endnotes

1. www.informit.com/articles/article.aspx?p=1671924.

2. Best: bugs that are "designed out" at ideation time.

3. www.cvedetails.com/cve/CVE-2013-2251/.

4. https://isc.sans.edu/diary/CVE-2013-2251+Apache+Struts+2.
   X+OGNL+Vulnerability/16382.

# 6 Deployment and Integration

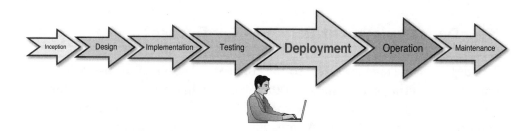

Inception → Design → Implementation → Testing → **Deployment** → Operation → Maintenance

S o the coding is finished, and it's time to deploy your shiny new application, integrating it into your business environment. What is the first step?

Okay, that's a trick question. The right first step in deployment is to do whatever you laid out for this stage when you *planned the entire project* all those many weeks/months/years ago. The point we are making here is that even though we are tackling this topic deep in the book's interior, and you might be carrying out this work years into the project, the concepts and questions here must be addressed as early as the *design* phase of the project. So, we hope, you've already been considering deployment and integration, and you've also been keeping an eye out for how things are likely to be changing in the deployed environment as you've been working.

Speaking of project phases, we need to distinguish at this point between the topic of this chapter and the next one. "Deployment and integration" is a one-time procedure during which the application and its associated peer processes and subsystems are installed, integrated, and spun up. Our next chapter—"Operating Software Securely"—is all about the steady-state "life" of your application, including its maintenance. Of course, nothing is ever quite so neat in real life, but we still like to consider these steps in that manner.

One more note before we dive in. There is not much material in this book about specific security products. We like it that way. In this chapter, however, because we are addressing integration, you'll find some discussion of some specific software products by real vendors. The references are there to teach a point, not necessarily as an endorsement. The various product offerings in this field change far too often for us to put a competitive recommendation in print. Suffice it to say, your mileage may vary.

## How Does Deployment Relate to Confluence?

The deployment stage is critical to the concept of "confluence" as we conceive it. During earlier stages of the project, what was flowing together were the thoughts and planning efforts of application programmers and enterprise security specialists. At this point, however, you will actually enable the interconnection of various streams of information and start observing convergence of confluence efforts talked about in previous chapters.

It is so common today—based on our experience, this might still be the norm—that deployment of an application begins and ends when the developers deliver a "tar ball," or other installable package, to the IT department. That package could include installation scripts, and perhaps even some basic installation documentation, but probably not much more. Oh, there has probably been a discussion with the IT staff about which server the software will be installed on, and connections made to back-end databases or front-end web firewalls. Perhaps the enterprise security team will be notified about the installation. But that's often as far as integration efforts go.

## A Road Map

What should be happening, of course, as we have been extolling, is ongoing cooperation between IT security and app developers to enable the detection of attempts to either tamper with key enterprise assets or apply pressure to the application along the lines of its weaknesses or key functions. Perhaps you even planned ahead to harden this system in ways that are specific to the application, as defined by the developers, who know what it does; those persons who know which company jewels it uses or affords access to; and, lastly, the experts who see every day who is attacking the enterprise, and how.

In this chapter, we cover in detail the measures you need to take to successfully deploy a "confluent" application. These steps include integration with the following:

- Perimeter firewalls
- Data-loss-prevention appliances and filters
- Application firewalls
- Identity management systems
- Intrusion detection logs and/or security incident and event monitoring (SIEM) systems
- Other key enterprise applications
- Real-time security alert mechanisms (e.g., an instant message to the enterprise security team)
- Real-time anomaly detection processes

We'll talk you through each step.

### Preparing for Deployment

You will know that the integration of your application has a chance to succeed if it proceeds something like painting a room. That work, done properly, becomes tedious long before you get to splash a brush against the drywall: You have to take everything off the walls, patch the nail holes, tape the doorknobs and light switches, and tarp the floor. Preparation for deployment is just like that.

You should start by trying to understand fully these factors:

- The application system and all its components, taking care to not omit infrastructure components like identity management
- The network environment in which it runs, including security sensors and filters
- Key enterprise assets (files, databases, and network queues) the application interacts with
- Privileges, in all their myriad contexts, that the application requires for using each of those enterprise assets

We suggest you then move on to topics such as these:

- Key security threats against the enterprise (e.g., who might try to do what and why) and business risk analysis
- Making use of intrusion detection, change detection, and anomaly detection systems
- More intense, real-time interaction with other applications and security appliances

We hope you are not too surprised to find at this point that today very little of the information you need for a successful deployment will come from the development team. They surely are a good place to start, though, and this cooperation is the main point this book has been advocating through all of its pages. "This is the key file," they might say. "If someone manages an unauthorized alteration of it, we are in trouble." At a minimum, the development team might be expected to contribute a list of sensitive files, operations, and valid users or user types, as well as a list of which systems or components of the network the application should be connected to (and from). Additionally, the development team should be expected to document access control mechanisms in use, which is most likely going to be one of the flavors of role-based access control.

That said, here are some basic questions that we recommend you address at the time you begin to make plans for deployment and integration of your application. Be advised, though, that if your analysis stops here, you will be mounting a twentieth-century defense against twenty-first-century attacks.

➤ **About the application system**
- What are the major components of the system (including modules, libraries, and chained-to executables)?
- How do they communicate with one another?
- Which system components were coded in-house, and which from third parties? Which are built on open source, which on closed source?
- What kind of security assurance was performed for in-house and third-party software?
- Which security and stress tests were executed by the team?

- Are there any known security weaknesses in the released version of the application? Be sure to check national vulnerability databases and other similar sources.

- What system resources does the application use, and how will it behave if and when those resources become scarce or unavailable?

- What database servers or other running applications does the software communicate with? Which user IDs are employed, how are they propagated in distributed systems, and how is access to files and records mediated?

- What kinds of log records will it create, and for what sorts of events or conditions? Where do these logs go, and how are they accessed and protected?

- What other kinds of alerts and notifications can the application produce?

➤ **About enterprise assets**

- What files does the application use, and in what mode (read, write, or read/write)?

- What database servers or other running enterprise services does the software communicate or integrate with? Which ones are enabled by default?

- Which key business activities of your enterprise are conducted by the application, or would be affected if it failed, or was corrupted?

➤ **About the network environment**

- Does the application run behind a perimeter firewall?

- Does the application run behind an application firewall?

- Are there security appliances on the network with which the application can communicate, or from which it can receive updates or alerts?

- Which other applications, processes, or servers on the network must this application trust, and to what degree? Again, include infrastructure components like identity management.

## Advanced Topics in Deployment

The basic analysis we just sketched out will help you lay a strong foundation for a classically secure deployment, and our experience tells us that if your enterprise does a good job addressing those topics, you will have better security than most of your peer organizations.

We see a new standard of care beginning to emerge, however: threat-based application security that responds to a rich set of captured conditions and events, perhaps in real time.

In the following sections are some ideas on how you, software developers and architects, can take that next step.

### Threat-Specific Deployment Decisions

At this point in the project, you should know where the weaknesses are—the skeletons in the closet—and here is the opportunity to set up methods in network space to protect the application and assets. Because rather than just detecting generic bad stuff on the network, IDS can look for specific kinds of traffic, to and from specific hosts and servers. It might additionally be helpful to consider non-signature-based IDS technologies, including network flow analyzers that are tuned to your application and can look for anomalous traffic. But because it helps to know what to look for, think about potential attacks and attackers specifically related to this application, using questions such as these:

- Is this application, either because of the service it provides or the assets it manipulates, known to constitute a particularly attractive target for security attacks?
- Who would benefit if this application were shut down by a denial-of-service attack?
- Would the attacks your security folks expect succeed against this application, with or without special shielding and filters?

You will also want to take advantage of specific business intelligence available to you. What about looking back at incidents that happened last year? What new insights can you get now with new information? We feel confluent applications can for the first time enable a holistic longitudinal view for defenders.

For example, if your software somehow facilitates, say, the manufacture of chocolate using secret recipes, the developers and deployment planners need to know the history at your site of phishing attacks, say, from Badlandia, Elbonia, or other countries famed for their chocolate confections—if that's the kind of attack that has been observed or is for other reasons anticipated.

## Contributing to the Big Picture

Your defensive shields might work great most of the time, but sooner or later incident responders will need to come in and use the information recorded by your business applications to reconstruct a chain of events. So think of your incident responders as the ultimate consumers of log data and alerts.

With help, they'll need to evaluate the business impact, and ultimately go to the executive team and explain what really happened. One key role of the responders, then, becomes building an integrated view of what happened: "The Badlandians were going after our chocolate recipes again, but we think we stopped them before they found out how we treat the marzipan."

That being the case, it becomes the responsibility of your applications to make sure that any intruders leave behind indelible "bread crumbs"— clues and pointers to exactly what happened, how, and when. Remember, these bread crumbs are going to be the things that our computer security incident response team (CSIRT) will need to use during any real security incidents. And beware that attackers often try to trick logging systems into logging things that merely seek to misdirect the CSIRT staff. So what sort of happenings should this application report?

Logging access failures are a given, of course. But we have found that very often the failed attempt that makes a log file is not in fact the first nasty access that has taken place, but merely the first attempt that was sufficiently over the top to cause a manifest error. As security investigators, we can't count the number of times we have wanted an answer to the question "What was the last thing the perpetrator did before accidentally setting off the alarm?" In essence, we sought to go back in time and replay what was happening, and to consider that from various perspectives. Can your application provide a way to dig out that information if needed? Of course, there is a fine line that one has to walk to avoid falling from one of the extremes, providing too little useful information, into another one, flooding the audit files with useless details.

Here is another tack to take. Can you draw information about your environment into the integration of this application, and tailor it so that this sort of context-sensitive judgment can be made? Suppose the application you're deploying handles payroll for your business. It is quite safe to assume that, after the application has been deployed, no one from the engineering department should even be trying to connect to a payroll application. And if they do, this should immediately trigger an alarm, because this would indicate the existence of a back door in the application.

The old security strategy "No worries, we'll run it from the data center!" doesn't seem good enough anymore to us. Instead, what we see emerging is a sense of enterprise responsibility, of network citizenship of a kind. "If you see something, say something," read the signs on the subways of New York. We recommend it as a policy for confluent applications.

## Integrating with the Security Operations Infrastructure

Without a doubt, the "bread and butter" of security operations in a modern data center is the logging and monitoring of security events, including Intrusion Detection Systems (IDS) and security incident and event management (SIEM) systems. This is because, when it comes to data center operations, a great deal of effort is put into operational monitoring of all the systems to ensure that they're all functioning as planned. The same holds true for security; security operations centers routinely centrally log and monitor vast numbers of security events reported to them from a myriad of IT components. Sometimes all of this data is aggregated by security information and event management (SIEM) systems.

And, as you might guess, doing this properly isn't anywhere near as simple as just dumping in a bunch of event log calls in an application. That simplistic "log it" attitude, although pervasive, won't accomplish anything useful in the long run. The principal reason for this is that developers generally write audit logs for the purpose of debugging a piece of code, not for performing the real business tasks needed when the security of an application gets compromised in a business context. The "audit" mind-set is very different from the "debug" mind-set.

So let's begin this discussion by looking at some of the basics, and then we'll see what we need to do to properly integrate our applications into a business operations environment.

## Status Quo

In pretty much every enterprise data center today, one can find a wealth of system events being logged. Most every system component can and does contribute to log information. Each component, however, carries with it its own perspective of what is being logged, why it is being logged, and so on. For example, a network router sees the world as a series of routing decisions to be made on any given data packet. As such, it logs the packet's source address (IP number) and destination address, the date and time the packet was seen, and so on. All of this is good and useful data to collect, but it isn't all we need. Even if it is logged, where does the data reside within the enterprise? Is it easily accessible and can it be correlated across other log entries to facilitate investigations of any sort—auditing or debugging?

If you were tasked with determining the business status of an application, you'd probably ask some basic questions such as these: Who is logged in? What accounts are being accessed? Has any money/information been stolen? Has anyone changed data without authorization to do so? These questions all have one thing in common: business. They are relevant to the business of an application. Looking at the network activity log traffic generated by a business application can't possibly answer any of these questions for us, because the data is vast and hugely complex.

So where do we look for the answers to these questions? We look at the only area of an application that would have the answers: the business logic. And in a service-oriented architecture (SOA), that business logic is typically housed in the applications themselves, and supported by the middleware, such as application servers, that those applications are running on. The only problem is that middleware and the applications themselves tend to be the ones that do the least amount of logging. Further, the Intrusion Detection Systems in use today aren't generally looking at business logs—they're focusing their attention on the network-level logs more often than not.

Today's data center operations usually include substantial intrusion detection logging and monitoring facilities. Many IT security staff tend to focus their attention on the lowest of "low-hanging fruit." The devices and services that most commonly are used as inputs to Intrusion Detection Systems (and security information and event managers) include those shown in Figure 6.1.

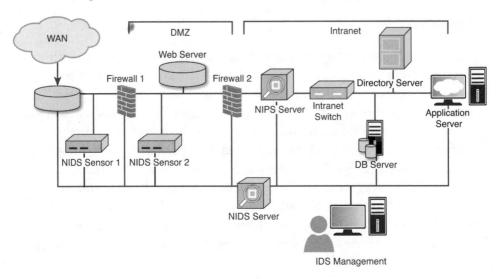

**Figure 6.1**　A typical SIEM and IDS deployed network architecture.

### Network Routers

Network routers are ideal for providing traffic analysis data via the Netflow protocol. Two factors make this so. First, Netflow data is very lightweight and does not add substantial overhead on either the router or the surrounding infrastructure. Second, routers tend to see all network traffic through a specific application domain, irrespective of policy decisions made by firewalls or other devices. On the other hand, their perspective on what they see doesn't well allow for "seeing" inside of an application, and not only in situations in which the application's data is SSL encrypted. Note too that in a typical edge or internal router configuration, Netflow data will be sent to one or more data concentrators, which in turn feed the SIEM system(s) in use.

### Network Firewalls

Firewalls are also seen as ideal components for providing network monitoring data to the SIEM. As they oversee network-level policy on a per-service basis, they can also quickly provide data on network requests that are accepted as well as those that are denied. Firewall logs are typically more detailed than Netflow logs, on the other hand. They typically include data on the source, destination, time/date, and network service—just like Netflow. In addition, however, they typically include information from the HTTP data—the requested URL, the user agent, and so on. As such, they can be useful to security practitioners in building a more complete picture of what a user is doing in any given network session. Still, though, they have only limited visibility into an application's business logic, notwithstanding vendor claims of "deep packet inspection" and such.

### Network Intrusion Detection Sensors

Network Intrusion Detection Sensors (NIDS) are security components, used typically by the IT security department to monitor a network for previously known intrusion patterns, or "signatures." They attach to a network and passively look into all the network data, searching for attack signatures. The problem with the attack signatures that are most commonly used is that the signatures are simply those of known attack tools/methods. They are in no way tailored to a specific application and its business needs. That said, a NIDS product's view of a network tends to be similar to routers and firewalls, although most modern NIDS products further have the capability to reconstruct fragmented packets as well as TCP sessions. This enables the NIDS devices to gain a slight advantage in seeing into an application's data, while still having a uniquely network-centric view of the world. Naturally, even having the capability to see into the application's data doesn't make it easy to detect application-specific attacks.

### Network Intrusion Prevention Sensors

Most Network Intrusion Prevention Sensors (NIPS) are essentially NIDS that are attached in-line (like a firewall) in front of a business application. As such, their view of the network is nearly identical to that of a NIDS device. The primary difference is a functional one: NIPS products can usually "prevent" a recognized attack by resetting a TCP session or otherwise merely dropping all of its network traffic, thereby preventing the attack from reaching its intended victim or for data to flow outward to an intruder.

### Web Application Firewalls

Web application firewalls (WAFs) are similar in their placement and architecture to traditional firewalls, but they make their policy decisions based on specific application-layer information. Typically, they can be set up to look for common known attacks like signatures of actual SQL injection attacks, or else they must be "tuned" or configured to know specific aspects of an application, such as all of its forms and the expected data types. As such, their view of the world is all the HTTP and HTTPS requests going to and from the web server. Like web servers, they can see all the encrypted as well as plain-text application requests and responses.

### Web Servers

By the time we get to the web server components of a typical web application system, we're quite far removed from the pure network view that the routers and such see of the world. Indeed, the web servers can see just a bit deeper into what is going on with a web application. They, for example, see every requested URL, every image file, and that level of application detail. However, theirs is a world made up largely of HTTP and HTTPS requests and responses, and not much else. On the other hand, they do see all the plain text of even SSL-encrypted requests and responses.

### Application Servers

For a common web application, it is the application sever that houses and runs the application's business logic itself, whether the application server is running a simplistic scripting language like PHP or a higher-level language server like Java or .NET/C#. In terms of truly knowing what an application is doing, there is no better place to look than in the application server. Often, though, the trouble is that the application server contains the least amount of operational security logging. The data that is there is often intended more to be used for debugging problems than for analyzing and responding to security incidents as they occur.

### Database Servers

Database servers generally contain an application's "crown jewels" in terms of the information they contain. Depending on the application, they might be used as dumb storage facilities, or contain very elaborate and complex business logic coded in some flavor of SQL language, such as PL/SQL, or an embedded version of a high-level language such as Java. Even though such applications are notoriously bad with audit logging, they too provide some degree of event logging in a normal business data processing environment. Their view of the world, however, tends to be in terms of data transactions: searches, updates, inserts, and so forth. Understanding meaningful business context from that perspective would be nearly impossible.

## Complications and Clouds

So we've taken a quick tour through the components of a typical application and what sort of logging value they can bring to the table. From the standpoint of getting a unified logging view of what is going on inside an application, the picture is rather bleak. And there are some factors that further exacerbate things.

Application server connections to database servers, for example, are commonly done using a single canonical set of database credentials. Thus, at the database server, often all transactions appear as though they were made by a single user. Back in the not-so-distant-past world of client/server applications, each database user would normally log in to his own account so that the database server would actually have multiple people logging in at once. Back then, we even had dedicated database administrators (DBAs) whose job was to set up and maintain individual users' database accounts and credentials.

If you further factor in loosely coupled business systems that communicate with one another via web services interfaces, the picture muddies even more. The previously given view of a business application represents a single user to a single application sort of approach. In today's increasingly complex business world, such simplistic architectures often are not the practice. Instead, we have web services or service-oriented architecture connections using protocols such as SOAP or REST (which, in turn, ride over HTTP network sockets). Web services connections are often server-to-server channels, for applications to exchange data among themselves—between business partners, supply chain systems, and so forth.

A more recent trend is with web services connections, especially so-called RESTful interfaces, between lightweight clients, such as mobile device apps, and servers. Here, too, the effect from our standpoint is that our applications' activities are further distributed, making it even more difficult to attain a single vantage point into what an application is doing. This can be further exacerbated when applications are deployed onto virtual-machine environments.

And still we're not finished painting the picture. One of the biggest trends in computing, as of this writing, is so-called "cloud computing." In cloud environments, the business transactions are hugely distributed, often across many companies' systems. Key enabling components for cloud computing are distributed identity and access management, which rely on new protocols such as OAuth. One of the effects of cloud computing is that it blurs the lines between the customer and the vendor. In Software as a Service scenarios, it is now the vendor's IT personnel who set up the infrastructure and monitor an application's instances allocated to the customers.

## What Is OAuth?

Consider this setup: You are a proud resource owner at application B and would like to allow application A to obtain access to that resource. The resource could be picture files within a picture-sharing application, an address book in your e-mail account, or pretty much any data or resource you control within an application.

Simply put, OAuth is a protocol to authorize application A to utilize some of a user's protected resources in application B. These resources are explicitly requested, and if authorization has been granted by the user, application A is issued an OAuth token and allowed access. Most important, all this is done without requiring that a user's passwords be shared with third parties or stored in other applications.

In the online world, applications A and B are typically two web sites that allow their users to transparently share features or data. Using the example in Figure 6.2, a user attempts to integrate his Twitter account into his LinkedIn profile. If successful, the user will be issued an OAuth token from Twitter that will enable him to access the profile, post and read tweets, and follow people, all without leaving the LinkedIn site. In this case, Twitter performs the role of resource server, LinkedIn is a client, and the resource is the user's Twitter account. Also note in the warning at the bottom that this authorization will not enable unlimited access to the Twitter account.

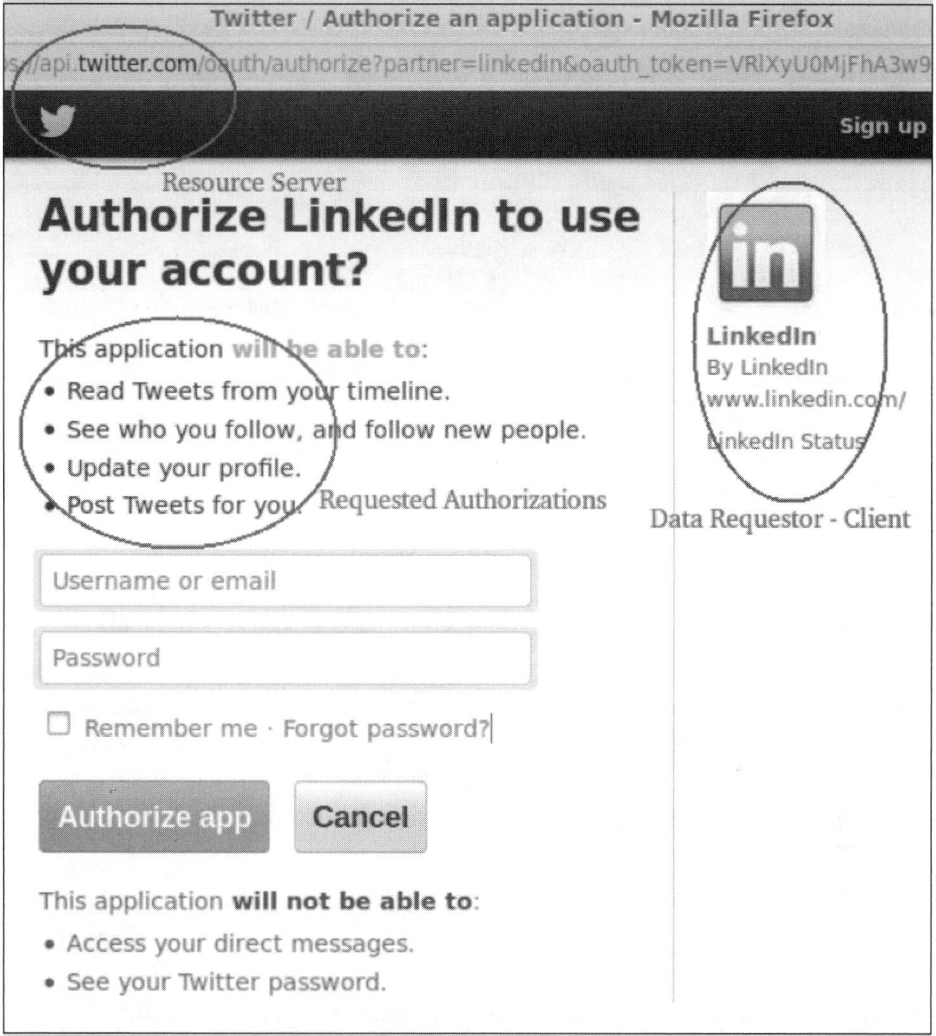

**Figure 6.2**   The user wants to integrate his Twitter account into his LinkedIn profile.

Technically speaking, OAuth exchange can involve two steps or three steps. The three-step protocol is used when user consent is requested, as is customary for web-based services. As shown in Figure 6.3, when the user provides his consent along with the necessary credentials to prove his identity to web site B (Twitter) using his browser, the Twitter's authorization server issues an OAuth token for accessing the requested scope from the requesting application (LinkedIn). This token is then submitted along with future requests for the user's resources on Twitter.

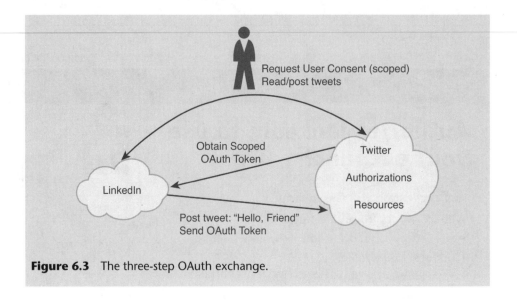

**Figure 6.3**   The three-step OAuth exchange.

Still, this general description of business application architectures is quite commonly found today. In describing the systems this way, we wanted to paint a clear picture of what sorts of components are found in modern data centers, and what types of event logging they provide to the operations staff for monitoring a system's activity. Clearly, the diversity of the components and the lack of a single point of visibility into an application make the job of truly monitoring a business application a hugely daunting one.

So can a well-written application help? A poorly written application certainly can hurt. Our data center operations folks are already drowning in a sea of data. After all, more weight isn't much help to a drowning person. Let's consider some things our applications can do to help.

We did address this issue at a design level in Chapter 4, "Implementation Activities," and again briefly in Chapter 5, "Testing Activities," but in terms of enhancing our operations, we should be going out of our way to provide clear, concise, and business-relevant logging data to the operations team.

To understand that, let's consider the use case for the log data. In an operational environment, the principal use case for log data is to acquire and maintain the situational awareness of what is happening in an application, much as we discussed previously. We referred to this in

Chapter 3, "Design Activities," as understanding the "Who, What, Where, When, and How" (WWWWH) of an application's security posture. That is to say, the business-relevant situational awareness. That log data itself is, of course, collected by the application's various components, which might make it difficult to determine the business context needed.

Often during incident response operations, the computer security incident response team is sent into a compromised environment to figure out what is going on—the WWWWH of the incident—and to report to the executive decision team with a damage assessment and a recommended course of action. It is important to note that many of these CSIRT operations are initiated after an incident has taken place, not during the incident. Thus, it is frequently the case that the CSIRT has only the log data to work with to determine the extent of the damage.

Bearing in mind the difficulties we discussed previously, let's consider how best our application can properly integrate into a production environment and actually enhance the overall security posture.

## Enhancing and Using Information Logged to a SIEM

As we described earlier, many production data processing environments include a SIEM capability. A well-integrated SIEM is the closest thing most enterprise environments have to a single vantage point of situational-awareness data. This is where the security operations staff seek to gain their top-level view of the security status of the enterprise.

But a SIEM is only as good as the information it receives. Traditional SIEMs gather log data from each of the sources we described previously. Sometimes it is worse as the signal-to-noise ratio decreases. But more information sources doesn't necessarily translate to better awareness. The problem, as we alluded to earlier, is that many organizations do little more than install NIDS, HIDS, and other event logging, using little more than the alerting provided by the products' vendors. Although this is an important first step, it really only provides protection against attackers who use canned or "off the shelf" attack tools and methods. It provides absolutely no tailoring to a real business application.

In other words, security tools with only vendor-supplied alerting cannot possibly know what is important to your business and its applications. They would view every SQLi, XSS, and so on as completely equal. The executive decision makers, on the other hand, have a completely different set of concerns. They want to know whether data has been compromised, stolen, and so forth. They want to know whether money is being or has been lost. They want to know the business damage assessment. Security tools used today typically provide very little of this sort of business knowledge to the business owner.

Getting that sort of knowledge and understanding from an application's logging requires careful attention to detail, and rigorous collaboration among the true stakeholders.

The SIEM should be one of the first places where the enterprise application development staff should seek to integrate their security log data, but it needs to be carefully planned out. Simply logging more data might well not help at all; in fact, it might make the situation worse than it already is.

For that reason, we consider it absolutely vital to engage with the key stakeholders as early as in the application's design phase in planning out what information to log and what information to not log. The first step in the process at this point must be engaging with the business owners, the CSIRT organization, and the IT security operations staff itself (see Figure 6.4)—and that is the bare minimum. Let's consider each of these parties and how they need to be included in the decision process. Also, keep in mind how the various data elements should be collected and collated to facilitate analysis.

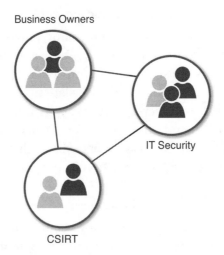

**Figure 6.4** Collaboration among key stakeholders.

### Business Owners

The business owners of an application need to provide all the high-level details of what the application does and how it does it. What data are important to them? What data are sensitive to them? What security breaches would be most troublesome to them? These sorts of questions—which undoubtedly were also asked during the architectural risk analysis or threat modeling process—are important to the development and operations team so that they can ensure that the correct data and types of data are being logged and assessed.

### CSIRT Organization

Since it is the CSIRT staff who are responsible for answering the WWWWH questions for the executive decision makers during an incident, it is important to include them in this decision process. They are the interface between the business operations and the executive team during incidents. Consider their use case in test scenarios—attack an application using a known methodology, and then see whether the CSIRT staff are able to reconstruct the events and build an accurate situational awareness picture. If not, what information was missing? In the testing, could the CSIRT staff determine with authority whether any business data was stolen or tampered with?

### IT Security

The IT security operations staff are typically the people tasked with operating the SIEMs, IDS products, and so forth. Their participation in the decision process at this point should be fairly mechanical: What is being logged? Where is the information being logged? Does the log data conform to any internal data formats, naming standards, and so on? They also need to ensure that IDS alerting is tailored to the business-critical events discussed previously. IDS products are generally very configurable in alerting monitoring staff on various events, none of which likely corresponds directly to your enterprise application. The problem is that the alert signatures provided by the IDS product vendors will essentially consist of known attack scenarios. In a properly designed operational environment, the application will also be logging business-relevant information, and the IDS products, SIEMs, and so on need to be "trained" to look for those alerts properly. In most operational environments, it is these custom rule sets that are the most meaningful, not the ones provided by the product vendors, at least if they don't fall prey to false positives.

These are the main stakeholders that need to participate in the decisions and process of getting the right information into the data monitoring environment, and making it available to those that need it, at the right time.

Let's consider this in a little more detail with a case study to illustrate some of the points.

## Netherlands ISP

One of your authors provided some input recently to a Dutch ISP and their effort to modernize one of their production business systems. In particular, their aim was to integrate some business logging into a production system so that security staff could more easily resolve potential security incidents as they were detected.

First, some background in the way the system used to work. The ISP's various systems had been built over many years, and they all did some degree of "logging." The problem was that the logging had been built from the perspective of debugging problems when they arose, not for the purpose of resolving security incidents. To further exacerbate the problems, Dutch privacy laws are especially difficult (for the purpose of logging system events)—for example, IP numbers are considered private because they can identify the holder's physical address, or so the laws were written.

The end result of all of this was that the security staff would be notified of a potential security problem, and would then have to painstakingly cross-reference event logs across multiple disconnected systems, often without success. This was the security use case they sought to address.

The modernization process they went through consisted of a few iterations before they got things right. The first step was to pick a single application as a test case for the log modernization. They decided on a system that is used for provisioning (from a web application) new DSL or UMTS (cellular data) services for end consumers. The existing system had a problem when someone would connect to the provisioning application and fraudulently initiate a new service. In the old system, due to privacy concerns, the logging would log little more than the postal code of the request—far from useful, especially in a densely populated urban area.

So the application was modified to log the postal code, the (new or existing) customer number, and some other basic information. When it comes to the needs of the CSIRT, remember the Who, What, Where, When, and How questions.

The ISP found this was a useful step forward, but it didn't yet meet all the needs of the CSIRT when they had to investigate a potential fraud event. It turned out there was a special attack/use case in which a customer could call one of the ISP's call centers and enter a new account/service via an operator. In those cases, the system was logging the user information of the call center operator, not the end consumer.

So they further modified their logging to include the customer ID number as well as the call center user's identity.

This process went back and forth a bit between the application developers and the CSIRT staff, until they found the right set of data to log that would store exactly the sort of business data the CSIRT needed when looking into cases of potential fraud in accordance with local laws.

From our standpoint, whenever you find the security staff and the development staff interacting positively like this, the results are far-reaching and have a great impact. We consider this to be a big success and a win for all involved.

## Third-Generation Log Analysis Tools

Third-generation intelligent log analysis tools can open a whole new window on security events across your enterprise if you take the time to design into your applications a comprehensive logging capability tuned to events of potential security relevance. Yes, good application logs have obvious advantages. But we see additional possibilities here.

You will find a side benefit, as you deploy one after another application that has been rigged in this way. Assuming that their designers heeded our advice from the design chapter, Chapter 3, it might now be possible for your applications to "communicate" in a security-aware manner, making adjustments for anomalies, overt attacks, and other events in real time by using third-generation filter applications to look for annotations and triggers that other applications have placed in the built-for-amalgamation log files.

Although it has always been theoretically possible on most major operating systems to conduct this sort of real-time dialogue between processes, many shops have found it just too tough to reliably integrate interprocess communication between business applications.

As an illustration, we will take a slight side trip here to talk about a specific software product, Splunk, a relatively new (as of 2013) piece of information technology utility that can be especially useful in the quest for confluence.

## Splunk as an Application Security Appliance

A Silicon Valley company named Splunk, founded in 2003, has in our opinion added a useful new wrinkle to the analysis of large data files. Its core product (also named Splunk) is advertised as an operational intelligence tool. According to its marketers, it "indexes and makes searchable data from any app, server, or network device, including logs, config files, messages, and alerts."[1]

Splunk has found a large market quickly for its mainstream use of log file aggregation and mining. From our point of view, however, it is even more promising as a tool for what we might call "confluent comprehension," situational awareness built up by assembling custom log entries from disparate business applications. Although we will give a short appreciation of it here, we of course commend you to the splunk.com website for definitive information.

We find Splunk extremely useful for exploring large log file data sets, allowing longitudinal examination of security logs looking for slow-burning events that might have stretched out over months or years. Additionally, it might well relieve you of the need for all those special-purpose Perl and PHP scripts that in the old days were necessary to digest and amalgamate the many varieties of log files needed by security practitioners. A further advantage (another "confluence" angle) is that since Splunk can easily adapt to multiple file formats, you can often make use of the log files or other emissions from your business applications as they exist, without rewriting the apps in order to normalize the log file entries to a canonical format.

To give you an idea of what Splunk looks like, one of us spent a few minutes getting a free personal license for Splunk and installing it on a home system. Without going into details about what the screenshot in Figure 6.5 shows, we present it here to give you a quick impression of the current Splunk interface.

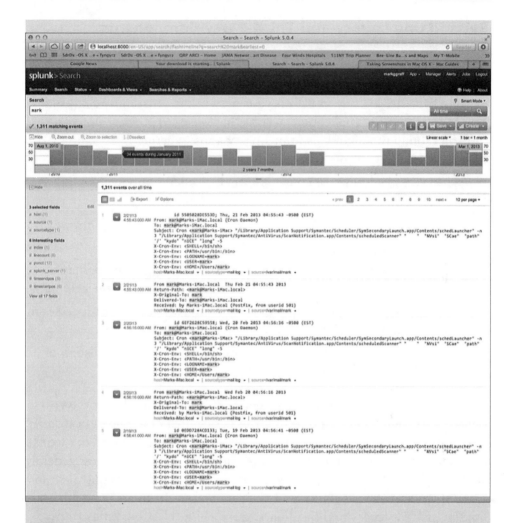

**Figure 6.5**  A Splunk example.

One final note: In 2011, Splunk introduced Splunk Storm, a cloud-based version of the core Splunk product, which "offers a turnkey, managed and hosted service for machine data."[2] We haven't tried that yet.

## Retrofitting Legacy and Third-Party Components

Although it can be relatively straightforward to design and code a new security-aware application, figuring out how to integrate it fully with existing software already in use on your network is often more challenging. This is true both for applications written in-house (whether or not you can still rebuild them) and also third-party apps (whether open source or closed), although your options in each case might be slightly different.

What you would like, of course, is for the legacy components to do the following:

- Create log entries for the same sort of events the new software does, following the canonical format
- Make use of real-time status information logged (or, perhaps, made available by interprocess communication) by the new apps
- Filter and/or block input coming from users or other processes in a manner consistent with your newer software
- Observe any new standards with regard to, say, whitelisting or blacklisting of web sites or users

We will share a few of the tricks here that we have used over the years. But we also want to say upfront that this is one area of application security that is still close to a black art. That is, there is a definite limit to the worth of formulaic advice when it comes to retrofits. These days, the best general advice we can offer is to install a web application firewall or equivalent in front of the app. A well-configured WAF will often do an amazing job of limiting risk for legacy and third-party apps, with relatively little effort.

Instead of (or in addition to) using a WAF, consider the following tips and principles:

- Make a best-effort retrospective design review, as described in Chapter 3. Puzzle out the data types and flow, key assets, and abuse cases, applying your standard threat models.
- Consider putting a virtual box around the system to limit input and output. You can prefilter input streams before they arrive at the app, and sanity-check outflows as well.
- Consider putting the app *into* a box—that is, running it inside a virtualized system that can check for contamination of the virtual system by malware.

If none of those approaches will work, you still might have a few options, if you understand your enterprise well. Here is an example that we think really showcases the advantage of a collaboration among application developers, information security practitioners, and enterprise network experts. Suppose you have an application that examines or interprets PDF files. It might well be vulnerable to malware hidden in certain file types. What about whitelisting the types of files that can be mailed into your enterprise? One of us has successfully deployed that stratagem at an enterprise level, so we know that it can be done. But if you can't sell that idea, could you put restrictions on the types of files that move into the subnet where your app runs, or over certain ports, using a local firewall?

The better you understand what the legacy software does, and the uses cases you need to allow, the better equipped you will be to devise solutions. These problems, in our experience, call out for a confluent approach.

## Notes for Small Shops or Individuals

Deployment is an area in which confluence is especially important, and here small shops might actually have the advantage. For example, in this chapter we advocate that special steps be taken to make sure that IT security and the applications developer communicate about sensitive files and information, and talk about what security events might take place after deployment and how they could be detected. In a small business, there could in fact not be two separate groups at all, but merely one or more people wearing multiple hats.

On the other hand, once again, if a small team is developing software for large enterprises, they must find a way to supply the necessary information for successful deployment just as the big companies do.

You also need to make a plan for how to respond quickly if a major hole is found in your product—or for that matter a small hole that could be used as a conduit to perform other attacks. This involves, for example, holding on to the build environment—libraries and so on—even after the product ships, so patches can be quickly developed and deployed. Maintaining these old development environments can be costly, especially for small shops, and so represent a challenge on how to do an adequate job with minimal investment. We see widespread use today of multiple virtual machines as a means of preserving build environments, and recommend the practice particularly for small teams.

# Mobile Deployment

At last, our PST comes to an area where they are feeling truly confident. After all, they've successfully deployed earlier versions of their app just fine.

The CTO again takes the initiative and sets up a preliminary meeting to discuss deployment security issues. The invited stakeholders are similar, but a little different than in previous planning meetings. In this meeting, the corporate computer security incident response team is heavily represented, for example. Whereas the CSIRT had been more or less a background player in previous meetings, providing occasional attack-scenario insights during the threat modeling, for example, now they are at center stage.

When it comes to security operations in the deployed environment, the CSIRT is rightly a central stakeholder in the process. They are the first responders when things go wrong.

So, not surprisingly, the CTO turns the meeting over to the CSIRT lead participant at the beginning of the meeting. The CSIRT's questions immediately start diving into how the mobile app will integrate with each customer's IDS and SIEM systems. "What data will be logged when an incident is suspected?" "What data exchange format will you be using?" "How will you quarantine any information to be used for evidence?" And so on.

Sadly, the tone becomes a familiar one. Our team just wasn't as prepared as they should have been. Truth be told, the vast majority of the logging that takes place within the greater app environment occurs on the server, and consists principally of debugging data to help the dev or ops teams debug any operational issues they encounter. They had never truly considered the CSIRT's use cases for responding to incidents. The data needed by the operators and by the CSIRT in those circumstances are very different indeed.

So to try to snatch victory from the jaws of (yet another) defeat, the CTO suggests that the teams try to find some middle ground they can all accept. Together, they build a checklist (and yet another major action item for after the product release) for this product release. The checklist goes like this:

- The dev team will interview the CSIRT, briefing them on the app's functional aspects and soliciting from them the sorts of information they would (and hence, the company's customers will) need for responding to incidents.

- From those inputs, an inventory of operational/security logging messages will be drafted and reviewed by the CSIRT.

- After the inventory is approved by the CSIRT, the dev team will create a customer-focused document describing all the security logging in the app, along with sample IDS rule sets for alerting the security operators to potential incidents.

- The dev team will additionally document an incident responder's guide that describes to the incident responders all the information contained within the app's architecture. This will include both mobile and server-side data stores.

- A feature wish list will be drafted containing future security enhancements for the app, such as customer tailored security alerting and encrypted/signed evidence containers that each customer CSIRT would be able to make use of during their incident response operations.

At the end of the deployment planning, our team is again feeling quite badly beaten up. Integrating their company (and their app!) into their new parent company has been a daunting process for them. The quick and easy victory they were hoping for clearly wasn't going to happen. On the other hand, they (quietly) admit that the changes they've had to endure have in the end been pretty positive.

## Summing Up

The deployment and integration phase of a project is the moment at which, to our minds, the concept of confluence becomes critical. Only if you make sure that your application "plays well" with its environment can you be sure you are taking maximum advantage of all the analytical skills, operational intelligence, and defense in depth that your business has to offer.

In particular, by ensuring that your application participates in a cooperative, collective real-time defense—tuned, second by second, to the slings and arrows launched by your adversaries—you can employ the principle of confluence in a true twenty-first-century cyber security strategy for the enterprise.

We will continue this theme in the next chapter, in which we turn the focus away from deployment and integration and toward its still more practical issues of day-to-day operation.

## Endnotes

1. Source: splunk.com, retrieved August 31, 2013.
2. http://en.wikipedia.org/wiki/Splunk, retrieved August 31, 2013.

# 7 Operating Software Securely

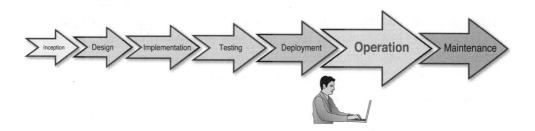

Inception | Design | Implementation | Testing | Deployment | **Operation** | Maintenance

All too often, data-center operations (whether in the cloud or still housed in a physical space) are viewed as being solely the purview of the IT and IT security organizations—and certainly not the purview of software developers. Indeed, there is often a necessary barrier in place between the software developers and the operations team. Checks and balances, after all, are necessary for business continuity and reliability. But that's not to say that software developers have no role to play at all in an application's operations. In fact, the growing DevOps movement highlights the importance of developers and operations staff working in concert.

To an enterprise's executive team, the notion of IT security is all-encompassing from a project's inception until the day it gets retired. The idea that there are typically separate teams that perform different aspects of designing, coding, testing, deploying, and so on is quite moot to the executives. To them, it is "simply" technology and our collective job is to "make it work." And "make it work" securely.

Put differently, every aspect of an application's security, throughout every phase of its life, is equally important to our employers, and should also be to us. And the production operations environment is the most real of them all for our software. That is where the actual business transactions and such take place. That's where the software earns all the time and effort we've put into it. And that is where the vulnerabilities (whether in the development or operational processes) are exposed. As a result, every person or organization involved in any phase of the process has—or should have—a vested interest in its well-being.

Given this reality, not only should developers (Dev) and operations (Ops) staff work together, but the info security folks must be included (and included from the beginning) too. Enter "Rugged" DevOps. Standard DevOps is the interrelationship between developers and the IT operations folks. Rugged DevOps means adding the role of infosec in the relationship between development and operations. It means identifying security as one of the areas in which Dev and Ops work together.

With this notion firmly in mind, let's embark on a journey through security operations and see where we might make improvements that address our notion of confluence. Note, of course, that this chapter is not intended to be a comprehensive guide to data-center operations. Instead, it is intended to highlight the link between security and operations in an increasingly complex and expedited operational environment.

## Adjusting Security Thresholds

We've spent some time here describing how to integrate business-relevant information into enterprise logging systems. By now, we know that merely logging the bad things isn't sufficient for a modern enterprise environment. Recall our description of three (low, medium, and high) "tiers" of security in Chapter 3, "Design Activities." No, for a modern business application to truly be enterprise worthy, it must be able to do quite a bit more than simply log the bad things—especially since you are likely not going to know whether something is "bad" until way downstream. As a result, it is vital to identify what to progressively log.

We need to be able to block the bad things, and log them, as well as take some evasive actions to actively protect the business data and processes our application processes.

As such, another tool in our security arsenal lies in defining thresholds for what to do when multiple events are detected within our application. For example, a user trying to log in to an application with a username of

";--" could well be attributable to a simple human typographical error once or even twice. It is unlikely we should bother reacting to such an attack. If the first attempt fails, subsequent attempts will also fail—that is, the attack is static. You might want to turn this into a dynamic attack in which the attack string is constantly changing, for example, "AAA1," "AAA2," "AAA3," and so on. But that same (or very similar) data observed 10, 15, 20 times could well be something that we're not willing to discount as human error. We might want to be able to declare 10 such "typos" as possible attempts to break in to our application.

On the other hand, if those ten events occurred over the course of ten months, perhaps they're just ten cases of human error. But ten events in one-tenth of a second could be something entirely different. It could be someone using an automated attack tool to try to break our application's authentication service.

Then there's the issue of what action(s) to take when a threshold is reached. If we've seen, for example, ten failed login attempts in rapid succession with usernames similar to ";--" then perhaps we will declare we're under attack—but now what? Do we lock the attacker's account? (Beware of DoS issues with such responses.) Do we report the attacker to the authorities? Do we launch a counterattack? The answers to all of these questions are policy decisions that the software developers typically won't be making, nor should they. These are more management-oriented decisions that should involve input from multiple teams. In fact, they are not even decisions that the operational staff will make. So here too is another instance that highlights the need for early and sustained collaboration among developers, operations staff, and the key business owners. Engage early with the appropriate decision makers to develop a set of policies and procedures that will be business appropriate and operationally sound for our application.

Clearly, there are many factors to consider in looking at events that might be logged by our logging system. Simply having a mechanism in place for detecting attack thresholds is by far the easiest part of the problem. The real issues are human ones, and those need to be considered and decided with due care. That being said, let's now take a brief look at one system that we could use to enable such decisions to be made: OWASP's AppSensor project.

## OWASP AppSensor

OWASP's AppSensor project is a framework for application-level intrusion detection and active response. It illustrates well the concepts we discuss in this section. Full project details can be found at https://www.owasp.org/index.php/OWASP_AppSensor_Project.

The AppSensor framework defines two primary modules: detect and respond. The detection module contains more than 50 unique detection points, and the corresponding respond module is then used to define how your application should respond when it hits the thresholds you define.

The detection points fall across pretty much every security aspect of an application, including authentication, access control, session management, and so on. Every time a detection point is triggered, several pieces of data are logged as well, including the date/time, the logged-in user, the activity type, and the entire HTTP request.

Responses are configured by configurable threshold, and can include warning messages, account lockouts, administrator warnings, and the like.

AppSensor is intended to work in conjunction with OWASP's ESAPI, and is relatively easy to integrate into an existing ESAPI-enabled application. Since it exists at the application level, developers have a great deal of control and flexibility in how to weave AppSensor into an application.

So now we should at least in principle have the ability to set thresholds for the security events our application encounters. Let's consider further the sorts of actions we might want to have our software take when these thresholds are reached—bearing in mind that the actual decision of what to do needs to lie within the scope of policy, and not merely with the technologists.

- Warning message

    At this level, a simple warning message is issued to the user and simultaneously logged for SIEM et al. analysis. The warning should be appropriately worded to act as a deterrent to further inappropriate behavior. It should also be fairly explicit to the user as to what policy or policies are believed to have been violated, and what possible actions could be taken should the inappropriate behavior continue.

On the other hand, warning a user who is attacking a system that his actions have been noted might not be something you always want to do. It does, after all, tip your hand by allowing your attacker to know that you're aware of the attacks.

*An appropriate warning message might look something like the following: Warning: Your actions on this application system have been detected as part of a possible security attack. Please cease and desist such actions, because they violate corporate policy #123 and are subject to disciplinary action to include termination.*

* Notification of the authorities

  When warning messages fail to persuade the attacker to cease and desist, we move on to another level of escalation by notifying the authorities. That is likely to simply mean ensuring that the IT security team is explicitly notified at this point. But in doing that, we might want to consider other prudent steps to take. For example, it might be useful at this point to tell the offending user that all actions taken are being collected and presented to the authorities. It might also be useful to start collecting and properly handling that information in the event that it must at some point be used as evidence against the offender. (That could well entail putting all logged actions into a digitally signed "evidence vault." Heavy use of digital signatures here is essential so that the digital evidence seal can be maintained to an exceptionally high degree of confidence. We might well need that tamper resistance if we need to present the information in court later.) And, if we are collecting that sort of potential evidence, we'll likely want to log everything the user is doing—to the extent that our application and associated systems include such functionality.

  Our user notification at this point could look something like the following (note that you'll most certainly want to coordinate all of these notification messages with your legal counsel):

*Warning: Your actions on this system are all now being logged and reported to the appropriate authorities for possible administrative or legal action.*

- Session logout

  Another action to consider taking is to disconnect and log out the offending user's session (perhaps after issuing a warning). When you're doing this, it is usually a good idea to enforce a "timeout period" during which the user is not permitted to log back in to the system.

*Warning: Your session is being terminated due to security violations. If you feel this has been in error, please immediately notify the IT security office at _____ to rectify the situation.*

- System lockout

  This action might be considered when an especially malicious attack has been detected that could impact other users or sensitive data if left unchecked.

*Warning: Your access to this system has been terminated indefinitely. Please immediately notify the IT security office at _____ to rectify the situation.*

- System (or partial) shutdown

  Although this is the most extreme case, it might well be necessary to shut down a system if a systemic or large-scale compromise has been detected and cannot be rectified in any other way.

*Warning: All access to this system has been terminated. The IT department is working to fix the situation as quickly as possible.*

Our main point with these examples is to provide some ideas for further consideration. What you end up doing with your application is going to depend on many factors, and might not align with what we've written here. What's most important, though, is that the choices you make be carefully thought out and planned by all the appropriate stakeholders. These decisions are not to be made lightly...or in isolation.

### Third-Party Components

Our focus to this point has been principally on application (and infrastructure) components that were developed or deployed internally. Unfortunately, very few real-world applications are quite this simplistic or ideally organized. Instead, they generally contain numerous third-party components that are vital to the proper functioning of the application system itself.

What makes these third-party components interesting and challenging from our standpoint is the question of how to properly include them in our security operations. After all, we generally are not afforded the opportunity of changing third-party code, unlike our own application code.

Building logging systems, security thresholds, and all those other important security activities we've discussed here isn't so easy to do when we can't get to the source code. So we're left with making some compromises, none of which is ideal.

So where do we begin?

A good starting point is to take a critical assessment of the inventory of all the security features and operational functionality of the third-party components. What logging data can each provide, for example? You can include such requirements in the contracts to provide the services. To what extent is the log data customizable? How can our SIEM make use of these logs and draw meaningful conclusions from what it receives?

Depending on the size and complexity of the third-party components we're using, this might well be a formidable task in and of itself.

Plus, while we're considering third-party components, let's not be constrained merely by the discrete components of a system (e.g., a database server); let's also consider the third-party code that our application is using (e.g., Java frameworks).

So it's best we start with a detailed component map of the entire application system. Identify all the components that were not built internally. Then, one by one, dive into the features of those components and see what they are able to provide us with to enhance our operational situational awareness of what our application system is doing. Understand that it's never as easy to accomplish as it sounds, but best practice guides pertinent to the third-party software should be helpful.

Next, consider augmenting log data with additional data sources. This is an area where a web application firewall (WAF) might actually provide significant value. Placing a WAF in-line with a third-party web application component can be an effective way of getting a far better logging overview of the system than just relying on what the third-party component can provide.

Unlike a traditional network firewall, WAFs parse and act on web application data. That is, they "see" all the business data going to and from a web application.

They can also provide enhanced input/output data validation by looking for common attack signatures, or even positively validating data field types throughout an application—given sufficient integration attention to detail and "training" of the WAF product. WAFs can also be useful to rewrite application functionality without requiring a full recode/test/ deployment cycle. But from our perspective at this point, they can often log application activities that third-party code fails to, and depending on the WAF product we select, we can likely tailor that logging to suit our needs quite effectively.

So augmenting an application's logging capabilities might be worthy of consideration.

Of course, the real starting point should occur before any components enter the organization. The first step ought to be determining how to convey the right message to the acquisition professionals. Who determines the contract details? Who selects the vendors? Who determines the trade-offs between price, quality, and security? These decision points are vital steps in the process, and the more team members who are involved in these decisions, the better.

## Collaborations

Clearly, building an operational IDS and SIEM environment such as we've described here requires substantial collaboration among various stakeholders, including IT security, operations, business, and software development. If IT merely integrates all the logging that the components make available, their view of the business aspects of the system will be incomplete. If the software developers choose to merely "log more," without regard for how the data will actually be used in practice, the result will be equally ineffective.

This is an opportune time to highlight how to integrate information security into DevOps. As mentioned at the outset of this chapter, DevOps is the integration of development and operations activities. That team works in an environment of constant deployments, where deployments are happening multiple times per day instead of every few months. In fact, as a large company, Amazon has announced publicly that they are doing 1,000 deploys per day. In an environment like that there is simply no time for security reviews that might take weeks to complete! Even a small shop that is doing 10 deploys per day cannot afford to wait for a lengthy post-development security review. Rather than testing being done after the fact, security questions and tests can be baked in and automated. With "Rugged" DevOps, security becomes an activity of the DevOps team. The rapid pace of these deployments requires that many of the manual operational steps that formed the basis of many security failures be automated. Several techniques exist for integrating information security with development and operations. We list these some of these techniques here:

- Graph it. Security is not a binary event. You are under constant attack—and everyone needs to see it. The visual reality will support the attitude adjustment that is vital to success. Developers, business owners, and operations staff must all be aware of the constant threat.

- Employ constant monitoring. If you believe you are under constant attack, it makes sense to have constant monitoring. Look for segmentation faults and server crashes. This could indicate bad code or it could indicate a successful attack or perhaps a soon-to-fail disk that could bring down a vital business process.

- Make sure that the postmortem process is blameless. Remember, the whole point of DevOps is that you have one team. If you develop and deploy as a team, the team takes responsibility for the entire process. This allows the focus of the postmortem to be on how to fix security failures instead of who to blame for them.

- Recognize your reach. The perimeter of your organization is not defined by the walls of your building. Remember the BYOD policies implemented months ago? Securing your systems now means securing the employees' systems. You need to help them practice good cyber hygiene across all the devices they use—those that are owned by the organization and those that are not. When you outsource/offshore applications, be certain to determine what the legal eagles say about who owns the data/logs/control.

## Dealing with IDS in Operations

Now let's deal with the topics of what can and should take place after an alarm is actually sounded, so to speak. IT operations staff deal with IDS, firewall, SIEM, and other logs constantly. When and how should the software developers participate in the process?

For the most part, the security operations should be "business as usual" and should require little if any input from the software development team. But those aren't the situations we're especially concerned about. The times to involve the developers are when the exceptional cases occur. But how can you anticipate these exceptional cases and know the exact times for collaboration? Well—unless you have a crystal ball—you can't. Thus the need for embracing a strategy that brings together all parties from inception to deployment.

Indeed, if we've designed, built, and integrated our system well, we should need to pull in the developers only to help handle the toughest of tough situations. But when those do happen, we want to be thoroughly prepared to handle them, and handle them promptly in a businesslike manner. By leveraging the principles of rugged software development— defensible infrastructure, operational discipline, situational awareness, and countermeasures, Rugged DevOps provides the foundation for the integration of security concerns to be incorporated throughout the process.

So what sort of things would we anticipate wanting the developers to help out with during security incidents? The big issue is a keen insight into how an application works so that we can more quickly review error messages or other information gathered in the course of handling an incident.

The operations staff and even the IT security staff can't possibly know the inner workings of an application as thoroughly as the software team should. When faced with novel situations and security alerting, often that knowledge of how the system actually works can help in quickly resolving whether the situation is indeed a security incident or perhaps a false alarm.

If it is then determined to be a real incident, a deep understanding of the system can further be useful in guiding the incident response team in coming up with the most effective recommended course of action to take.

And bear in mind here that this needs to be a true collaborative effort rather than a paper-based partnership. The operations and incident handling team should seek to engage the software developers—who in turn need to be candid and forthcoming in considering what is taking place in the software. This is no time for placing blame or trying to cover up errors. To be effective, the team needs to communicate and collaborate openly and fully.

Doing all of this means planning for failures. We need to make sure that everything is going to be in place for the developers and the operations team to collaborate during difficult situations. Consider the following list of issues you'll likely face:

- Configuration management

  Developers are usually busy working on the *next* version of the software, not the version that is currently in production. At a bare minimum, they need rapid access to the exact versions of all the software and all of its components, exactly as they exist in the production system. (Ideally, although this is expensive, you will have a completely duplicate environment.) That is basic configuration management, but there are nuances here that will cause challenges. For one thing, the developers are most likely thinking about the software mechanisms and functionality that is under development. If substantial changes are being implemented, getting them to go backward in time to consider the production versions might be problematic.

- Test beds

  The QA test team is no doubt already well versed in setting up software test beds to test software systems. During a security incident, things might need to be just a bit different, however. For example, the test bed most likely needs to include all the security operations infrastructure found in the production environment, including the firewalls, IDS, SIEM, WAFs, and so on. In other words, the purpose of a security incident test bed is quite different from that of a functional testing environment. The functionality being tested isn't the business functionality of the software, but the security operational functionality. What set of circumstances can result in the following error condition, for example?

- Test tools

  Similarly, the tools needed in the security test bed might well be quite different from those in a traditional functional test bed. We might need various types of instrumentation to capture network traffic, introduce faults into the system, inject "poisonous" data into the system, and so forth. The tools we'll likely want to deploy are more like what would be used in a penetration test than a functional test of the software.

- Staff availability

  Security incidents don't happen at convenient times. (It has long been our experience, for example, that major incidents all seem to begin on Friday afternoons.) When you need to bring the developers in on an incident, you're going to need to know how to find them. Although this sounds quite straightforward, in practice it often isn't. And the failures won't necessarily be the trivial ones like "what's her home phone number?"—they're more likely to be those like "he no longer works here" or "we don't have a contract in place to bring that team back onboard." Plan for failure; make sure you'll be able to reach out to the key staff when you need them. And practice. Run drills.

These are just a few considerations to plan for. The important issue is to understand that the developers can be useful to the operations and IT security teams when things go wrong. They can bring a level of awareness of the application's inner workings that the operations staff can never attain. That knowledge can be enormously helpful in debugging difficult security situations.

## Typical Security Events

Let's now consider a handful of hypothetical security events and how a collaborative approach to resolving them might work in practice. Remember that collaboration is the operative word. The DevOps movement is about collaboration...real collaboration that starts at inception and flows throughout the process...a confluence of disciplines, if you will.

- Repeated authentication failures

  In this first and simplest scenario, the operations team has been seeing on their SIEM a series of repeated authentication failures for one specific user of a system. They assume that the application itself is blocking the attempts and escalating its response process internally, but because the messages persist, they call in the application developers and perhaps some other key application stakeholders. The developers might quickly recognize that the account experiencing the failures is used by a partner for a Business to Business (B2B) connection over a web services channel between the business partner and our company. A quick phone call to the business partner confirms that they've recently made some changes to their software, which resulted in incorrect SOAP credentials being passed to our application inadvertently, and the situation is resolved.

  The fact that this connection was a server-to-server connection precluded the warning messages and such from being noticed by a human, and the business partner's software was simply retrying to connect over and over, without success.

- Access control failures

  Next, our operations team is being deluged by access control failures in their firewall and IDS logs, but with no corresponding alerts being issued from the application itself. The log messages indicate repeated attempts to connect to a specific path and URL, along with some nonsensical command-line data. They search for known attack signatures and malware that could be the culprit, but find nothing. So they bring in the emergency response team, who in turn call in the developers to help with the diagnosis.

  The developers look at the URL and realize that it is a legitimate one, but from a version of the software that had been deprecated several months ago and replaced with a new version. Next, they stand up a test bed with the old version of the software and dynamically test the URL with its command data.

  The results of this test point to a data poisoning weakness in the deprecated software; had it still been in production, the attackers would have succeeded in getting an encoded cross-site script attack through the data input validation and possibly doing further damage. What's worse, the attack was clearly written and tailored specifically to this software; someone with inside knowledge of how the software worked likely wrote it.

The incident is escalated and handled as a potential criminal attack.

- Log overflow

  In this scenario, the operations team is suddenly getting hit with log overflow problems—in which the event-logging system is being bombarded with repeated alerts. This goes on to the point of causing some logging components to fail. The log messages themselves don't seem to have anything to do with security issues, but the repetition is causing disruption. So the IT security team is called in to see whether the problem might be security related.

  After an initial assessment of the problem fails to find the root cause, the security team assembles a larger emergency response team, to include the software developers of the applications involved.

  The developers look at the errors being logged, and are quickly able to pinpoint where in the source code the logs are coming from. They then perform some basic unit tests on the modules implicated in the problem.

  Through this testing, they are able to pinpoint a logic error in their code that was resulting in a log call inside of an infinite loop—much to their embarrassment.

  They fix the code, test the patch, and then push out an emergency fix of the application to the production environment.

- Log injection

  During an incident response operation on a real incident, the CSIRT organization discovers a log entry indicating that there had been a privilege compromise on a critical business application. But even though the logs clearly show the compromise, the application system's logging is unable to corroborate the information. Which one is wrong?

  To explore all possible causes, the CSIRT calls in the software developers to offer their assessment of the information in the logs. At first glance, they concur that the system had been compromised, but they agree to take on some tests to verify the functionality of the logging infrastructure.

After setting up the test rig, they conduct some fuzz tests of the logging system. The input to the logging is by way of the username being entered, so they build a test rig to fuzz that interface in an HTTP POST request. They fuzz all the data targets in the HTTP request.

When they review the results, they discover that the software wasn't adequately validating the input, and that an injection attack could alter the logs by injecting a CR/LF and an otherwise legitimate-looking log entry into the logs. They then test that specific attack and verify that they can use it to inject arbitrary data into the event logs through their application. The application is quickly (and quietly) patched and returned to production.

- SQL injections

  The IT security team discovers a new SQL injection tool out on an Internet forum. Being concerned, they run some unannounced penetration tests of a few key applications in the data center using this new tool. This is best done in a test-bed environment.

  The penetration tests result in error messages being logged to the logging systems, via the IDS sensors, warning of the SQL injection attacks.

  So they call in the software developers to help verify that the tool will or won't be a problem if a real attacker uses it to target the company's business applications.

  The software developers are then able to quickly do a static analysis of their production code on all the Internet-facing applications to verify that they all use parameterized queries for all SQL calls. They further build a fuzz testing tool that exhaustively steps through each and every input to the Internet-facing application interfaces, and verifies that none of them is susceptible to the new tool's attacks.

- Other data injection attacks

  SQL injection might well be the big bad injection attack that makes all the headlines, but it's far from the only form of malicious data injection attack. At a core level, any structured data (or interface) can potentially be injected with malicious data if input and output data is left unchecked, or is inadequately checked.

All an attacker needs to do is to understand the structure of data being used by the application—for example, XML formatted data. Knowing that structure, the attacker will attempt to enter malicious data designed to enable the attacker to "jump out" of a particular context and into another. For example, data going into an XML element could contain a ">" character, which would allow the attacker to enter any arbitrary XML data element or syntax. The attacker will attempt to encode the input data in an effort to trick a poorly written input validator to accept the input, but the end result is the same.

When an injection weakness is found, or believed possible, the team will again want to build a fuzz testing tool to exhaustively test various possibilities for a specific data element or interface.

## Identifying Critical Applications

A common problem faced by IT operations and security staff is that they lack the business insight to be able to identify and prioritize the business value of systems they operate in a data center.

Put differently, network attacks can often result in a deluge of log data being sent to the operations team via the IDS and SIEM infrastructure. Faced with the very real problem of "which fire do we put out first?" many IT security operations teams are not able to make the right business decision—or make it quickly enough. And if not careful, they can get suckered into responding to the noisy (highly visible) attack, and miss the "under the radar" sneak attack.

So let's consider how the operations team might identify and prioritize a list of critical applications, and what role the software developers might need to play in that.

### Identifying Critical Components, Data, and Other Assets

The first step a security team should take in identifying critical assets is to take an inventory of all business "systems" in an organization—including their architecture and component diagrams! Note that we are not referring here to individual computer systems, but the collection of computers—likely distributed—that are essential to the operation of any given business application. They can include databases, application servers, storage arrays, and all sorts of other technical components. Increasingly, the landscape might well be further obfuscated when considering cloud services as part of an individual business system.

In an ideal world, the inventory we are speaking of here will be built and maintained throughout a system's life cycle. However, in reality it's quite possible the inventory never existed or was built during the application development stage and will need to be developed ex post facto. This can be a laborious and difficult prospect to undertake, but the good news is that going through the process will doubtlessly benefit the entire organization in the long run.

When trying to build an inventory ex post facto, we generally try to discuss a system with the business owner as well as the system architect, if such people exist and/or are still with the current organization. Start by interviewing these individuals (or teams) and asking them how a system works. Be sure to include the start-up and shut-down process. We've found a large whiteboard to be among the most useful tools when trying to build this mental image of a system and its components.

During the interview process, be sure to also identify the types of data a system processes. Include user information, payment information, and anything else a system uses.

From there, it is generally possible to build up a working image of how a system functions and what its most critical functions and information assets are. Remember, though, that this information must be maintained and kept up-to-date.

## CSIRT Utilization

In most medium-size to large organizations, the CSIRT is the team responsible for the first response to security incidents as they occur. They are the ones who have to make sense of an often hugely confusing set of logs, symptoms, and anecdotal hearsay and actually find out what is taking place on a system, and in great technical detail. The CSIRT almost never has all the data—or the right data—it needs in order to determine these things. Yet they are usually the ones that the executive decision makers will turn to for a candid assessment of what's happening during a security breach.

As such, when it comes to the security functionality in a piece of software, from its event logging to its set of evasive actions it can take when it is determined that an attack is taking place (or has taken place), the CSIRT should be considered to be the primary "user." To clarify, the end users of a system are the functional users, but the CSIRT should be considered to be the consumer of security functionality.

Some of your authors have many years of experience on various CSIRTs and can categorically say that it is truly rare that a software team even speaks with a CSIRT, much less collaborates with them on the security functionality of the software. In some organizations, the CSIRT must approach the Ops team to request log data. And as the investigation unfolds, they must continuously go back to the Ops team for more and more data. This can cause friction between the groups because it distracts the Ops team from current priorities to satisfy the CSIRT requests.

We feel strongly that a key opportunity is being completely missed here. Particularly in the case of enterprise software, the CSIRT can and should have every feasible opportunity to assist in specifying the security functionality of software under development (or maintenance). With the continued trend of distributed access to centralized enterprise applications, teamwork is paramount to the CIO/CSO mandate of maintaining system security.

## Notes for Small Shops or Individuals

The ideas expressed throughout this chapter are ideal for small shops. DevOps is, in fact, the process of bringing together individuals or staffs who focus on different parts of the development-deployment life cycle. In small shops these individuals are often embodied in one person. By default, the developer and the operations staff (and often the business owner) are the same individual. In this case, we do not need to spend time convincing you that they should talk. But the activities to be performed and the details to be considered are still worth noting.

## Mobile Operations

By now, our PST is starting to fall into more of a rhythm. In anticipation of this discussion, the dev team has gone out and acquired some reading material on the topics of vulnerability scanning and penetration testing. After all, they're expecting the operations portion of the process to be pretty straightforward. Right?

They're partially right, anyway.

The first jolt of reality hit the team when they were asked how they planned to integrate into each customer's SIEM. What hooks are available? Are they publishing sample IDS alerts for Snort or other popular and/or open-source IDS products? How would they ensure that any logs sent from the mobile device would be kept protected from prying eyes (and network eavesdroppers)?

Sadly, our team again recognized the signs that they were in over their heads. This was becoming a familiar plot, and they would clearly have to give things more consideration than they had in the past.

Since so many of the issues surrounding operations integration were related to logging, that's where they focused the discussions at this point. It turned out that the app does plenty of logging, but all the logging is designed to help make debugging and diagnosing bugs easier. They had gone to quite some lengths to verify that no personally identifiable information (PII) is in the logging, which is a good thing from a HIPAA compliancy standpoint. Nonetheless, absolutely none of the existing logging was intended for the purpose of aiding incident responders in their work.

To that end, the next thing our team did was to meet with some of their company's CSIRT staff. They asked the CSIRT folks what sort of information they would need if the mobile app was involved in an incident. The big issue was accountability. The CSIRT would need to determine the classic issues: Who, What, When, Where, and How.

So together they set out to design the most basic core set of alerts that could go to a customer's operations logging systems. To complement these alerts, sample Snort alerts were built so that existing IDS products (like Snort or based on Snort) could easily take action if they received any alerting from the mobile app.

Next, they built in a mechanism for customers to import their own server's X509 certificate(s). Those public certificates would be used to encrypt any logging originating on the mobile client before transmitting any logs.

This seemed like a reasonable set of first steps to take for the product before it is shipped. For future releases, they would build a road map that would include taking evasive action against identified attacks and other steps.

## Summing Up

Here we highlighted the importance of linking security and operations through a "confluence" approach that should begin at the project outset. Rugged DevOps, or DevOpsSec, is an inherently confluent concept that brings together the infosec staff with the software developers and the operations team to address the organizational needs of an increasingly complex and expedited operational environment. And don't forget to include the business owners early and often in these conversations. They have the business logic. Together, they can make the right business decisions quickly and securely.

# 8  Maintaining Software Securely

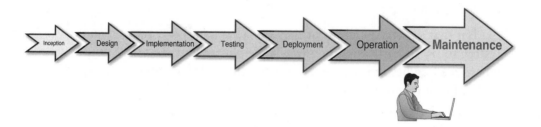

It's quite easy to think of software maintenance as the Rodney Dangerfield of software development: It gets no respect. Let's face it, in most enterprise environments, the maintenance team for a particular piece of software often is not the elite crew of developers at the tops of their careers. Why not? Simply put, it's because developers typically want to be working on the next big piece of new software. They often disdainfully view maintaining software as grudge work.

Although we don't disagree that this is indeed the status quo all too often, we feel that it's disappointing and that it misses some hugely important security issues. Let's explore that notion a bit more deeply.

Let's start by exploring the traditional mission of the maintenance team. In many enterprise environments, the maintenance team fixes bugs and adds (minor) features to existing software. In some cases, the maintenance team might also be responsible for fixing relatively minor security bugs. The bigger issues are often addressed by the senior developers. In fairness, we've also encountered companies that employ substantial sustaining engineering teams to maintain and enhance their products. These tend to be companies with mature products that have been around for a while, but they bear mention here, because they don't fit the more stereotypical image we've presented.

The maintenance team thus has a "punch list" of bugs that they work through, hoping the list will slowly get appreciably smaller over time. The bug list generally includes at least some form of prioritization, such as "high," "medium," and "low," and those bugs certainly aren't all related to security. For the security bugs, it is worth considering using an open-source scoring system such as the Forum of Incident Response and Security Team's (FIRST) Common Vulnerability Scoring System (CVSS) to help with the prioritization.

But that's pretty much what they do. They analyze a bug, do some testing to try to replicate it in a test-bed environment, and then pinpoint where the bug lies in the code base. Then they implement a patch—perhaps with a bit of research work to determine just how to do the fix.

For an extra treat, the maintenance team sometimes gets to implement new features into an application. These don't tend to be the big flashy features—those are left for the next major release that the core development team will implement. No, the sorts of feature changes left to the maintenance team often consist of little more than aesthetic changes such as user interface changes, rather than changes to an application's existing business logic.

Of course, when you put it this way, maintenance doesn't sound very fulfilling professionally, does it? It's no wonder that the people on the maintenance team tend to be junior staff or newbies on a specific project. They first have to prove themselves before being "called up to the majors" where they might actually get to touch real code development.

Do you see how this might be a problem, from a security perspective? The principal problem is that the maintenance team in all likelihood lacks the experience and, more important, deep understanding of the application itself—the nuances of how the code interacts, which are extremely hard to document, and the variations of which are very difficult to describe.

In fact, one of the toughest things a maintenance team must accomplish is to attain that deep understanding of an application. To do the maintenance process well, the maintenance team really should have a comparable level of understanding of an app as that of the original designers and implementers.

And yet, the time it would take to get to that level of understanding is the one thing that most maintenance teams aren't given. They're often maintaining many applications, and have tight and often conflicting deadlines of their own to meet. Exacerbating things is that senior management usually views maintenance as little more than a cost drain. As a result, it is common practice for the maintainers to be "thrown to the wolves" and be expected to do their jobs without much in the way of big picture understanding of an app. Anyone who has ever looked at someone else's code—or even his own code months after it was written—knows well the difficulties of the situation.

It should come as no surprise, then, that we've seen many security bugs introduced inadvertently during the maintenance cycle. In this chapter, we'll describe some ways in which we can try to avoid just that.

## Common Pitfalls

With the previous mission and all of its challenges in mind, maintenance teams are prone to inadvertently introducing security problems with their new and modified code. Let's look at some of the problems we've encountered in our collective experiences.

- Third-party components

  Almost all software today makes use of some external components. In many cases, those components don't include source code, due to licensing issues and such. In many such cases, the third-party software simply doesn't get updated during maintenance cycles. Similarly, when those same third-party components themselves receive major updates, it's common for the updates to not be included because they might well require retooling of the application itself. And factor in that security fixes in third-party products are often published openly on various Internet forums and sites. Either way, a full regression test would be required in the extreme.

- Frameworks

  Similar to the preceding issue with third-party components, software frameworks often don't get updated during maintenance cycles. But with most frameworks, they are compiled into an application—not merely linked in during a build process. Thus, changes to software frameworks require an even deeper reach into the build process. As such, they are even less likely to see updates than are simple libraries.

- Design skew

   To successfully add new features to an application, it is often
   necessary to build a deep understanding of the application itself,
   from its design on down to specific implementation details. When
   the maintenance team lacks that knowledge, or doesn't have the
   time to truly understand the application they're working on, mistakes tend to happen. Things like programmatic access control in
   an application's business logic, for example, can be overlooked
   or—worse—disabled in order to get a new piece of code to function correctly.

Further, there are in reality at least two categories of problems that
can be introduced by the maintenance team. Consider, if you will, the
two principal missions: bug fixing and adding new features. When the
maintenance team is fixing bugs, they will at least start by diving "into"
someone else's code, and make corrections to it after they've identified the
problem(s) causing the bug.

By comparison, when adding new features to a piece of software, the
maintenance team will often be adding new code to the existing code
base. Although that new code will of course need to be connected with the
existing code, it is nonetheless new code. At times, the original code might
be "refactored" so that it can perform its original purpose and support a
new feature.

It stands to reason that the latter scenario can be more prone to
introducing architectural security problems into an application. If the
maintainers, for example, lack the knowledge of the security components
used throughout the application (e.g., input validation, output escaping,
access control), it's quite possible that they would either implement simply
what they consider to be the best practice, or omit a security control
entirely.

On the other hand, when the team is repairing someone else's code, a
different type of problem can creep in. If the existing code, for example, is
using an access control library and the maintenance team is not familiar
with that library, removing it from the code is a simple human mistake to
make. This sort of thing can often happen while maintainers are trying
to debug a piece of code, and can easily be overlooked when they are
reconstructing the code to its original state.

# ESAPI AccessController

To consider this scenario, let's start with an access controller method straight out of OWASP's own ESAPI documentation. The method discussed here, enforceAuthoriza- tion, is used to grant or deny access to any given object within a Java application.

When a maintenance team is trying to add functionality to a piece of code, and they cannot figure out how the method works, it is trivial for them to make a "tempo- rary" fix to the enforceAuthorization method to bypass the access controller. The problem can creep into the code in different ways, but if they never fix the temporary workaround, the application's access control will not function as planned.

Here's the correct enforceAuthorization method:

```
public void enforceAuthorization(Object key,
Object runtimeParameter)
    throws org.owasp.esapi.errors.AccessControlException {
    boolean isAuthorized = false;
    try {
        AccessControlRule rule =
        (AccessControlRule)ruleMap.get(key);
        if(rule == null) {
            throw new AccessControlException(
                    "AccessControlRule was

not found for key: " + key,
                        "");
        }
        System.out.println("Enforcing Authorization
    Rule \"" + key + "\" Using class: " +
    rule.getClass().getCanonicalName());
        isAuthorized = rule.isAuthorized(runtimeParameter);
    } catch(Exception e) {
        throw new AccessControlException
        ("An unhandled Exception was " +
                    "caught, so we are recasting it as an " +
                    "AccessControlException.",
                    "",
                    e);
    }
    if(!isAuthorized) {
        throw new AccessControlException
        ("Access Denied for key: " + key +
```

```
                           " runtimeParameter: " +
        runtimeParameter, "");
    }
}
```

Now, this is all well and good until the maintainers stumble onto the code and can't figure out how to integrate new functionality into the existing access control design. One outcome might look like the following example:

```
public void enforceAuthorization
(Object key, Object runtimeParameter)
    throws org.owasp.esapi.errors.AccessControlException {
    boolean isAuthorized = false;
    try {
        AccessControlRule rule =
        (AccessControlRule)ruleMap.get(key);
        if(rule == null) {
            throw new AccessControlException(
                        "AccessControlRule was
        not found for key: " + key,
                        "");
        }
        System.out.println("Enforcing Authorization Rule \"" + key +
➥"\" Using class: " + rule.getClass().getCanonicalName());
 /*        isAuthorized = rule.isAuthorized
        (runtimeParameter); */
    isAuthorized = true;
    } catch(Exception e) {
        throw new AccessControlException
        ("An unhandled Exception was " +
                "caught, so we are recasting it as an " +
                "AccessControlException.",
                "",
                e);
    }
    if(!isAuthorized) {
        throw new AccessControlException
        ("Access Denied for key: " + key +

    " runtimeParameter: " + runtimeParameter, "");
    }
}
```

In this simplistic example, the maintenance team has clearly commented out the returning Boolean `isAuthorized` and made it true under all circumstances. Although this will certainly result in their code passing the authorization test, it clearly breaks the access controller design.

The preceding scenario is realistic and must be avoided. It can creep into code easily when the maintenance team is not adequately trained in the technologies being used in an application, as well as on the application itself. In situations in which it's feasible, having the original dev team review major proposed code revisions could be helpful, but that's often not feasible for a myriad of reasons.

## Case Study: Debian OpenSSL Versus Valgrind

An example of security defects being introduced during maintenance can be found in the Debian Linux community, from a few years ago. Further details can be found at http://blogs.fsfe.org/tonnerre/archives/24.

In 2006, a group of well-intended Debian developers used Valgrind, a popular code profiling tool, to go searching for bugs in OpenSSL. They found one, or at least thought they did, and it didn't end well.

What they found was an uninitialized memory buffer in a function. Believing it to be a bug, they commented out the offending code, which resulted in a downstream problem in OpenSSL when a random number generator started producing predictable random numbers—surely, a kiss of death in any crypto code.

The problem crept in because the maintenance team didn't understand the OpenSSL code they were patching. It turned out that the buffer was deliberately not initialized, and that its contents were being used to at least partially seed a pseudo random number generator. (As an aside, we are more than slightly surprised that crypto code would rely on "random" memory contents to seed a random number generator, but that's another issue.)

The impact of this seemingly legitimate patching process was that all SSL and SSH certificates generated on vulnerable Debian Linux systems between May 2006 and May 2008 were insufficient and needed to be revoked and regenerated. This was a major black eye for the Debian OpenSSL team, of course, because OpenSSL and SSH are key security components of its server software.

No doubt there are many similar anecdotes to be found wherein maintenance teams inadvertently introduced security weaknesses into code.

## How Does Maintaining Software Securely Relate to Confluence?

In many ways, the software maintenance process is a miniature development and deployment process in and of itself. At that level, it is as relevant to our notion of confluence as the rest of the topics in this book are. In a very real sense, the maintenance cycle is uniquely suited to act as something of a feedback loop to our core development efforts. Let's delve into this topic in some more detail.

A common maintenance scenario occurs when a security defect is found in a piece of software. The problem is verified in an engineering support cycle, and sent (urgently) to the maintainers to fix the problem and deploy a fix.

Now, there are two major issues that come out of that, at least from the perspective of maintaining software. First, as we've discussed previously, the software development industry doesn't often successfully learn from its past mistakes. Well, here is the ideal place for that to happen. Let's not simply treat this as a single problem that requires a point solution to be developed and deployed. Instead, let's seize the opportunity to really study the underlying root cause of the problem, and let's treat it as a systemic issue that needs to be addressed in a far broader sense. We recognize that this can be difficult to accomplish for various technical, management, and social issues.

Second, in a small percentage of situations, we'll actually be dealing with an as-yet-unknown security defect. In those cases, the burden on the maintenance team is even greater, because it needs to analyze the software carefully and determine how it was attacked. If the successful attack is in fact a new attack methodology, the maintenance team should work with the organization's security team to fix the problem, and to get word out to the broader security community regarding a newly discovered attack methodology.

To accomplish either of these objectives requires substantial integration among the security and development teams. Further, the maintenance team generally doesn't consist of software security experts, and they might well have a tough time connecting the dots and truly understanding the bigger security picture in play. We'll address these points further in the following.

## Learning from History

We've previously bemoaned (see Chapter 1, "Introduction to the Problem") how bad our community is at learning from its past mistakes. Here is our chance to correct that.

When we are correcting our software security defects, we have a perfect opportunity to buck the trend and learn from the underlying mistake. But to do that, we need to first truly and deeply understand just what the underlying mistake is. Is it, for example, a simple implementation mistake made by a developer who didn't understand a security issue? If so, was it a "once and done" mistake, or can we observe a trend in the errors we're correcting? Or, on the other hand, did it represent a more significant and deeper problem with the software's design?

Yes, there are many aspects of learning from history. On a fairly simple level, we can use the defects corrected by the maintenance team as a feedback loop. For example, if they are spending substantial time fixing input validation problems that have led to cross-site scripting (XSS) defects, the development team should consider taking appropriate actions, such as additional or remedial training on input validation for its members. They might also take extra efforts to address XSS defects during code reviews. They might step up the fuzz testing performed on data inputs during the security testing processes.

These are all reasonable responses to finding an increase in input validation failures in a piece of software. They require the maintenance team to study the security defects they repair, however. They need to be keeping statistics of the defects they repair, for example. They need to be coordinating those defects and their corresponding remediations with the security team. They also need to deeply understand the root cause of each security defect. Was it an input validation failure? A trust failure? And so on.

These things all matter substantially in the feedback loop process. Although simple implementation bugs are relatively easy to remediate and move past, they might still represent process failures that should be fixed in the development process. Likewise, design flaws might well not be so easy to remediate, but they most assuredly need to be deeply understood and addressed at a design level.

Next, consider just what type of feedback you expect from your maintenance team. In some cases, it might be sufficient to simply know that a defect has been fixed and tested, and is now ready for production. However, to truly learn from mistakes, it is important that someone in maintenance or in the developer group study the inputs coming from the maintenance team and take appropriate actions. What is needed here is an effective feedback loop among the code developers, the security team, and maintainers.

Doing this effectively will no doubt require an ongoing dialogue between the developers themselves and the maintenance team—and likely too, the security team.

Additionally, consider the case in which a security defect represents an as-yet-unknown weakness and attack. This situation spotlights the need for the maintenance team to work closely with the security team. While analyzing a defect, the maintenance team should be seeking to replicate the issue in a testing environment. After they've studied the weakness and how it can be exploited, they should be including the security team in a dialogue. It will most likely be the security team that validates a weakness to be an as-yet-unknown one.

We should note here that by "as-yet-unknown," we are referring to a security weakness and attack that hasn't been seen in this or any other application—not merely a new SQL injection weakness in the current application, for example. The latter would need to be fixed, but is hardly a new issue to the security community.

For those circumstances, the need to dive deep into the problem is even further underscored. In most circumstances, the maintenance team should likely work closely with the security team and coordinate their findings with an internal or external computer security incident response team (CSIRT) that specializes in vulnerability handling. The CSIRT should, in turn, work with affected product and technology producers to rectify the problem.

Among the major issues faced in taking on this sort of activity is the need for reporting confidentiality. Although it is useful to work with an external CSIRT in these circumstances, the development team should take all steps possible to ensure that the weakness in our application itself is not made public, at least until a patch is available.

The major point we're trying to make here is that simply fixing an endless queue of SQLi and XSSi problems in an app is useful and meaningful, but the maintenance team should be helping the organization continuously improve. And further, the maintenance team needs to be vigilant regarding weaknesses that are potentially completely new to the community. Those can well be game changers, and someone needs to be spotting them if and when they are found.

## Evolving Threats

Another area in which we must rigorously coordinate our software security activities is in keeping up with ever-changing threats. Even in the absence of any form of patching or adding features to a piece of software, things change over time. And here, of course, we're mostly focusing on changes in the security posture of the software, but functional changes also occur. Let's explore.

From a security standpoint, the software components that were included in our software's build environment—the libraries, frameworks, and such—are from time to time updated with new functionality, as well as security patches. When a security patch becomes available for one of the components on which we built our software, we need to update our own software and perform the appropriate regression testing.

At times, the updates include major revisions to our dependent software components. That translates to spending significant time verifying our software in a maintenance cycle. It might even include a relatively major amount of recoding in the event that an API is revised along with a major software component release.

More often than not, most software organizations don't revise their software when a software framework is updated with new functionality. Unfortunately, the same all too often holds true when a software framework is updated with security patches. We must not fall for that, even when updating our software requires a substantial amount of retooling.

In this regard, we would be well advised to follow the lead of our data center operations. In most modern data centers, security and IT staff have clearly defined software update and patch procedures. When a security patch is released, they more often than not have a test bed where they can test the update and then deploy it onto production servers via a change management process. Unfortunately, this patch process generally covers only operating systems, application servers, web servers, and the like. Rarely, if ever, does that patch process include software frameworks that were included in an application's build environment. It is up to the software developers—and maintainers—to take that burden on. That being said, when a patch is necessary for performance issues, having a proper test bed environment complete with realistic traffic generators and such becomes absolutely essential.

Furthermore, on the topic of keeping up with evolving threats, the burden doesn't end with merely keeping up with patches. In fact, it goes much further than that. We must also monitor changes in attack methodologies and ensure that our own application is properly protected. This is another area that must not occur in a development organization without close collaboration from the security organization.

The approach we like to see is holding periodic meetings among the security and development organizations, to include software maintainers. During the meetings, recent threat changes should be discussed, especially those that involve a substantial state change in observed attacks. Of course, high-priority changes must also be addressed via out-of-cycle meetings, but for the most part, the recurring meeting process should be adequate.

Let's describe this situation by considering an attack that took place recently. The attack (described in the summer of 2012—reference http://9to5mac.com/2012/07/13/apples-in-app-purchasing-process-circumvented-by-russian-hacker/) enabled the attacker to circumvent Apple's in-app purchase mechanism for iOS apps, enabling the attacker to make purchases for free. To carry out the attack, the attacker presents a fake x.509 certificate to the iOS device, which itself has a fake x.509 trusted CA certificate installed. Further, the local network's DNS is altered by the attacker to serve up incorrect DNS resolutions for IP numbers and hostnames. The resulting environment tricks the iOS app into thinking an in-app purchase was approved. A patch was quickly made available by Apple, and that resolved the problem. However, app developers using the in-app purchase mechanism all had to update their software, or else risk being hit by these fraudulent $0 transactions.

The in-app purchase problem put the spotlight on various issues surrounding using SSL for financial transactions. Among many proposed solutions to bolster the venerable SSL protocol was a methodology known as "certificate pinning," which involves ensuring not just that an SSL certificate is properly signed by a trusted CA root certificate (it was in the attack), and that the DNS resolution correctly mapped the certificate to the server (it did in the attack), but that the SSL certificate presented is the exact certificate the software is expecting.

Now, this methodology of certificate pinning can certainly solve some SSL-related problems, but it also isn't a general solution to all SSL woes. For one thing, an app that uses certificate pinning cannot work through a corporate network proxy system.

Nonetheless, in the scenario described previously, we suggest that the software developers meet periodically with the security team to discuss this new form of attack and its cures. If certificate pinning turns out to be an appropriate solution for a specific app, clearly it would be the developers, and specifically the maintainers, that would have to implement the solution in the organization's various software applications.

On the point of confluence, we feel that this scenario is not likely to succeed without careful and considered collaboration between the software development and security organizations (see Figure 8.1).

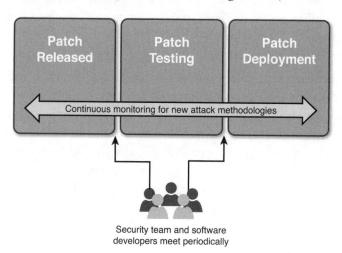

**Figure 8.1** Collaboration among the maintenance team.

## The Security Patch

Implementing a security patch is a special case of maintenance. Why? Well, let's consider several factors.

- Impact of failure

  A security patch isn't a simple functionality patch. Failing to install a security patch can have disastrous results for the software and the organization that runs it. As a result, every security patch needs to be carefully scrutinized and deeply understood. What is the attack vector and its preconditions? Are they relevant to our deployment of the software? Why or why not? How about the nature of the weakness itself? What does exploiting the weakness enable an attacker to do, and how would that impact the business our software is supposed to be performing for us? Understanding all of these issues can be done only by someone (or a team) that has a thorough understanding of the software as well as the patch and its underlying issues.

- Out of cycle

  In most data centers, there is a strict patching schedule. It is usually a result of years of experience in its organization, and properly done, it follows the business's production cycle in order to minimize any adverse impacts when things go wrong.

  However, that finely tuned patching schedule and process sometimes needs to be adjusted for high-priority security patches. Doing this is hugely disruptive to everyone in the organization, from the testers to the actual data center operations staff. As such, any out-of-cycle patching really should be reserved for the true exception cases. And when you do need to make use of them, it can sometimes make sense to bundle in a few other patches anyway, since some level of testing will need to be done in any case—there might be an economy of scale to be had in such a case.

  That makes the decision of when to declare a security patch worth all the disruption an especially difficult one to make, and one that absolutely must not be made lightly.

- Comprehensive

  With traditional functional patches to software, an organization can elect which ones to install based on whether a bug is being experienced, whether a new feature is desired, and so on. Such is not always the case with security patches. In fact, the majority of security patches do absolutely nothing in the form of enhancing a piece of software's (intended) functionality. Instead, they simply prevent some undesirable action from taking place. Yet, in many cases, we have little or no choice to make in terms of whether to implement a patch.

- Rush

  From the standpoint of the organization developing a security patch, as well as the standpoint of an organization deploying a patch, it's often the case that the patching must be done in an otherwise rushed manner. Security patches often aren't merely out of cycle, but they need to be deployed urgently. Sometimes, this means there is limited time for testing a patch. Other times, it simply means that the people involved might not have the time to be quite as careful as they normally would. Still, we should all be aware of the perils of rushing things, so give careful consideration to temporary workarounds in lieu of rushing a patch. Even disabling some little-used functionality can in many cases be preferable to having to rush things. Plus, when patches do need to be rushed, it's even more important to have a reliable rollback process should the patch cause problems when put into production.

There are no doubt other factors that make security patching different from traditional software patching, but these things by themselves make security patching especially delicate. There's more than plenty at stake in a security patch for the software developer as well as the users.

One thing is for certain regarding security patches: This is no time for a loose understanding of a security defect. To develop a security patch requires the maintenance team to study the problem in excruciating detail. They need to know the defect itself, as well as all the nuances surrounding exploiting the defect.

In many environments, developing a security patch is well served by a small group of dedicated software developers. Any and all proposed solutions to a problem should be carefully considered from every possible angle: performance impact, efficacy of the patch, compatibility with other software products, and so on. This is especially true in environments that rely heavily on web services and other server-to-server communications. Next, the patch itself should be implemented and reviewed by multiple thoroughly informed developers. Then and only then should the patch proceed to testing.

Testing a security patch should also involve an extra level of scrutiny not always afforded to otherwise normal software. At a bare minimum, the patch should be tested to ensure that it actually fixes its respective security defect. The test for the vulnerability should, of course, be well documented and thereafter included in the entire suite of security tests the software gets subjected to during every testing cycle.

Another consideration in patching a security defect in software is to consider similar defects in the same software. Often developers tend to repeat patterns, including failed patterns. Before a patch is unleashed on the user community, the software should be examined for similar circumstances that have led to the current defect and patch (see Figure 8.2).

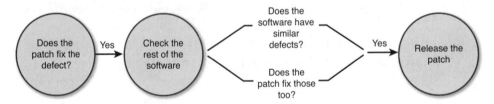

**Figure 8.2**   A process flow diagram.

## Special Cases

There are a few special cases that are worth exploring separately here, because they are substantial and can be quite difficult to handle.

- Third-party software

  There will no doubt be situations in which, upon considerable testing and analysis, you determine a software defect to be in a third-party library or another dependent component in your software. What are your options at that point?

You could notify the third-party provider of the flaw and hope that they fix it in a timely manner. You could even follow a responsible disclosure[1] process and prepare to notify the community of the defect. Perhaps you even have a contractual relationship with that third party and you can compel them to provide the fix within the constraints of a service-level agreement with them. (In the latter case, you can surely count your organization among the lucky ones.)

You could also omit the third-party code and write the same functionality from scratch. Chances are that's not a viable option, though, and that you selected the third-party code for good and valid reasons.

Another option is to rigorously test the software to determine with confidence the inputs that cause the software to fail. Next, write some "wrapper code" that you'll interpose between your own software and the third-party code. That wrapper code's main function will be to prevent the fail case(s) from being passed to the third-party software, thereby making it "safe" again, at least temporarily.

Of course, if you go the route of writing some wrapper code, you're going to also need to be rigorous in doing code reviews to ensure that you're using the wrapper code everywhere you're invoking the third-party software.

Another benefit of the wrapper software is that you can add some system logging at that layer of abstraction, so your operations staff will be able to have some accountability whenever the third-party software is being used.

• Open source software

Another scenario is when you find security defects in open source code that your software relies on. In some ways, it is similar to the third-party library scenario, but there are some important subtle differences that we should consider carefully. First, though, let's consider the available options.

Since the source is open, you have the source. It's more than likely you can find the bug and fix it yourself, as part of a normal maintenance cycle. That's the easy part. Well, it's easy assuming that you've built things from source code and have the appropriate build environment, which often is not the case. The next part is where things might get dicey, depending on your organization's policies. Can or should you submit your patch back to the open source project? In many cases, the answer is yes. But you need to verify before you do it. There might well be intellectual property policies in place that inhibit you from making open source contributions.

On the other hand, if you are unable to contribute your patch back to the open source project, you'll most certainly need to add it to a checklist of things to verify each and every time a new version of the open source software is released and used within your organization. That can become cumbersome and overly burdensome very quickly, so be sure to point that out when seeking permission to contribute the patch to the open source project.

At the very least, if you're submitting a patch to an open source project concerning security weakness, it's probably a good idea to leave your organization's name out of it. There's no need to draw that kind of attention to your company.

- Legacy software

  Our third special case here has to do with legacy code. By that, we are referring here to software that is in production but has essentially zero chance of being upgraded or repaired. Quite possibly, the source code or suitable build/test environment no longer exists, or you don't have access to it, or perhaps the developers are no longer available to your organization. (And it is entirely possible that all of those things are true.)

  Nonetheless, in your testing, you have uncovered a security defect. This case is fairly similar to the case of a third-party library in which the third party is unwilling or unable to provide a patch. (Perhaps they're no longer in business.)

  Similarly, you can write your own code to provide the core functionality that the third-party code previously provided. Or you can write a code wrapper and ensure that it is always followed.

## How Does Maintaining Software Securely Fit into Security SDLCs?

At a simplistic level, we could consider a maintenance cycle to be a miniature version of a full development process. As such, it would be easy enough to blithely assume that the maintenance cycle will follow our prescribed SDLC, right? Well, kind of sort of, but that really doesn't accurately capture the maintenance process's begin and end points, at the very least.

And further, only the Microsoft SDL directly addresses security patches, so the maintenance cycle is largely ignored by the major security SDLCs.

Let's start by considering the differences of a maintenance cycle versus a full product development cycle.

- Part of an existing project

  By definition, our maintenance cycle will be focusing on one component (at a time) of an existing development project. That means—or should mean—that there's already a design of some sort in place, in addition to all the other artifacts associated with a full development effort.

  Does that mean the maintenance team should design their intended fixes? Should they do a threat model of them? Indeed, many of the things that we've now come to expect from a full development effort just don't add up here.

  Nonetheless, if the maintainers follow a process of "everyone go deep" and just start coding, that doesn't work well either.

  So where do we draw the line?

  At the very least, the maintenance team should study the existing design and ensure that their work isn't going to interfere with the design—unless of course it must, in the case of a design weakness.

  And the code built in the maintenance process should certainly undergo rigorous code review and testing, as we've discussed. Perhaps code review and testing should, if anything, be even more rigorous for maintenance code than for the original production code.

- Micro focus

  In a similar way as described previously, when we're maintaining code, we're generally looking at a very small aspect of the project. In some cases, a very small aspect. Fix a bug, add a feature. These things don't generally require a big-picture view of an entire project. However, they are well served by a deep appreciation for how the maintenance code will fit into the bigger picture.

- Code review

  As we've discussed, maintenance code should be thoroughly reviewed. Period. Now, that's not always easy to accomplish, but it needs to happen.

  However, let's consider that a bit deeper. Because it's likely that the maintenance code was written by a relatively junior team of developers, there are some aspects of this code review that we should really stress. For one thing, consider conformance with corporate or organizational coding guidelines. If you have an existing cookbook of security mechanisms and how to implement them, it's important that the maintenance code is being properly developed. (And don't overlook the training benefits of that sort of code review.)

  Next, the code review should verify that the implementation is tightly synchronized with the product design and architecture. For example, did the maintainers use the same access control mechanism prescribed throughout the product? Did they use the same technologies used throughout the application, and in a consistent manner?

  Although these things might well not have a material effect on the functionality of the maintenance code, they very much can impact the future maintainability (and stability) of the code. Allowing noncompliant code to creep into the code base can over time cause a tremendous amount of confusion and extra work for all, not withstanding potential vulnerabilities.

- Testing

  Testing maintenance code is another important topic to consider. For a bug fix, the first thing to test is whether the new code fixes the bug. For a feature addition, we should verify that the functionality has indeed been added as required. That's the simple stuff.

But if we look deeper, there are other things we need to ensure during the test process.

## Mobile Maintenance

By now, our PST had come to realize that they'd be doing battle at every step of the process. Their key to success was to find a reasonable set of compromises that everyone could accept, and to plan for a more robust and resilient future.

So when it came time to discuss product maintenance issues, the dev team was prepared for the worst. On the plus side, though, they pretty much realized that the maintenance practices they'd need to adopt were essentially a microcosm of their entire software development process. Whew!

They were pretty much able to define a maintenance process with fairly minimal fuss, given their other experiences up until this point. At least, with only a few exceptions.

One exception case involved a "technology watch" process in which they'd ensure that someone was watching out for component/dependency updates with security consequences. These would include new versions of frameworks they used to build their software, but only updates that included security fixes. For each security fix, the maintenance team (with supervision) would look into the problem and its resolution, and make a determination as to whether it affected their product.

## Summing Up

Code maintenance is all too often overlooked from a security perspective, but as we've described here, it's also an opportunity for major defects to be inadvertently introduced. It's important for all software producers to take the time to ensure that their maintenance cycles get the same amount of security attention as their normal software development efforts.

It's a common practice to pass maintenance tasks to a junior team of developers. In many environments, it's even considered a rite of passage to spend time doing maintenance. Just be sure that your maintenance team has appropriate guidance, functionally as well as from a security perspective. Be sure to do rigorous security reviews of their work, looking for some of the common pitfalls we've described here. It can save you a lot of grief in the long run.

## Endnotes

1. Numerous attempts have been made for years to define a single process for researchers and product vendors to disclose product vulnerabilities in a mutually agreeable fashion. Although none has been truly standardized, most parties follow a process of negotiated disclosure that each party consents to. http://en.wikipedia.org/wiki/Responsible_ disclosure.

# 9    The View from the Center

W̲inding up now, we describe here how the various concepts of confluence presented in this book can be integrated into an enterprise-wide, holistic approach. Taking the point of view of a Chief Information Security Officer (CISO) in a medium-size corporation, we illustrate how a centrally positioned leader, as suggested by Figure 9.1, can help build—or exert influence in favor of—a confluent information security model.

**Figure 9.1**  CISO as director of the process.

Source: http://commons.wikimedia.org/wiki/File:Director_chair_icon.png

To do this, we will revisit, from a more central perspective, topics covered in earlier chapters from the point of view of either developers or enterprise security practitioners. We describe how a C-level executive (you, perhaps—now, or in the future) with typically broad areas of responsibility can help introduce confluent practices into the following areas:

- Application development, by influencing both architecture and the SDLC
- Security incident visualization and response
- Security awareness and training
- Policies, standards, and guidelines
- The role of other departments

Along the way, we will discuss how to build the case for confluence at every level of the enterprise. Specifically, we cover relationships between you as the CISO and applications developers; security practitioners (your staff?); supporting departments, such as Human Resources, Legal, Media Relations, and Purchasing; your vendors; your peer executives; your boss, up to and including the Board of Directors, if you have one; and any regulators, whether inside the company (an internal audit department, for example) or out (e.g., the Securities and Exchange Commission of the United States).

We also present our idea for what we call a *confluent network,* an innovative architecture that would combine data flow from both business applications and security appliances (such as firewall boxes) to communicate security events in real time—and make adjustments to your enterprise's defenses in response. We talk about resource budgeting and strategic planning too, with some ideas about how to pay for all this activity.

Having described what you *might* do, we move on next to figuring out what you *ought* to do. We supply here some ideas about how you can assess the current state of your enterprise with an eye toward confluence. Although there are not specific out-of-the box tests we can recommend, there do exist a few measurement tools and techniques that can get you part of the way.

Whatever your current role is—a software developer, say, or an information security practitioner, a manager, or an executive—the central view we present in this chapter of the integrated potential of confluence will help lock in for you the key obstacles and touch points along the path toward information security confluence in your environment.

## Ideas for Encouraging Confluent Application Development

Let's assume you have a role to play in shaping how software is produced in your shop. What are some concrete steps you can take? Consider forming a Software Security Group (SSG). Let us make the case, amplifying on our earlier description in Chapter 3, "Design Activities."

### Confluence Factors

The recurring topic of this book is confluence between product development teams within an enterprise working directly with the operational security (i.e., those Information Technology and Information Security folks who deal directly with security threats to enterprise infrastructure). There are lots of potential interaction and cooperation points between those camps, because their members typically possess a quite distinct set of skills and have been trained to view software products from very different angles. Unfortunately, those points remain mostly underutilized (or unutilized completely), as has been explained before.

Developers tend to think constructively, along the lines of functional specifications and what the product aims to achieve. Good software engineers, however, are trained to perform deep architectural analysis of software systems at hand and have the necessary skills to deconstruct them into abstract modules and components. Additionally, software engineers are the first to see the emergence of software components (or entire products), because they are the ones working on design specifications and actually implementing them.

Operation security personnel, on the other hand, are faced with adverse environments and evaluate the products from the viewpoint "what kind of additional havoc can it introduce?" As such, their first instincts are destructive, aimed at finding problems with the software product and trying to clamp down on potential issues arising from its introduction. This leads to a quite different mentality, trained in performing threat analysis and violating design assumptions, since this is the behavior they have to expect from the systems users (regardless of evil intent or not) and be prepared for. Note that this is just the kind of "abuse case" thinking we advocated in Chapter 3!

The best way to bring together those camps would be the creation of a bridge team of a sort, one that could incorporate security awareness of IT/IS folks and be well versed in development issues. All the models and frameworks reviewed earlier also point to the necessity of forming such a team, commonly referred to as a Software Security Group, as a prerequisite for establishing a successful security program. In his analysis of Build Security in Maturity Model (BSIMM) results, Gary McGraw argues that creation of a successful security program is primarily a management issue, requiring a lot of shepherding and support from the top, because purely grass-roots initiatives tend to have only a very limited scope and impact within an enterprise. This conviction is also deeply shared by the authors, who defend the importance of the collaborative approach to software security throughout this entire book.

## About a Software Security Group

The notion of an SSG has been around ever since introduction of security assurance into the development process. Such a group typically handles program management tasks related to the introduction of security processes into the development organizations, as well as owning additional areas such as security vulnerabilities response, and security research and analysis. SSGs are best composed of people with mixed backgrounds, those who came from development as well as operational teams.

If you are the CISO, building and managing a Software Security Group might be a task among your set of responsibilities.

The mixed background of its members makes a Software Security Group an excellent confluence tool for an enterprise. On one hand, those of its members with a development background have a good understanding of software development processes and realities in product development organizations. On the other hand, they work hand in hand with people from a security operational background, with its specific requirements and skills. This positions the group right at the crossroads between the development organizations and IT/IS realms, helping both parts of an enterprise actually connect and communicate. Thanks to its internal expertise in both software development and security operations, SSG should be able to find good interaction points for introducing IT security policies and involving security operations folks into the development process at the right moments, as well as help development teams understand specific requirements and the mind-set of security operations folks.

A Software Security Group does not have to be very large. The typical ratio among BSIMM participants is about 1 member per 100 developers. Unless it is a security consulting business, SSG represents a pure overhead, so the existence of additional head count has to be justifiable to the top management.

Depending on the enterprise's approach, this ratio can be achieved either by beefing up the central team and using its resources to team up with every product development group, or by keeping the central team relatively lean and distributing security expertise by creating so-called "satellite teams." Using this latter strategy, as CISO you would formally assign security-minded developers to security oversight roles within product development teams. The former approach is not very scalable, because it requires SSG members to go to really low-level details for all parts of the security assurance process, doing it hand to hand with the product development teams.

The satellite team approach allows SSG members to stay focused on high-level aspects of the security assurance process, relying on the security-minded folks within the development teams to handle the low-level details of the process implementation within their units. Of course, the overall success of the second model greatly depends on the quality and diligence of these part-time security resources available within the product development organizations.

The Software Security Group model has been used by your authors in the many enterprises we've worked in. It's the best way we have found to influence both security architecture in general (by establishing, say, design standards and reusable modules for authentication) and the design of individual applications, by way of security design reviews embedded in the development, release management, and change control processes.

## Other "Encouraging" Ideas

Whether you actually are a Chief Information Security Officer or are just pretending to be one for the purposes of this chapter, we need to ask you a question. What incentives can you put in place to cause your colleagues (as well as vendors and collaborators) to really do all these wonderful things you've been reading about?

As an experienced manager, you already know that you have several tools in your motivational kit. The three methods that over the years have yielded the best results for us, as encouraging confluent behavior, are these:

- Praise and bonuses
- Peer competition (e.g., "traffic light" model with green, yellow, and [yuck] red cores for all)
- Policies and guidelines, or contracts for product vendors

The utility of praise and bonuses is easy to see. We would just point out that this approach might be particularly pertinent in the area of encouraging confluent behavior, in that it gives you a way to call attention to aspects of the daily work that might otherwise not be noticed. By calling out a developer or manager for special achievements with regard to not only software security but also collaboration, let us say, with the enterprise security group, you might open the minds of some members of the development groups to new opportunities for reward and advancement.

Similarly, the principle of peer competition is very well established. We would like to emphasize here the effectiveness in certain corporate cultures of publishing charts and other metrics in full view of senior management, showing the extent to which various groups and departments are participating in your information security programs. A word to the wise: We advise that you never surprise a manager with a chart displayed before senior management that shows him in a poor light. In our experience you can often get gratifying results by previewing that performance chart that gives a "less than success" impression, and giving the object of your disapprobation an opportunity to improve before the final report is presented.

Policies and guidelines could well be, depending on the size and culture of your organization, the most effective single way you can encourage (or in fact compel) confluent behavior. It is such an important element of a successful program that we discuss the topic in its own section a little later.

## Toward a Confluent Network

One key area of information security that relates to the concept of a confluent enterprise at the most basic level relates to incident situational awareness and response. Whether you have direct responsibility for the security architecture of your company, or merely are in a position to assert influence on its design, we feel it is imperative for you to consider from the central point of view the role confluence can play.

In chapter after chapter throughout the book, we have examined in parallel how your business applications and the security appliances scattered throughout your network play complementary roles in securing it. When this collaboration is fully realized—as it has not yet been, so far as we know, although the OWASP AppSensor project (discussed in Chapter 7, "Operating Software Securely") is an intriguing approach—we foresee a state of real-time protection that might be the best bet to provide the millisecond-range defensive responses we believe are needed in today's enterprises.

We present here our vision for a confluent enterprise in which business applications have been trained to circulate a stream of significant security events. Combined with similar streams of events contributed by servers, desktops, routers, and security appliances such as firewalls, these ringed flows will create a circulating river of confluent security data in which all network elements will participate.

Here is a short list of events we anticipate appearing in the circulating stream:

- Unsuccessful login attempts
- Unsuccessful access attempts (this could be on the host, file, record, or even field level)
- Successful logins and logouts
- "Layer 7" attack attempts, such as SQL injection
- Changes to the security environment for infrastructure, such as web proxies or DNS handlers
- Sudden ramp-ups in byte flow rates that might indicate the beginning of a denial-of-service attack

The point of such a river of security data, of course, is to be able to dip into it and make adjustments in real time to the security posture of the enterprise. We expect to see many differing ways of managing these adjustments implemented over the next decade. One could use a master/subordinate design, in which a single monitoring process would sample the data and issue directives to step the security state machine through its paces. Bear in mind that something that might appear small in one context could be seen as a much higher priority in another. One could use collaborating observer clients, and a voting mechanism to avoid deadlock and other theoretical problems of real-time management. Whatever the implementation, the ability to tighten and loosen security strictures within milliseconds in response to a security event might be the most promising potential result of the confluence concept set.

In Figure 9.2 we show how key elements of your enterprise might participate in this confluent network. Applications and various security appliances are shown as *Emitters*. The events from applications, firewalls, and other network elements flow together into a stream of raw security events (solid lines). Each participant process can also, of course, sample the event stream, and react algorithmically by adapting its behavior.

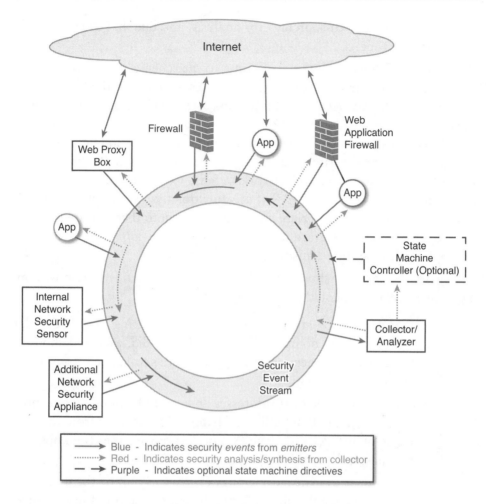

**Figure 9.2** Key elements of the enterprise in the confluent network.

We also show a *Collector* process, which monitors the raw event stream and analyzes the aggregation. This collector, which might have access to longitudinal event history and previously collected logs, as well as security policy settings, could issue synthetic events, shown in red. One example of a synthetic event might be, "We have detected a 10 percent rise in SQL injection attacks from former Soviet Socialist Republics over the past three minutes." Although we show a single process, it might well be prudent, as we mentioned earlier, to operate several instances of a collector, with varying algorithm or policy bases, and institute a voting system among them. (A sort of "crowd-sourcing" for analysis, and one that usually improves over time.)

Finally, we show an optional addition to the scheme, which we call a State Machine Controller. This controller takes a feed from the Collector (and perhaps the raw feed as well). It emits state machine directives, shown as dashed lines in the diagram. We envision these directives as embodying high-level adjustments with human oversight to the finite state machine that represents the security model of your enterprise. A sample directive might be, "We are shifting to Network Defense Condition 3," or, "We are calling a 'security Code Red.'" If this functionality was implemented, devices that had the appropriate intelligence built into them would be able to execute the pre-agreed defensive (well, perhaps *offensive*) actions associated with the state transition.

There are, of course, hundreds of other possibilities. Consider now how a confluent enterprise could react to such a stream:

- If SQL injection attacks suddenly start appearing from Badlandia, and we are not doing business with Badlandia, we could choose to disregard connection attempts that are geo-located from that source.
- If a certain range of IP addresses appears to be flooding our input gates, we could limit either the bandwidth accepted from the range of addresses, or even the sorts of transactions (lookups, purchases, requests, etc.).
- In response to many suspicious occurrences that by themselves did not reach a threshold alarm, the enterprise could react to the multifaceted context by raising a general level of security conservatism, with preprogrammed implications for behavior.

What would it take to make this vision[1] a reality? You could start by modifying your business applications to emit events, and your security infrastructure to be able to absorb, parse, and make use of varying formats of telemetry data. (Many of them might already emit Syslog events, a good start.) The next step would be to give them the ability to react to such events as well, possibly as amalgamated by a Collector process. A fully confluent arrangement as illustrated previously would seem to require modifications to security appliances, by their cooperating manufacturers.

Our general point is that we believe that future enterprise systems will behave this way, using the principles of confluence we have enunciated throughout the book to produce a new level of security readiness and enterprise protection.

## Security Awareness and Training

We have discussed throughout the book several opportunities for training with respect to confluence. Here is a summary.

- Basic training for developers about security threats and secure coding concepts (we expect there's a good chance your company does this already). Programming language–specific training with hands-on labs is most effective here, in our experience.

- "Confluence" training for developers that covers the fundamentals of information security defenses, such as firewalls, Intrusion Detection Systems, data loss prevention methods, and various kinds of monitoring and blocking. The object here would be to show your application developers how your enterprise security staff thinks about what happens on your network.

- Basic training for your information security practitioners about what software is (you'd be surprised!) and how software is developed at your shop. Cover the SDLC (be prepared to cover several different sets of practices, as discussed earlier in the book). Be sure, too, to explain your release management practice.

- "Confluence" training for the InfoSec staff. The curriculum here should include commonly used libraries, frameworks, and third-party packages; common architectures (two-tier, three-tier, etc.); a selection of methods your apps use to perform security tasks such as authentication, authorization, and error or anomaly reporting; and, especially, a list of security events (login attempt failures, file access attempt failures due to access rights issues, etc.) that your applications usually perform. You must also cover "business logic" issues, such as where your customers come from (company-wise and by geography), what they buy, and, yes, what your company sells!

Let's say you have made the sale on security training, and the courses are available. (No small feat...so, good work!) How do you ensure that the target audience actually receives the training? Well, you will want to ensure that proper policies, standards, and guidelines are in place; sufficient resources are allocated; and methods of determining training success are defined (and staffed, and funded). We provide suggestions in each of these areas in the text that follows. Read on.

## Policies, Standards, and Guidelines

As we said earlier, policies and standards and guidelines are an essential tool for managing security at an enterprise level. So we see three questions: What sort of policies do you need? How should you enforce them? For that matter, how should you create them?

### Some Policy Suggestions

We recommend you consider creating and maintaining policies in the following areas:

- Software quality—bug tolerance, allowed time to fix, etc.
- Training
- Security requirements for third-party software and hardware, plugged into Purchasing
- Supply-chain controls
- Release management
- Configuration management
- Change control
- Protection of important data and assets such as customer records

Your policy elements in those last three areas (as well as other stages of your application development and operation) should all include the engagement of information security practitioners. If you have a full-fledged Software Security Group, as described earlier, your policies might want to call out that group bought specifically as the interface to security.

The best policies, of course, are of limited utility unless they are enforced. You have several options available to you here. You could require training in the policies, for example. This leads almost to a recursive consideration: How could you compel people to take the training about the policies? We say: Put an end to the madness. Find a way to measure compliance with your policies, and make a measured threshold of compliance a systemic part of the performance review for everyone in the position in your company to affect the success of your content's program. That's the best solution, although some of these things are subjective and some are more quantitative.

We can't leave the topic of policies behind without trying to save our esteemed readers some scar tissue in this area. We will make two points, based on long experience.

First, to paraphrase what Gene Spafford and Simson Garfinkel said all those years ago, "If you are responsible for security but do not have the power to enforce policies, your real job is to take the blame."[2]

Second, your information security policies are more likely to succeed if they have been reviewed by—or, better yet, are the product of—a deliberative body composed of key stakeholders in your enterprise. In our experience, collaboratively developed policies are better accepted, better understood, and, well, just better. After all, if your specialty is information security, you might actually not know everything there is to know about how the business operates or what really happens throughout the company when the work is being done.

## The Role of Other Departments and Corporate Entities

We take up now the topic of how to build the case for confluence at every level of the enterprise, and across the key departments with which you interact.

As a CISO, you might find that you interact with every corporate entity, daily or almost daily:

- Human Resources
- Legal department
- Media Relations
- Purchasing
- Networking and Information Technology

- Development managers
- Manufacturing
- Chief Information Officer
- Chief Operating Officer
- Chief Executive Officer
- Board members
- Industry regulators
- Internal audit
- External oversight and review bodies
- Vendors

We expect that you will find that the various departments encounter different aspects of the confluence challenge. For example, you might interact with Human Resources in the areas of employee training and corporate policy, and the Legal department relating not only to policy but also to vendor contracts and purchasing controls. You might well find yourself working with the Purchasing department in several respects—to find appliance equipment or software that is most easily adapted to confluent purposes, or to help secure your supply chain against various nefarious attacks.

Working with other executives probably offers the best opportunity for you to progress in the area of confluence between application development and information security practitioners. Whether it is by mandating training, agreeing to policy changes, or contributing to the design of a confluent architecture, your fellow executives (both inside and outside of IT) are key to executing your vision—if you communicate effectively. Should you give them a copy of this book, or merely summarize it for them?

In your reporting structure, all the way up to the Board of Directors (if you have one), you will need to make the case successfully that the best approach to defend against the constantly increasing threat is to get people to pool their information and create effective defenses that can react quickly to attacks. In our experience, although middle managers might object and obstruct because they worry about losing resources or incurring delays in their projects by making the sort of changes we suggest in this book, your authors have yet to encounter a top executive with fiduciary responsibility for the safety of the company and its assets who was not willing to devote resources to the kinds of programs and policies we advocate. There will be trade-offs, no doubt. But let's be sure they are well informed trade-offs using the sort of collaborative approaches described in this book.

Generally, we have found the same willingness to support a confluent approach in dealing with regulators, internal audit, and other similar oversight bodies. Although one must pay due attention to checklists and inventories of security controls, it is our perception that the more general responsibility an entity holds for the security of an enterprise, the more amenable it is to a holistic approach. Your mileage may vary.

## Resource Budgeting and Strategic Planning for Confluence

One topic we have not talked about much in this book so far is how to get funding for the various confluent initiatives, programs, and other activities you might want undertake or encourage. Let's consider first how you might find money to support confluent application development.

Begin by making a list of the things you want to do that cost money, with estimates. (One common basis for costing out training is to estimate it by the pupil, but we've seen it done several ways.) Your main job right now is to get a handle on What, When, and How Much.

Here are a few expenses to consider:

➤ Training

- Basic and confluence training for developers, as discussed previously
- Basic and confluence training for your information security practitioners, again as discussed
- Symposiums and other professional development venues

➤ Meetings/Events

- Colloquia. There's no substitute for getting people together in the same room. Depending on how many people are involved, you might need to invest in a formal get-together involving conference sites, hotels, meals, guest speakers, gift bags, shuttle buses—the mind (the budgeter's mind, especially) reels.

- Meetings. On a smaller scale, if one or two dozen individuals are involved (or you can logically split the staff into groups of this size that have a continual need to work together), you might be able to arrange regular meetings or videoconferences. If that's the case, consider what costs might facilitate attendance and attention. Will you pay for meals or snacks?

### Software Licenses

Although we have not identified in this book any software packages we especially recommend, it might be part of your responsibility as CISO to specify development tools that promote application security, such as static code checkers. Whether or not you do that, your department might carry the budget for security software licenses. We would advise you to also identify tools that facilitate *collaboration* among the various groups as part of the information security budget.

### Capital Expense

As in the case of software licenses, we cannot recommend as this book goes to press any security specific appliance or other piece of equipment. We can only point out that as confluence-compatible appliances begin to appear on the market (as we believe they will), you will want to consider such features and budget accordingly. We expect with some confidence that firewalls, Intrusion Detection Systems, data loss prevention tools, and other similar security equipment will adapt to the need for signaling security events in a lingua franca and reacting to a stream of events in a policy-directed way.

### Consulting

As you build your confluence program, you'll want to factor in appropriate amounts for consulting budgets. The first investment might be in assessment projects.

### Finding the Money

Okay, who pays? The details, of course, will vary according to how money is budgeted and accounted for in your enterprise. But in most companies, the question will come down to, "Whose budget will it come out of?" (Better, of course, would be, "What part of whose budget covers this?"

But we'll assume that some other, less far-sighted person other than our Esteemed Reader planned the current budget.)

Here are three approaches that we have seen work, at our own companies and in other case study instances:

- Directly from the information security budget. This would probably take the form of a strategic initiative, a project that has a definite beginning and end and a well-defined goal that can be measured. For example, you might package an effort to begin at the beginning of the fiscal year (Q1, say) and last six months. A measurable goal might be training 90 percent of a group of developers and a similar percentage of information security practitioners about key software development concepts and business logic principles.

- As a special initiative or pilot effort—maybe a quality boost project—in the budget of one or more development groups. The goals in this case might not relate to training. We could see a target of improving a quality measure by a certain percentage, so long as it isn't merely a one-time budget input.

- As an embedded element of the SDLC, probably built into the development budget. We envision this option as the desired end state. Of course, in a perfect world all of these costs would already be built into the steady-state operation of your enterprise, but we have seen very few companies to date that are that far along. If yours is, however, try to include a Confluence Effect Factor in the basic loaded expense calculation (salary plus benefits plus training, plus extras) for employees with job descriptions in a class (e.g., application developer) relevant to our topic.

Having laid out three options, we'll take the author's way out and say that the choice of funding model is "an exercise left to the reader."

## Assessment Tools and Techniques

After an enterprise has established a security assurance program of its own, sooner or later its security and executive management—you, potentially— is inevitably faced with a question of how well it stacks up against the industry and competitors. This question might come up as a result of an internally conducted audit, in response to a customer inquiry or as fallout from a security-breach investigation. Regardless of the initial motivation, top management will want to have at its disposal an effective tool to compare against its industry peers and determine gaps and priorities for its own program.

You have many options here, and we will discuss just a few for you. You could start with a simple, what-have-we-got-and-how-does-it-look process survey. You could employ a formal Capability Maturity Model (CMM) for a structured review of your software development processes. You could even commit the organization to, or engage in, a full-blown, formal risk management framework such as an ISMS (see sidebar).

Since we were just discussing funding models, by the way, we'll point out here that there are at least two money-related questions that arise when considering assessments. First, how would you as the CISO pay for the assessment study itself? Second, and probably harder, how would you pay for the work needed to address whatever deficiencies are uncovered?

Funding for the study itself would probably come from your information security budget. Perhaps it could be part of an external due-diligence audit. Moreover, if you are lucky enough to have in your company an internal audit department (practitioners pause for ironic laugh here), you might find the money there. Generally, whichever internal group pays for effectiveness studies or audits of security function would be a likely source. If your company lacks either sort of security oversight group, consider approaching the development teams for funding.

Paying for process fixes and indeed new functionality (as a result of the study) will require more inventiveness. Harkening back to some ideas from the preceding section, you might need to either propose a new strategic initiative to allocate the resources, or convince the executives responsible for overseeing development that their processes are deficient (or defective, or inadequate) with regard to modern security requirements. Do you speak the language of ROI (return on investment)? You will need to, because improving processes past the point of tangible return is not good business. It's not enough to identify areas of potential improvement in your software development processes. The gains you might glean from making recommended improvements must be weighed against the very real opportunity cost of, for example, features not implemented or developers not hired as a result of the investment in process you envision.

Software assessment is a huge topic, complete with controversies, competing factions, and commercial interests. We are not going to dig into it too much, or take sides (although we will venture to present a few lessons from our own experiences in the area). Our recommendation is to *do something* to get a sense of where you stand, considered both in the abstract and as compared to peer organizations.

## Information Security Management System

In our opinion, the best generic term for the sort of management tool we have in mind here is Information Security Management System (ISMS). This term comes out of the work done by the International Organization for Standardization (ISO), together with the International Electrotechnical Commission (IEC) on Information Technology standards. An ISMS generally describes a set of policies and other controls instituted to help control IT risks.

Now the ISO/IEC universe, as it relates to information security, is enormous—far too big for us to cover adequately in this book. Parts of it are proprietary too. We'll just skim the surface in this chapter and give you some pointers for more information. It will be well worth your study.

One ISMS is the ISO/IEC's "27000 series" of standards, sometimes known as "ISO 27K." There are several standards in this series; the two that we are most concerned about are 27001 and 27002.

Another ISMS we will just mention here is the Standard of Good Practice (SOGP) from Information Security Forum. A third discipline, in use within the United States Federal government, is FISMA, the Federal Information Security Management Act of 2002 (renewed in 2009). A fourth, which is under development as we write this chapter in the summer of 2013, is an emerging "Cybersecurity Framework" being developed by the National Institute of Standards and Technology (NIST) under Executive Order 13636, Improving Critical Infrastructure Cybersecurity, for voluntary use by critical infrastructure owners and operators, and their partners, within the United States.

All the ISMS frameworks we've just discussed are worthy of your study, and also extend far beyond the scope of this chapter, since they cover comprehensively all elements of information security, whereas our focus is mostly software development and enterprise defense.

For additional overview, with some details, you might check out the Wikipedia entry on Information Security Management Systems at http://en.wikipedia.org/wiki/Information_security_management_system.

We'll present a high-level view here of a few evaluation methods or standards you might want to consider. We'll start with a couple of simple yet formal methods we know firsthand, and then give a broad overview of one Big Solution, the canonical ISO/IEC 27001/2 standards.

## Build Security in Maturity Model (BSIMM)

The best assessment tool we know of for quickly assessing the state of your application development practices, and forming a basis for a plan to improve it, is the BSIMM process from Cigital. We say that out of firsthand experience: one of your authors is a satisfied BSIMM customer.[3] (BSIMM is free—as in have at it—but you can also do as one of your authors did, and hire Cigital to conduct the study for maximal return.

In describing BSIMM we are going to quote liberally from the BSIMM web site, which is at http://bsimm.com.

### Vendor's Description

BSIMM (pronounced "bee simm") is short for Building Security in Maturity Model. It is a measuring stick for software security, based on a study of real-world software security initiatives. The best way to use the BSIMM is to compare and contrast your own initiative with the data contained in the model about what other organizations are doing. You can then identify goals and objectives of your own and look to the BSIMM to determine which further activities make sense for you.

Cigital built the BSIMM entirely from observations made by studying 72 real software security initiatives. The BSIMM does not tell you what you should do; instead, it tells you what everyone else is actually doing. This approach stands in sharp contrast to "faith-based" approaches to software security.

BSIMM version 5, the latest, describes the software security initiatives at 67 well-known companies—all told, efforts to secure the software developed by 272,358 developers. On average, the participating companies have practiced software security for nearly 6 years (with some initiatives being brand new at first measurement and the oldest initiative being an impressive 18 years old in 2014).

The most important use of the BSIMM is as a measuring stick to determine where your approach currently stands relative to other firms. Note which activities you already have in place, and use "activity coverage" to determine their levels and build a scorecard. In our own work using the BSIMM to assess levels, we found that the spider-graph-yielding "high-water mark" approach (based on the three levels per practice) is sufficient to get a low-resolution feel for maturity, especially when working with data from a particular vertical or geography.

One meaningful comparison is to chart your own maturity high-water mark against the averages we have published to see how your initiative stacks up.

Figure 9.3 shows the BSIMM "Earth" graph (a depiction of where the aggregated data from all 67 firms land).

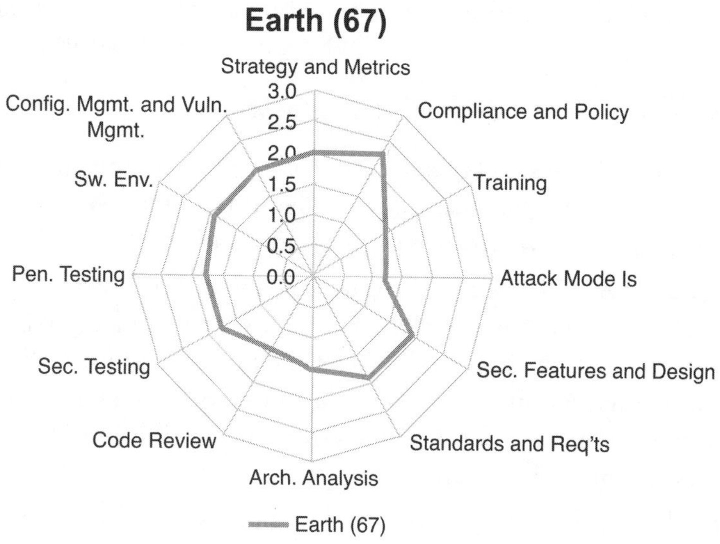

### Earth (67)

**Figure 9.3** A plot of aggregated data from all firms: the BSIMM "Earth" graph.

The 12 program elements measured by BSIMM are as listed here:

- Compliance and policy
- Training
- Attack models
- Security features and design
- Standards and requirements
- Architectural analysis

- Code review
- Security testing
- Penetration testing
- Software environment
- Configuration management and vulnerability management
- Strategy and metrics

Of course, we don't have the space here to describe BSIMM in full, but we hope you'll take away the idea that it represents a very useful, statistics-based way to evaluate how your software security development efforts stack up against those of some of the best companies in the world. It's a great way to find out where you should be focusing your efforts.

### Software Assurance Maturity Model (SAMM)

Shifting gears a bit, we will lay out here a fully open, nonproprietary model developed under the auspices of OWASP, the Open Web Application Security Project. (See www.owasp.org for information about OWASP.)

The official SAMM 1.0 guide arrived in March 2009 (beta released in August 2008), and it had clearly benefited by learning from past experiences (including those of SDL) over the preceding four to five years. In particular, measurability (expressed via Maturity Levels) and metrics provide important tooling for building a road map adoption of a security assurance program by an organization.

The model's authors emphasize "building blocks," the nonprescriptive philosophy of the model, in which each organization is expected to define its own objectives and begin picking corresponding practices to build the adoption road map.[4]

The SAMM project's development has been (and still is) funded and led by representatives from Fortify Software (now part of HP) with very active community participation. An important differentiator of SAMM (as compared to SDL) is its vendor neutrality, which was one of the stated goals of the project from day one. Acceptance as an OWASP project has further underscored its perception as a generalized industry framework for common usage.

SAMM defines four main business functions:

- Governance
- Construction
- Verification
- Deployment

Instead of centering the entire process around a typical software development life cycle, it rolls all development-related activities under the general umbrella of "Construction," making it just one of the verticals in the overall model (see Figure 9.4). This reflects a more balanced approach to security assurance, viewing a software product as the end result of many activities, which commence long before the product requirements phase and do not finish with its release.

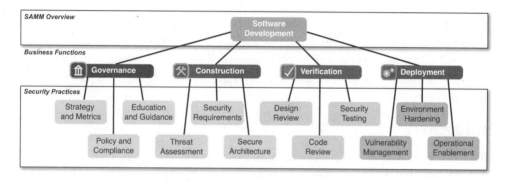

**Figure 9.4**   Software Assurance Maturity Model.

Source: https://www.owasp.org/images/7/71/SAMM-Overview.png

Each business function in SAMM consists of three security practices, which are considered independent activities constituting overall assurance program. Overall, there are 12 such practices organized by business function:

- *Governance:* Strategy and Metrics, Policy and Compliance, Education and Guidance
- *Construction:* Threat Assessment, Security Requirements, Secure Architecture
- *Verification:* Design Review, Code Review, Security Testing
- *Deployment:* Vulnerability Management, Environment Hardening, Operational Enablement

These objectives and associated activities allow for assessing the current state of security assurance programs in various parts of an organization and developing road maps for reaching the desired state, which might not necessarily correspond to the highest maturity level, at least in the short to medium term.

Speaking generally, SAMM is a higher-level framework, aimed primarily at the organizational structures responsible for managing corporate security assurance programs, but not so much at the folks "in trenches," who will be called upon to implement those programs. Although the nonprescriptive nature of SAMM creates a lot of flexibility at the organizational level for planning a security assurance program, that very same quality represents a liability when it comes to implementing it at lower levels, since it lacks explicit guidance and abundant samples.

For instance, the threat modeling practice will be very difficult, if not impossible, to introduce into a development organization unless a good deal of collateral and consulting is made available at the same time. Similar considerations apply to other practical elements of the program across all business functions.

## ISO 27001/2

The Big Solution, as we said before, is the international standard set ISO 27001 and 27002. There are only several thousand enterprises worldwide[5] that have certified even part of their security operations to these standards, but the list is growing.

The details of standards themselves are proprietary, so we'll just take a cursory look here. For more details about the 27001–27005, you can naturally check into the official ISO site at www.iso.org/iso/home/store/catalogue_tc/catalogue_detail.htm?csnumber=42103.

As described by ISO,[6] these are the content sections of the standard:

- Management Responsibility
- Internal Audits
- ISMS Improvement
- Annex A: Control objectives and controls
- Annex B: OECD principles and this international standard
- Annex C: Correspondence between ISO 9001, ISO 14001 and this standard

For an alternative set of descriptions, which (as of this writing) are free (but copyright-controlled), you could check out the ISO27k toolkit at www.iso27001security.com/html/iso27k_toolkit.html.

For our money, the heart of this set of standards is 27002.[7] It outlines hundreds of security controls you might want to deploy, including many that are perfectly pertinent to potential areas of confluence.

Based on public sources,[8] the domains covered by ISO 27002 include (we've italicized the areas we consider most pertinent to confluence):

- *Security policy*
- Organization of information security
- *Asset management*
- Human resources security
- Physical and environmental security
- Communications and operations management
- *Access control*
- *Information systems acquisition, development, and maintenance*
- *Information security incident management*
- Business continuity management
- *Compliance*

If you want a comprehensive set of controls and processes, we recommend that you investigate the ISO 27001-27005 series. Be aware that implementing the full set of controls—and ensuring that the processes are carried out reliably year after year—could represent a significant investment in time and money (on the order of millions of U.S. dollars over several years for a medium-size enterprise).

## National Institute for Standards and Technology (NIST) SP 800-53

We couldn't leave the topic of information security program evaluation and security models behind without a mention of SP 800-53, a Special Publication of the United States National Institute for Standards and Technology (NIST).

Now in its third version (released in 2009), this venerable document, titled "Recommended Security Controls for Federal Information Systems and Organizations," was never intended to be a vehicle for information security program evaluation—but it became just that, in many countries around the world. Your authors are personally aware of half a dozen companies and institutions that developed software and questionnaires designed to help an enterprise score itself against the controls that NIST recommended, graded by risk level of the assets involved.

The scope of this document, like the ISO 27001 family of standards, goes far beyond issues of secure coding. It describes hundreds of potential controls, at various levels of intensity and effectiveness, distributed among 18 control families. Of those 18 families, we have 12 of them italicized in Table 9.1 that we consider most relevant to an understanding of the state of confluence, from a central, CISO-like vantage point.

**Table 9.1**   Control Families from SP 800-53

| Identifier | Family | Class |
|---|---|---|
| *AC* | *Access Control* | Technical |
| *AT* | *Awareness and Training* | Operations |
| *AU* | *Audit and Accountability* | Technical |
| CA | Security Assessment and Authorization | Management |
| CM | Configuration Management | Operational |
| *CP* | *Contingency Planning* | Operational |
| *IA* | *Identification and Authentication* | Technical |
| *IR* | *Incident Response* | Operational |
| MA | Maintenance | Operational |
| *MP* | *Media Protection* | Operational |
| *PE* | *Physical and Environmental Protection* | Operational |
| *PL* | *Planning* | Management |
| *PS* | *Personnel Security* | Operational |
| RA | Risk Assessment | Management |
| *SA* | *System and Services Acquisition* | Management |
| *SC* | *System and Communications Protection* | Technical |
| *SI* | *System and Information Integrity* | Operational |
| *PM* | *Program Management* | Management |

Here is what NIST says about SP 800-53:

> The objective of NIST Special Publication 800-53 is to provide a set of security controls that can satisfy the breadth and depth of security requirements levied on information systems and organizations and that is consistent with and complementary to other established information security standards.

> The catalog of security controls provided in Special Publication 800-53 can be effectively used to demonstrate compliance with a variety of governmental, organizational, or institutional security requirements. It is the responsibility of organizations to select the appropriate security controls, to implement the controls correctly, and to demonstrate the effectiveness of the controls in satisfying their stated security requirements. The security controls in the catalog facilitate the development of assessment methods and procedures that can be used to demonstrate control effectiveness in a consistent and repeatable manner—thus contributing to the organization's confidence that there is ongoing compliance with its stated security requirements.

The document itself can be found in the historical (and historic) NIST Computer Security Research Center (CSRC) warehouse, at http://csrc.nist.gov/publications/nistpubs/800-53-Rev3/sp800-53-rev3-final_updated-errata_05-01-2010.pdf.

## Mobile Plans—Postmortem Interviews

We have now taken you with us all the way on the meandering journey of how our acquired mobile team has fared in their new parent organization, following a new product release from beginning to end. As we're considering the CISO's view and perspective in this chapter, we felt it appropriate to interview the CTO and the development team leader here. To accomplish that task, we've asked them for their candid feedback on the process they've just endured. First, our dev team leader:

> *Well, I have to say this process has been unlike any we were prepared for when we agreed to be acquired by Peabody Medical. We had the impression we'd be able to continue our app development process pretty much along the status quo we were used to. We sure were in for a culture shock on that!*

*That said, although the Peabody CTO has been quite a stickler for how he wanted things to be done, we were all able to make some important compromises in the interest of getting this app release out the door in a reasonable amount of time and cost. So, from that perspective, I'm pretty happy with things, but I can sure sense that the way we work is going to continue to change pretty drastically as we plan our next one to three years of work ahead.*

*All those compromises we made were for this release, and aren't going to carry the day going forward. We're going to have to take a far deeper dive into what the CTO has been proposing in the way of a secure software development process, and decide what's going to be feasible to do.*

*That said, I suspect we've been able to suitably impress the CTO with what we're able to deliver, so perhaps there will still be room for fair compromise going forward. I guess we'll know soon enough.*

By contrast, the Peabody Medical CTO (who also shoulders the CISO responsibilities at Peabody) had this to say:

*This was painful for all of us. Candidly, I was more than a little concerned when our Mergers and Acquisitions (M&A) team told us we'd need to fast-track this acquisition. We just didn't have enough time to properly do our due diligence on them. Sure enough, one of the things we missed was verifying the maturity of the Scherr-Mantis software development processes, especially from a software security standpoint. We knew going in about the weaknesses in their (now our) infrastructure protections, and a somewhat lackadaisical approach to protecting their (now our) laptops. We had budgeted for and were able to put in place some mitigating controls, including aggressive scanning and patching and a mature network monitoring stack. But we hadn't spent the time to dig deep on their development methodology. I suppose we got exactly what we deserved.*

*Well, what's done is done, and we dove in and gave it our best. Clearly, we had to handle an epic set of cultural changes between their dev team and our way of doing things. Fortunately, we were all able to work together and find compromises we could accept for this release. Following the acquisition, it was absolutely vital that we got the new product out the door and to our customers as quickly as we could. From a business standpoint, that was paramount. I'm proud that the entire team was able to see that and make things work.*

*But now we have to take a critical look at our processes and decide once and for all just how the team formerly known as Scherr-Mantis is going to fit into Peabody Medical. We all want this to succeed, so there's no doubt going to need to be some give and take from all sides.*

*What I'm most concerned with is setting our goal and then coming up with reasonable steps we can take to get to that goal over the next one to five years. I realize we're not going to be able to miraculously change things overnight, so let's take small steps to get there iteratively.*

*To lay out the vision for our goal, I'm going to turn to the BSIMM as a measuring stick to compare ourselves against others in our industry, as well as outside of our industry. I'll then sit down with the dev team and we'll together agree with what we're going to implement, and how we'll get there.*

*It's going to be a pretty painful process, but I'm adamant about it. We will do it, and I am not willing to accept no for an answer.*

We interviewed one of the IT security guys from the acquiring company as well. It sounds as though there is some fairly fundamental work left to do.

*I have to confess I still don't understand the data flows for this thing. I've had it explained to me what the app does; but the briefing was by one of the sales guys and I don't understand the details of our product lines as well as he does, so I couldn't follow all the explanation. We added Intrusion Detection boxes on the subnet junctions, tuned the web application firewall a bit, and slapped endpoint protections on the developers' machines. But where does the data come from, where does it go, and what bad thing can happen? That's the meeting I am waiting for.*

We will give the last word to one of the Peabody developers, who all in all didn't seem too impressed.

*I am not sure I see the point. I am still sitting in the same chair, doing the same job, with the same laptop—well, actually, the security guys rebuilt the laptop. But if it makes us safer, or the big boss thinks it makes us safer, I'm cool with it as long as they don't screw up the build scripts too much.*

Hey, that last line might make a better bumper sticker than the one we were planning, "I Brake for Confluence." What do you think?

## Notes for Small Shops or Individuals

If you operate or own a part of a small shop, this chapter should be particularly pertinent, since it's all about looking at the problem from a central point of view—and that is where you live. The entirety of the enterprise is open to you. So here's a case in which small size can be a real blessing. Could it be that you are the CISO but didn't know it?

Of course, getting the resources together to follow the recommendations we have made here—maybe the biggest challenge will just be getting the time—is sure to be a challenge. Most of the ideas and models we've presented are free, though, so if you can get the work done you might well end with a more accurate assessment than the bigger shops as to what steps toward confluence will have the biggest payoff, how to get started, and what each will cost.

## Summing Up

Summing up our last chapter of the book, we will pass up the chance to make our case for confluence once again. What we hope you take away from this last, central point-of-view analysis is a sense of how achievable this dream might be in your enterprise.

As we complete the five-year journey that this book represents, and as a follow-on to 25-plus years of security efforts that have led up to its beginnings, we are more convinced than ever that the detailed suggestions we have presented in this and previous chapters provide a glimpse of a more secure future for our companies, our data, and ourselves in the Information Age. The great World War I statesman Georges Clemenceau said, "War is too important to be left to the generals."[9] In our age, information security is too important to be left to the firewall manufacturers and antivirus makers—or even, left to their own devices, the most conscientious of application developers.

# Endnotes

1. If, by the way, you perceive a resemblance to the operation of the mammalian immune system, we agree with you (and commend for further study analyses of such processes as the clotting cascade).

2. *Practical UNIX and Internet Security,* ISBN 1-56592-148-8.

3. And we note also, in passing, that the editor of this book series for the publisher is actually one of the progenitors of BSIMM (it's a small world, isn't it?). But the independent evaluation of BSIMM we present here is based on our own firsthand experience with it.

4. To our minds, this facet of SAMM represents a stark contrast with the highly prescriptive approach of core SDL models, although the SDL Optimization Model did move it closer to the SAMM's way of thinking.

5. As of December 2012 (the latest date for which statistics are available), the total was 7,940 ISO 27001 certificates, according to the International Register of ISMS Certificates. Over half (4,152) of certificates to date have been awarded to enterprises in Japan, followed by 573 in the U.K., 546 in India, 461 in Taiwan, 393 in China, 227 in Germany, 112 in the Czech Republic, 107 in Korea, 103 in the United States, and (rounding out the top ten) 82 in Italy. Note that some enterprises have multiple areas of certification. Source: www.iso27001certificates.com.

6. You can dig this information out of the official ISO website too, but we found the simplest explanation at www.27000.org/iso-27002.htm.

7. Are you interested in the history? As we follow it, 27002 is derived from the older U.K. standard published as BS7799 by BSI (the British Standards Institution) in 1995. ISO published the now-international version as ISO 17799 in 2000. Then in 2005, the same essential standard was recast into ISO/IEC 27002, as part of the 27001-27005 set we mentioned earlier. An updated version was released in 2013.

8. http://en.wikipedia.org/wiki/ISO/IEC_27001, retrieved December 2, 2012.

9. "La guerre! C'est une chose trop grave pour la confier à des militaires." As quoted in *Soixante Anneés d'Histoire Française* (1932) by Georges Suarez.

# Index

**THIS PRODUCT**

informit.com/register

Register the Addison-Wesley, Exam Cram, Prentice Hall, Que, and Sams products you own to unlock great benefits.

To begin the registration process, simply go to **informit.com/register** to sign in or create an account. You will then be prompted to enter the 10- or 13-digit ISBN that appears on the back cover of your product.

Registering your products can unlock the following benefits:

- Access to supplemental content, including bonus chapters, source code, or project files.
- A coupon to be used on your next purchase.

Registration benefits vary by product. Benefits will be listed on your Account page under Registered Products.

**About InformIT — THE TRUSTED TECHNOLOGY LEARNING SOURCE**

INFORMIT IS HOME TO THE LEADING TECHNOLOGY PUBLISHING IMPRINTS Addison-Wesley Professional, Cisco Press, Exam Cram, IBM Press, Prentice Hall Professional, Que, and Sams. Here you will gain access to quality and trusted content and resources from the authors, creators, innovators, and leaders of technology. Whether you're looking for a book on a new technology, a helpful article, timely newsletters, or access to the Safari Books Online digital library, InformIT has a solution for you.

**informIT.com**
THE TRUSTED TECHNOLOGY LEARNING SOURCE

Addison-Wesley | Cisco Press | Exam Cram
IBM Press | Que | Prentice Hall | Sams
SAFARI BOOKS ONLINE